The Once and Future Ocean

NOTES TOWARD A
NEW HYDRAULIC SOCIETY

BY PETER NEILL

For Jackson &
Kateryn

buddies scientists!
The sea connects us all

March 2016.

LEETE'S ISLAND BOOKS, SEDGWICK, MAINE

Library of Congress Number: 201591994
ISBN 978-0-918172-57-0 (cloth)
ISBN 978-0-918172-56-3 (paper)
Copyright © 2015 by Robert Neill III
Leete's Island Books, Box 1, Sedgwick, Maine 04676
First Edition
www.leetesisland.com
Publication of The Once and Future Ocean is made
possible in part by the generous support of the
J. Aron Charitable Foundation, Inc.

For all Citizens of the Ocean, Worldwide

Water remains a chaos until

a creative story interprets its

seeming equivocation as being

the quivering ambiguity of life.

— IVAN ILLICH

CONTENTS

Contents

ACKNOWLEDGMENTS

If every book is a progress of accidents and influences, then this one began on a miserable day in Cambridge, Massachusetts, when I ducked into a used book store to escape the sleet and rain. I found there, in the $1 bin, a copy of *The Ocean, Our Future*, published by Oxford University Press, the final report of the 1998 Independent World Commission on the Future of the Oceans, chaired by Mario Soares, the former President of Portugal. While that year was the United Nations International Year of the Ocean, the Commission was not a function of that body, deliberately independent lest it be influenced by whatever was the official UN policy, if any, for the future of the oceans.

The Report remains, in my view, the single, most prescient and thoughtful set of observations and recommendations yet presented for global consideration of what has become an even more pressing challenge in the intervening years. There have been subsequent such programs, one as recently as 2015, but none have been as clear-minded and considered regarding what is possible, what is necessary, and what specifically can be done to engage the public in response to the inevitable contribution to be made by the ocean to the future of human survival. Among the penultimate Commission recommendations was the creation of an Internet-based place of exchange of information and educational services about the ocean defined as "an integrated, global, social system." Reading this small book, with the storm outside and the future before me, I knew my life had changed, and the World Ocean Observatory was born.

President Soares deserves a second acknowledgment, for that very same year he assembled and chaired the Committee for the World Water Contract, a similar independent commission that defined and declared water access and sustainability as "a source of life" and "an inalienable individual and collective right" essential for the health and welfare of all mankind. What an astonishing achievement for a statesman, to convene the best and the brightest to think independently and creatively about conservation of the most valuable element of Earth—water, in all its circles and cycles of conveyance worldwide, as the natural source and community resource upon which we all depend. Few have made such an important contribution to the modern civil conversation; when I met him in Malta some years ago, I confess I blurted out my gratitude with tears in my eyes for such important work that has gone mostly unappreciated.

I needed to perform due diligence, to see if this was an idea already claimed or intellectually useless, and I went in search of counsel from ocean leaders, among them Patricio Bernal, a member of the Independent Commission and then Secretary of the UN Intergovernmental Oceanographic Commission; Dr. Robert Gagosian, then President of the Woods Hole Oceanographic Institution; and Julie Packard, founder and Director, then as now, of the Monterey Bay Aquarium—all three recognized for their ocean accomplishments and well-versed in the world of ocean research, policy, and politics. To my dismay, all three endorsed the potential value of the project and encouraged me to move forward, encouragement without which I might not have persevered and for which I am grateful.

Sadly, this bright idea did not find favor with the leadership of the South Street Seaport Museum in New York where I proposed to integrate it into the exhibit and educational programs of a maritime museum devoted to the very historical themes the Observatory would address in their present and future iterations. The idea needed a new home, and from 2002 through 2014, the World Ocean Observatory was welcomed and nurtured by Kim

Elliman, President of the Open Space Institute, and thereafter by Alix Thorne, Chair of the Ocean Classroom Foundation. Their support was essential. My thanks.

Funding was of course a necessity, and a small group of individuals stepped up to contribute, some for more than a decade, the basic resources required to keep a small budget adequate to a very big idea. This central financial support was essential as I resolved to remove all barriers, financial and otherwise, that might intervene between the information and those who required it. Those supporters, as individuals or through associated foundations, include Charles Swenson, Ed and Pamela Taft, Alix Thorne, Daniel K. Thorne, Peter Gates, Peter Davidson, Rebecca Clapp, and Peter Aron. Indeed, the J. Aron Charitable Foundation has provided a generous subvention for the publication of this book. My gratitude for their constancy and trust is profound.

The work of the World Ocean Observatory is as varied, relentless, and volatile as the ocean itself. My colleague and sole co-worker, Trisha Badger, W2O Managing Director, has made the intricacies of the new technologies simple and effective, the capacity to expand and innovate seemingly without limit, and the quality of the work time a joy. I simply have never worked alongside anyone so skillful, flexible, imaginative, and fun as Trish. It is a privilege.

There is a further wonderful group to thank, those who have contributed so professionally to the making of this publication in all its phases and formats: Karen Davidson, dear friend and elegant graphic designer; Jane Crosen, close reader and copy-editor extraordinaire; Casey Neill, in-house reader, official W2O troubadour, and author's career counselor; Libby Chamberlain, first reader and argument organizer; Krisanne Baker and Michele P. Mannion, diligent reference checkers; Matt Murphy and all the staff and volunteers at WERU Community Radio, Blue Hill, Maine, where World Ocean Radio, for which much of this manuscript was written, found its home; the many helpful staff and sales team at Independent Publishers Group who have placed Leete's Island Books where and how they best can be for more than 30 years; and the patient and experienced client representatives at R.R. Donnelly who are as interested in the quality of the short run as they are in the quantity of the long. All errors and omissions are, of course, my own.

Finally, there is my ultimate friend, advisor, partner, and captain, Mary Barnes, whose support and love, continuously taxed, are seemingly without end.

These are the acknowledged perpetrators of accident and influence who have brought these ideas to light. To what purpose? You, the *Citizens of the Ocean* to whom this book is dedicated, are the perpetrators to come, to take what is provocative and possible from among these thoughts and to put them to meaningful use for yourselves, families, friends, and strangers worldwide who will inevitably come to the ocean for the full spectrum of its beneficence, who will care for it and give back to it, plan a new world around it, and sustain it for generations to come.

The sea connects all things.

Peter Neill
Sedgwick, Maine
January 2016

FOREWORD

Paul Andrew Mayewski
Explorer, Glaciologist, Climate Scientist
Director and Distinguished Professor
of the Climate Change Institute,
University of Maine

It was not that many years ago that we thought, as a collective society, that the environment was something to conquer and that it was literally timeless, marked only by occasional slow transitions from cold, harsh glacial to warm, mild interglacial climates. We thought that our current interglacial (approximately the last 11,500 years) was not only mild, but also a climatically quiescent period. After all, civilization has emerged and advanced in this mild era, yielding widespread agriculture, the construction of sophisticated centers of civilization, and the marvels of technology. We saw the environment as an endless resource from which and into which we could march, despite understanding of the natural balance that maintains the environment, and despite understanding its weaknesses, the role we play in its ecosystem, and its capacity for absorbing our involvement.

Within the last two decades we have learned that the environment is not timeless; that it does have limits that, if exceeded, have consequences; that past civilizations have disappeared during the relatively mild climate of the last 11,500 years from even small changes in the timing, frequency, and magnitude of the atmospheric circulation systems that deliver moisture, heat, and pollutants; that even small changes in temperature can lead to dramatic rearrangements in sea ice extent, extremes in heat, cold, drought, and flood; and that humans and the ecosystem cannot tolerate changes in the naturally based levels of air and water quality that mandate our health and evolution.

In the last few decades we have experienced environmental

wake-up calls as we have become aware of the risks to health, life, and our economy in the form of acidification, lead, radioactivity, and other toxic substances, and a world that is not gradually warming, but is instead experiencing abrupt changes—like the 8-degree-Fahrenheit rise in annual average temperature of the eastern Arctic in barely five recent years, in addition to drought and forest fires in California and Australia, and drought-initiated unrest in the Middle East and much of Africa. The humanitarian, geopolitical, and economic consequences are immense, and the onset of much of the climate change underpinning these consequences has been massive and abrupt.

While all of this clearly forewarns of further gloom and doom, we are in the best position ever to address the future. We know more about the environment than ever before. Perhaps most importantly, we know that the environment can change abruptly, in less than a few years, and remain in a new state for many decades to follow. This is critically important, because without this knowledge we would be proverbial sitting ducks, assuming nothing would ever change. We know that we have it in our power to mitigate change that we have imposed. The most encouraging examples include legislation by many nations addressing acid rain and reduction in the use of chlorofluorocarbons, lead, and some other toxic substances; remarkable attempts at habitat preservation; and the awareness and attempts to legislate reduction in the rise of greenhouse gases that have set us on a course into elevated temperatures unsurpassed in hundreds of thousands and millions of years. Integral to all of our understanding and attempts at mitigation and adaptation is the perspective we now have of where our environment and in particular climate have ranged over tens to hundreds of thousands of years. The resulting double-edged-sword result is that we now know that we live in an era of world climate that is unique in Earth's history, a period of our own making super-imposed upon but rapidly altering natural climate variability, where extremes in weather are projected to cause greater and greater stress amidst a rising ocean that will cause civilizations to migrate or disappear, and shifts in water availability that will sadly result in massive migration in both underdeveloped and developed regions.

We now understand our climate dilemma: it is not a political debate, it is a scientific fact. We have wasted too much time at too many levels debating scientific facts that the vast majority of climate scientists have proven many times over. We must move forward with plausible scenario planning that invokes the strong potential for abrupt climate change. We are already seeing amazing advances in areas essential not only to our adaptation to emerging climate change, but also to the vision of a world that is more efficient, cleaner, and offers enhanced quality of life in the form of transformational advances in renewable energy, water management, food resources, and much more. But we need many more innovative advances and the stimuli to continue.

We need one more critical component—a new philosophy

based on a new value system to guide us toward and through the complexities of mitigation, adaptation, opportunity, entrepreneur-ship, and the quality of life that humans and the ecosystem require to maintain not just a viable condition, but a condition that will be stressed even more from increasing population.

Enter Peter Neill and *The Once and Future Ocean*. In the eloquent style of a professional journalist, Peter offers an amazing view of the necessity of and the basis for *a new hydraulic society* where water replaces oil as our world currency.

As the book opens, Peter Neill provides us with a paradigm for the ocean that is not very commonly considered in popular literature—that the ocean extends from mountaintop to sea bottom—and as a consequence the ocean is that great filter through which all of water passes. The ocean holds our greatest percentage of the world's protein reserves, acts as a major sink for our pollution, and offers life for a vast array of known and unknown creatures, plus potential for new cures to human and ecosystem diseases.

The Once and Future Ocean is not just a pleasure to read, it is a potentially critical stepping-stone in our hoped-for passage through the climate-stressed future we have now entered. In the spirit of Rachel Carson's *Silent Spring,* Peter Neill opens our eyes. He already has more than one million followers spread worldwide through the World Ocean Observatory (W2O) website, so his concept of "a new hydraulic society" has great potential in a world looking for solutions to the major security risks posed by climate change as we enter the age of climate change decision where the stakes are as high as they can get. He offers us a very basic premise from which we can locally and globally move forward:

> *If we can understand the peculiarities of our plumbing and habits at home, then we can fix them. The same holds true for a municipal water system. And the same holds true for a watershed. And the same holds true for the ocean, the greatest water system on Earth. Understanding the problem allows us to invent a solution. If we can understand how our patterns of water use and profligate waste are connected, perhaps we can look to solutions evident and possible through planning with (and valuing) water.*

After all, don't we all, rich and poor, have the right to clean air and clean water? If there aren't enough assurances in place, then don't we need more to protect the very essence of our lives (water) and that of the ecosystem that surrounds us? The answer rests in giving clean air and clean water as much value in our society as we have given oil. In fact, much more value, since we can live with less oil, but we cannot live with less water and we cannot exist, much less thrive, by polluting the nexus of all of our fresh drinking water—the ocean. The solution, to paraphrase Peter Neill, is in fact systematic use of *watermarks*—a holistic and pervading approach to the balance of water use by all entities.

I. Introduction

THE SEA AROUND US

I n 1951—more than half a century ago—Rachael Carson published *The Sea Around Us*, a classic compendium of the ocean's history, its workings, and its central role in the health of our world and those who live in it. The book is short, concise, informative, and eloquent. It is not a polemic, although its reputation as a classic of environmental literature might suggest that purpose. The text clearly struck a chord, won the National Book Award, has progressed through multiple reprintings, and remains a seminal work, indeed the impetus for subsequent awareness, expanded ocean research, and greater public interest and engagement in the surrounding ocean.[1]

Carson worked at John Hopkins University and the Marine Biological Institute at Woods Hole, Massachusetts, and went on to serve as marine biologist at the US Fish and Wildlife Service and to write additional books to include *Under the Sea Wind, The Edge of the Sea*, and of course, *Silent Spring*, that *was* a polemic and sounded the alarm over the harmful effect of chemical pesticides in agriculture.

Carson, and subsequently Jacques Cousteau, brought the ocean into our classrooms and living rooms. Cousteau's popular, long-running television series took us into the ocean, under the sea, to explore the underwater topography, the brilliance of coral reefs and biodiversity, and the physical workings of marine systems—tides, winds and currents, vast cycles of underwater movement and exchange, earthquake and tectonic shifts, and the life cycles of creatures heretofore beyond our imagination. Carson and Cousteau introduced us to the rewards and dangers of ocean observation and exploration, and their influence shaped more than one generation to become environmental scientists, marine biologists, oceanographers, and conservationists.

This legacy has driven decades of new investigation. New research institutions and programs have been founded in the United States and around the world. Governments have created and funded agencies and projects that have extended our observations by expedition, satellite, and arrays of drifting, fixed, and submerged monitors—a powerful network for the assemblage of data, experiment, and reports that have established an informed baseline of ocean conditions against which future study can be compared. Carson and Cousteau inspired an exponential increase in ocean observation and set in motion the first efforts to transform that information into conservation action.

The period that followed added the ocean to the scrutiny and mission of land-focused conservation groups—World Wildlife Fund, The Nature Conservancy, and the Natural Resources Defense Council—as well as motivated the creation of new organizations such as Conservation International, Oceana, The Ocean Conservancy, and Mission Blue that both extended their advocacy and programs worldwide and applied their resources more directly to ocean issues. Their work, and that by numerous other global organizations and government initiatives, has raised ocean knowledge, consciousness, and planning to its highest level.

But is it enough? Recently, I listened to a radio interview

with a well-known and very well-informed ocean advocate and philanthropist who was describing the world ocean crisis in its many forms. He painted a dour picture indeed. It was a call-in show, and so I dialed in with the question, "Now that we know the problem, what do you suggest we do about it?" He indicated that that was the essential question, and then proceeded to give a very disappointing answer—don't use plastic bags, don't eat fish, don't drive your car, hope for the best! With all due respect, that's just not good enough.

If the second phase of the Carson/Cousteau legacy was observation and information that has defined the questions, then the next phase must be invention: the definition of new ideas and application of different answers. We are all seeking. I hear it again and again, at ocean conferences, in speeches and books by ocean experts: presentation of the overwhelming problem followed by silence, not solutions. It is as if we are sailing along the edge of an abyss; we have the skill perhaps to keep going, to extend our way for a time, until we fall off into darkness, or we can apply that skill to our ship and change course, away in a new direction. It is dangerous and uncertain, but I submit that we have no choice but to set forth.

II. Where to Begin

The Exhausted Land We Live In

To understand the crises affecting the world ocean, we must first understand the condition of the land around us. For decades, alarms have been sounded to alert us to the exhaustion of the Earth. We have experienced a continuing increase in population; in demand for energy, food, and fresh water; and in the pollutants derived from our physical, chemical, and biological responses to those requirements. We have come to expect an annual raise, ever increasing quality of life, and sustained returns on our investments unrealizable without undisciplined personal credit, under-collateralized debt, and unregulated consumption of natural and human resources. Like any *ponzi* scheme, we have borrowed against assets once tangible, now increasingly limited, even ephemeral, and can no longer rationalize, postpone, or deny the consequences.

For me, pollution is excess: too much chocolate, too much alcohol, too much fertilizer, too many chemicals, too much waste, too much unregulated gain indifferent to the needs of an ever-growing community. That we have become divided over money, land, resources, and power, locally, regionally, nationally, and internationally, by disputes over all of these is surely no surprise.

We can measure that excess now: in diminished wells and

corrupted waterways, in the acidified air, in the price of fuel, in the exploitation of labor, and in the failed economic and social aspirations now impacting the entire world.

But what about the ocean? I submit that the ocean begins at the mountaintop, and descends to the abyssal plain; that is, everything that occurs on land—be it development, manufacturing, agriculture, or financial enterprise—descends to the sea. It passes in, on, and above the earth in fluid streams of decision, action, and transaction, behaviors that reveal our system of values, be they economic, personal, social, political, or moral.

Thus, specifically, those behaviors impact the downstream, be it effluents that generate red tides along the beaches, or nitrate runoff that atrophies and suffocates life on the ocean floor, or emissions that rise and fall into the sea to increase the acidity to modify the food chains and to disrupt the breeding and survival of marine plants and animals upon which the system depends. We often think of the ocean as a place apart, a maritime wilderness, infinitely self-healing and immune to our polluting excesses. But that is not so. Just as we know the situation on land, we now know through observation, research, and experience that the ocean is also threatened by exhaustion: myriad organic pollutants, declining species, poisoned wildlife, excavated mangroves, developed wetlands, dead coral, and more. We know that the glaciers are melting at accelerated rates; we know that extreme weather is damaging our coasts in ways unforeseen by our designers and builders. We know that coastal communities continue to grow into urban centers making exponential demands on supply of food, water, and energy. We know that many of those settlements have been devastated by tsunami, hurricane, typhoon, and shoreline inundation that has cost millions and displaced thousands of environmental refugees with no place to go.

To understand the crises affecting the world ocean, we must accept, not deny, these facts, and use this knowledge to mitigate and adapt short-term to these challenges. But long-term, the problem is more demanding, and may require very different answers to the very difficult questions we face.

On what new premise will we base this response?

Moral Pollution

When asked to define pollution, I usually reply "excess," advocating that not all things are polluting in or of themselves, but become so in excessive quantities—thus natural sugar is a body health requirement, but too much sugar contributes to excessive weight gain, debilitating diabetes, and other unhealthy outcomes that accelerate disease and death. Too much chocolate, too much untreated waste, too much pesticide, too many emissions, too much acid in the air and sea, too much money—all these things, in the extreme, compromise stability, security, and survival.

Is there such a thing as moral pollution—an excess of principle or ideology that can have similar spiritual or social effect? For example, if one believes in a certain religious concept to the exclusion of all others, can this fervor not corrupt moral balance and lead to extreme acts of suicidal terrorism that go against, indeed inhumanely disrupt, a society prepared to acknowledge, respect, and integrate different religious views and practices as part of societal norms, a successfully integrated community, and accepted tenets of civilization? We may ask this question every day in response to events around us.

In the context of the ocean, indeed of our relationship to the natural world in general, the operative extreme relates, in my view, to greed and its associated derivatives, corruption and hypocrisy. If greed is the rapacious accumulation of wealth regardless of consequence, then we have examples of it everywhere: in the behavior of some, certainly not all, governments, politicians, corporations, entrepreneurs, and individual confidence schemes that dilute, corrode, exploit, and contravene all attempts to modulate the unrestrained making of money and to exempt this conduct from regulatory structures designed to protect the rest of us from theft, fraud, bankruptcy, and other forms of financial and societal compromise.

The corporation is one place to look for such phenomena. Perhaps you recall the classic declaration of the fictional investment banker, Gordon Gecko, from the film *Wall Street*, that "Greed is Good!" The statement was extreme, but honest. Gecko did not care at all for any consequence of investment in corporate behaviors other than short-term return. Just an exaggeration of fiction? Well, not really, as we so often hear chief executives of corporations publicly justifying extreme strategies in terms of maximum return to shareholders, measured in ever-decreasing intervals that theoretically influence stock price and, coincidentally, the CEO's performance bonus from year to year. That the strategy might lessen mid- or long-term impact on the sustainability of the company and its investment value over time seems irrelevant. This attitude explains the ever-increasing articulation of opposing proposals in annual meetings, and shareholder-initiated actions to challenge such behaviors, report profits differently, or modify or curtail certain technologies, products, market opportunities, accounting practices, lobbying activities, executive evaluation and pay, and other strategies that determine what the proposers see as excessive, unnecessary consequence, indeed as poison that pollutes both the landscape and the community.

Corruption and hypocrisy are inevitable by-products of this

way of doing business. Millions are spent to influence politicians to provide government subsidies, tax loopholes, statutory exemptions, regulatory exception, and other, almost invisible, but very profitable modifications that exclusively benefit the funders. Given the role corporations now play in political campaigns, political action committees, business associations, lobbyist firms, and special-interest organizations, we can explain the steady stream of ethical reprimands, indictments, convictions, and precipitous decisions not to stand for re-election that are a result of this corrupting political process.

The concurrent hypocrisy is frequently stunning, not just in the self-justifying statements of politicians caught in their contradictions, but also revealed in the actions of the contributing executives themselves. A most egregious example concerns Rex Tillerson, CEO of ExxonMobil, one the largest and most profitable corporations on Earth. At $40 million per year he is one of the most highly paid executives in the world, one of the most articulate defenders of consumption-driven energy policy, one of the largest corporate beneficiaries of US Government subsidy, one of the most vociferous deniers of climate change and the negative impact of automobile emissions and energy production facilities on air and water quality, and one of the most fervid proponents of hydraulic fracking for natural gas. ExxonMobil has aggressively promoted the manageable risk of the fracking process in the face of documented impact on fresh water supply, the surrounding, typically agricultural community, the regional landscape, along with the introduction of contaminates and potential health hazards into aquifers, groundwater, and the further impact of leaked polluted water entering the watershed to poison streams, rivers, and the ocean. Recently, according to the *Wall Street Journal*, Mr. Tillerson joined a lawsuit against another energy company setting up a 160-foot water tower to support a fracking operation on land adjacent to his private $5 million Wyoming horse farm, as a plaintiff citing increased noise, heavy truck traffic, and other negative impacts on his property values.[2] What does this say to the citizens of the places where his zealous corporate enterprise has disrupted *their* lives, depleted *their* spirit, ravaged *their* landscape, and polluted *their* land and water without apology or concern? This is moral pollution at its most egregious, for which there is no redemption.

The Sea Connects All Things

For many, the ocean is a place apart, a vast wilderness extending beyond our physical and psychological horizons, at once alien and indifferent, fascinating and compelling, and about which we know very little. But consider these facts: the ocean covers 71 percent of the Earth's surface; the ocean is a central element in the recycling and purification of fresh water; the ocean provides 40 percent of the world's protein, especially in developing nations; more than 200 million people worldwide are dependent on the ocean for their livelihood; 65 percent of the world's population lives within 100 miles of an ocean coast.

The reality is that the ocean is essential to human survival, a primary source of food, water, climate, and community—immediate, universal, and undeniable. In short, the ocean is the determinant ecology in which we live—the sea connects all things. If, indeed, all life is dependent on the ocean, then this understanding calls for its new definition as:

- an interconnected, global ecosystem that integrates natural process, habitat, and species with human intervention and impact;

- a comprehensive social system that integrates human needs and actions; and

- a complex political system that connects all peoples world-wide through economic interests, cultural traditions, and cooperative governance.

Thus, when we envision the ocean as a wilderness, we are ignoring the reality of the ocean as a domesticated place where humans have left their mark throughout history by exploration and exploitation, immigration and trade, and the exchange of custom and culture. To look today from a satellite, one can see that the ocean is marked constantly by the tracks of ships, the tools of globalization through marine transport as old as the ancient Chinese in the Pacific, the Phoenicians in the Mediterranean, and the Vikings in the Atlantic.

What has changed over time, however, is the impact of human population growth whereby the use of the ocean has increased exponentially so that today the ocean evinces a shift from abundance to scarcity and from accommodation to conflict.

This is well exemplified by the crisis in fisheries. Research has documented the collapse of certain species such as cod that once formed the staple diet of much of North America and Europe[3], a result of a complex of causes to include unrestricted catch, the advent of new, efficient gear and technology, and the unwillingness of fishers, both artisanal and industrial, to work cooperatively toward a sustainable harvest. This problem was further compounded by the difficulty of regulation, a resultant lack of jurisdiction outside of national economic zones, the inability to monitor or enforce quotas, and the failure of governance to address the challenge.

There are many other examples. What underlies them all,

however, is the understanding that just as there are social causes to these problems, there must also be social solutions. We can complain and accuse and litigate, much as we do for similar behavior on land, but the true solution lies with our determination to deal with both the cause and effect of our need to domesticate Nature—whether terrestrial or marine—for human use, and to engage in the dialogue and change required to conserve and sustain all natural resources for the benefit of all mankind.

I sign all my email messages with the phrase: *the sea connects all things*. What interests me is that the responses don't necessarily indicate agreement or understanding of what is a powerful, certain declaration. What does the sentence actually mean? Is it so obvious that it does not merit reaction? Or is it so profound that it defies understanding? Of course, it is both—obvious *and* profound. Is that a contradiction, a paradox? Or is that reality?

Let's take the sentence apart.

The sea—easy enough at first glance—but if you think that the sea is confined only to a stretch of beach and watery horizon, if you think that the sea is only a regional body, if you think that the sea is only a seventh of the world inventory, then you have not fully comprehended the completeness of the meaning. The sea is all these combined, 71 percent of the Earth's surface, the one ocean on which the continents and islands float, the substance that surrounds and supports the nations, in turn the terrestrial platforms on which we build human institutions.

Connects—also straightforward in the dictionary:
1. To bind or fasten together.
2. To establish communications between.
3. To cause to be associated.
4. To associate mentally or emotionally.
5. To join or unite.

These variant definitions can be easily seen to have physical and psychological, social and political connotation. Used in our sentence, the verb declares without equivocation a unifying action, a transitive link between parts conjoined. It is not about inequality or separation at all, but rather about the absolute synergy between places, peoples, actions, and ideas.

All things completes the equation. *All things* includes that absolute synergy in all its variety and time, all natural phenomena and human endeavor as we know it. Is it legitimate to say so? I think yes, in that the sea has always been *there* since the beginning, as asserted in the evolutionary record, historical accounts, social actions, myths, and spiritual beliefs. *All things* means every thing.

If you are persuaded by this parsing, then you will agree with the obvious and profound understanding of the ocean as the determining system that informs every aspect of our living—from the water we drink and bathe in, to the food and land we cultivate and live on, to the financial and intellectual exchange between us, to the values we apply to live together—sometimes successfully, sometimes not.

What we should fear then is the *disconnection* between the ocean and our lives. And that is exactly what we are facing today. Unthinkingly, purposefully, we are disconnecting ourselves through deliberate actions that interrupt the natural cycles of water and weather, deprive us of protein, deconstruct the natural barriers that protect us, and divert and exhaust our resources and energies from the essential requirements for survival in our changing time and place.

This matters. This behavior is ignorant and foolish. Why do we choose this path when it is so obviously and profoundly contradictory and paradoxical? We are not living in reality; if so, we would not enable delusion. We are not being practical; if so, we would assure that our needs would be sustained for generations. We are not being smart; if so, we would apply our intelligence to long-term means over short-term ends. We are not even thinking about ourselves and the ones we love; if so, we would know that our own future is at risk if we do not change our behavior.

The sea connects all things. It is a very simple sentence. Think about it. Change in our lives typically follows a sudden understanding, a clear realization that one thing is different from another, better than another, that transforms our thoughts and liberates our actions. Dare I ask again? Think about it. If you can accept this first premise, then let the complicated work begin.

What then is the challenge?

There is no dearth of information about the present state of the ocean—the plight of marine species of all sorts, the degradation of water quality worldwide, the measurable changes in sea level, temperature, and pH, and the inability of policy-makers, regulators, and political leaders to agree or unite around national or regional governance in response. The headlines are continuous; the demonstrative events depressingly sequential; the evidence of failed response to date only partially offset by a few isolated, momentarily encouraging events. The public and private organizations focused on ocean issues seem to have become paralyzed by the opposition and denial, and intimidated by the special interest invested in no change. They pursue formulaic responses that may attack one problem, but leave the rest, directly and intricately connected, to the side, as if one swallow ought to be enough to empty an entire glass.

My despair and cynicism about the outcomes of the climate talks in Copenhagen, Mexico City, Durban, Rio, and Paris are evidence of this failure. The designations of hundreds of thousands of acres of open ocean as marine protected areas, as encouraging as they may be, are nonetheless marginal in that they do little more than symbolize our concerns, in an area far, far away, where despite such declarations and treaties, illegal fishing still occurs, vast gyres of consumption debris still accumulates, and everywhere back home the public still goes about the business of polluting land and sea as usual.

The challenge, then, is to change our attitudes and behaviors about the ocean through the following fundamental realizations:

- There is one integrated world ocean that unites rather than separates the land, the nations, and the civilizing masses.

- The land and the sea are directly connected and synergistic—naturally, socially, and politically.

- The crisis, whether we admit it or not, is that the land is exhausted by consumption, and the sea is not far behind.

- The solution is not to sustain systems inadequate to the conditions, the growing population, and the political confusion, but rather to apply new systems organized around alternative attitudes and values, new strategies for living, and revolutionary behaviors based on the changing natural phenomena we have created.

- We must invent our way out. The solution to be proposed here is to build *a new hydraulic society* based on water, its cycles, its essential value, and its meaning for change.

And so here, with these premises in mind, I am resolved to formulate a new, rearticulated presentation on the status of the world ocean: how we should understand it; what new tools we must use to respond to its changing conditions; and what specific new strategies and actions must be applied to progress successfully away from the status quo toward a new ocean ethic and revolutionary set of behaviors.

A Self-Healing Place

We have long perceived the ocean as a self-healing place. Fair enough, given for centuries its implacable capacity to receive and assimilate the detritus of our living ashore. We have deposited into it our waste of every kind, in growing, exponential volume. We have not hesitated, deliberately or accidentally, to discard our sewage, garbage, toxic manufacturing by-product, chemical effluent, lost ships, even our dead. It was not so long ago that obscure pipes from somewhere protruded into the sea to release foul, inexplicable streams of poison, and we gave this, if we were even aware, no second thought. Nor did we consider that the towers of our power plants or the tailpipes of our cars might release invisible emissions into the air that would not waft innocently above the land, but rather dissolve into water as acid concentrated enough to change the basic pH of streams and lakes, even the ocean itself, to interrupt the food chain and kill every living thing therein.

What difference could it make? The ocean is so vast. How could these incremental bits and pieces of human activity ever add up to such an outcome? And, even if so, what ultimate effect could be imagined that would dissuade us from the benefits of the industrial revolution, technological advancement, and improved quality of life? As with the raw materials we extracted from the land for this extraordinary human progress, how could the ocean, so enormous in its extent, ever be finite or taxed to its limit?

Our assumption was that Nature existed only to meet our needs. We were to apply our imagination and energy to the transformation of natural resources into energy, implements, systems, and wealth. In sum, to feed, shelter, and improve our lives in an ever-increasing radius of expectation and well-being.

These resources were perceived as infinitely available for us to consume, at first for our basic needs, then for our desires, and now ultimately for our entertainment. There was no envisioned limit to fuel, water, or the productivity of the land and sea, and so why not take whatever, forever, without hesitation?

To be sure, these are not observations or alarms newly made or sounded by me. We have heard these laments for decades, and we have attempted to deal with some of the effects with regulatory legislation to protect clean air, clean water, and coastal wetlands. Nonetheless, we have proudly dammed and relocated rivers from their natural flow, decapitated mountaintops to be screened, transported, and burned—all to sustain a voracious appetite for energy, consumption to feed consumption, a cultural gluttony that has gone mostly unlimited. Yes, now even those once well-meaning attempts to limit the demand in the name of conservation and public health are going by the political wayside as a result of consequently diminished supply, increased cost, and the corporate influence of those who feed on the feeding.

The Point of No Return

Every voyage reaches that place where the distance to the new is shorter than the return to the safety and comfort of the old—the point of no return. Literally, on a ship, it is a function of exhausted supply of food, water, and human energy. Turning back represents failure of resolve and the impossibility of destination. Sailing on is fraught with peril—those sea monsters drawn by sailing captains in the margins of their charts on which safe ports and known hazards beyond may not all be marked.

I submit that we are at that point now, perhaps beyond. If, for example, we were to halt all CO_2 and greenhouse gas emissions into the atmosphere today, it would take half a century for the acid base in seawater to return to historical norm. It would take decades for dead forests, coastal areas, and coral reefs to regenerate to their former state. If we were to cease all fishing for cod, it would take years for those fish to return to their prior bounty. In some instances, it is already too late, those species having passed into extinction.

Can I prove this? Well, publicized observation, research, and experience would argue for it as fact. Scientists have been measuring the changing pH of the ocean for some time now, as well as the consequences on marine life worldwide. Coral reef experts indicate that some 10 percent to 30 percent of the world inventory has been killed or critically corrupted by global warming, dynamite fishing, and development.[4] And indeed, we have stopped fishing for cod, either by moratorium or simply because the supply is just not there. How much more evidence will be needed, example-by-example, until we are forced to admit that the time for decision has come?

Am I alone in this conviction? Well, no, not at all. This awareness can be found in classrooms, laboratories, policy institutes, nonprofits, and many government agencies around the world where national ocean policies addressing these problems are put forward, sometimes legislated, sometimes implemented, not always enforced. To continue our ship analogy, these are all strong members of the crew, skilled in many aspects of sailing, but not in charge, and subject to the decision-makers, the officers, and, yes, the owners, whose objectives may be very different, indeed indifferent, to the knowledge, safety, health, or wealth of those on deck or aloft.

Would it not be far better if the captains and owners came on to an alternative course by themselves? Would it not be more effective if they could realize that there are still places to be discovered, and even fortunes earned, by a different set of premises or a better course of action? It does not seem likely. The captain's word is law. Mutiny is not an attractive option.

Analogy aside, the world environment today is victim to those fixed premises of the past and to the laws devised to uphold them. The owners, the captains of industry, and the politicians who continue to serve them will not change course unless they have to. Witness the continuing subsidy and expansion of the oil and coal industry, the resistance to comparable support for alternative technology, the protectionist fears when other countries act or innovate against the status quo, and, finally, tragically, the armed conflict that has often within it an unarticulated justification for the protection of national interest as the most interested so define.

Nonetheless, the environmental community has been hard at work to define an alternative concept beyond the point of no return. It's called "sustainability," and over the past 10 years or so, the world policy "crew" has cleaved to this idea as a collective framework for action. In the United Nations, and in the worldwide policy *apparat*, sustainability has become the accepted, over-riding new principle around which to organize the next stage of the journey, the future planning and strategies for responding to critical challenges to land and sea.

Sustainability

Sustainability, then, is the principle we hear most often in discussions of how to deal progressively with the social and economic challenges resulting from the world's radical population growth, global economy, and voracious appetite for nonrenewable natural resources to meet those needs over time. The most common usage derives from the 1987 United Nations *Brutland Commission*

Report that defined sustainable development as that "which meets the needs of the present without compromising the ability of future generations to meet their own needs."[5] From this has emerged an industry of academic proposals, new standards and accreditations, non-governmental organizations and policy institutes devoted to full amplification of the concept in the form of environmental management, financial analyses, planning processes, and the inclusion of poverty alleviation, social justice, human rights, and cultural traditions as factors also essential to the response. In some cases, sustainability may be expressed by a formula relating population, affluence, and technology as measurable elements of an equation, or to a newly inclusive accounting system, or to a calculation of previously ignored factors reduced to an index; in others, it seems more like an idealistic, unobtainable philosophical concept that at least offers hope, however illusionary and illusive.

From the specific perspective of the ocean, sustainability as a doctrine may at first seem beyond the more narrow and obvious applications regarding fisheries and sustainable seafood: species protection, regional quotas, gear restrictions, and regulated market forces; or aquaculture, a means to increase alternative supply against insatiable demand; or coastal management and marine protected areas, schemes to protect inshore artisanal fishing, coral reefs, seed ground, and sheltering habitat against extreme weather, sea level rise, and the predations of resort and high-rise developers.

But if you step back and take the broadest ecosystem view, the ocean becomes an enormous contributor to any new strategy of resilience, maintenance, and enhancement of global biodiversity and capacity, essential to the life-support system of the Earth from the beginning, but ever so much more needed now. As we continue to deplete underground aquifers, to increase irrigated land, to disrupt and pollute streams and rivers, the ocean becomes even more valuable as a primary component of the *world water cycle*, a necessary circulation, filtration, and purification system, and an inevitable source of desalinated drinking water to meet future global demand. As the ocean is essential to our need for fresh water, as water security and food security are linked, as food security and the alleviation of poverty are linked, and as alleviation of poverty is key to civilization, justice, and peace, the ocean simply cannot go the way of the earth, be brutalized, ignored, taken for granted, or abandoned.

The ocean is the true commons, a vast reservoir of natural capital without which the mechanics of the Earth will break down. There is much talk of a *green economy*, a shift away from relentless growth fueled by forests, minerals, and fossil fuels—resources stolen from the past and the future—toward renewable energy, pricing that incorporates the true value of ecosystem services, and development based not on consumption but rather on utility and quality of life.[6] All those new ideas for changed behavior on land are welcome and must be supported. But the green economy will not succeed without the *blue economy*: the ocean as a redeeming source of renewable protein, energy, fresh water, and biodiversity with unimagined implication for the future of human survival.[7]

The blue economy has a chance to succeed because the ocean is open and free. No one owns it, no one can fence it, no one can master it, no matter how hard they try. To be sure, governments will still assert their exclusive economic rights along their coasts, corporations will still seek to impose their extraction values offshore, but it will not be enough; it will only postpone the inevitable and prolong the decline. When we learn to see the ocean as integral to the land, when we design physical places, make financial and social decisions, and take political action based on that symbiosis, then we may well have achieved the means by which to build a world that is truly sustainable.

Globalization

Globalization, like sustainability, is one of those contemporary terms that can define many, sometimes different explanations, policies, and actions. The more these words get used, the larger or more diffuse their inclusive meanings. At a recent maritime heritage meeting, a Swedish historian was discussing his definition of globalization, and asked the audience if we felt that this was only a modern phenomenon, not a function of history. A Dutch respondent stated didactically and emphatically no, it was not historical, but was instead a modern invention of technology and political circumstance. He was so certain.

But is he correct? It seems to me that globalization began the first time any intrepid sailor left the security of land for an unknown ocean destination—Phoenician, Viking, Polynesian, Asian, no matter who, where, or when the reality of departure defined the expectation of arrival, even if there were only stars to guide the way. If the Phoenicians initiated what became ship-borne trade routes, if the Vikings came ashore at L'Anse aux Meadows in the Americas, they and their global counterparts began the system of connection that now binds the continents and nations in a net of exchange and financial transaction that we call "globalization."

Are there other maritime tipping points that we can cite to counter our assertive Dutchman? Let's start with the very familiar steam engine, with its early application on the water and its ensuing revolution of ship technology and construction that exploited existing connection radically and transformed global capacity for types of products and volumes transported. Its invention underlies the dramatic expansion of immigration the world over, and transformed exploration and naval warfare into a resultant phenomenon called "empire."

A second maritime example is the undersea cable. Many people understand the facility of global communications to be a function of satellites, but in fact it is primarily sustained by yet another network, albeit invisible on the ocean floor, that connects the continents and has developed from early telephone connection to vast data transfer capacity that underlies up-to-the-minute information exchange, market trading, and Internet-based communications such as email and social media.

A third example is the Global Positioning System (GPS) technology, satellite-based but essential to modern marine navigation, location services for trade goods and shipping containers, and real-time recording of ocean data collection, sampling, research experiment, weather prediction, underwater exploration and mapping, and navigation of underwater vehicles be they submarines, research submersibles (manned or remotely operated), or free-swimming drones or robots.

All these ocean-expressed functionalities are definite contributing factors over time to our globalized world. There are certainly other historical examples, just as there are new manifestations to come. What might we imagine for the future?

Here's a surprising thought to consider. Unlike any other place on Earth, a vast portion of the ocean remains outside the limits of national jurisdiction. The 15- to 200-mile territorial extension of proprietary rights that frequently overlap, in the Mediterranean for example, in an impossible scribble of claims on maps and conflicting national policies, cry out for new forms of social communication, consensus agreement, jurisdictional negotiation, and successful tools for governance.

The open ocean may seem less complicated, but as an enormous area, inclusive of a magnitude of political aspirations, natural resource values, and sources of conflict, it remains nonetheless a unique and unresolved component of the globalizing world. Successful adjudication of this situation stands as an essential challenge to equitable resolution of the circumstances, demanding for success significant review and reconsideration of values and strategies different from the conventional approaches which have not even served the alongshore reality well.

We return to terminology—to globalization and sustainability. It does not necessarily follow that globalization is a counter-force to sustainability, even if many might claim that the demanding integration of worldwide need for goods and services lies at the root of the apparently insatiable consumption-based attack on environmental conservation and sustainability on land and sea. But if, as we face the pressure of some final approach for governance of the ocean outside national jurisdiction, if we face this as an opportunity to rectify and define our response to the value of the commons, then we may achieve yet another tipping point whereby maritime enterprise and ocean resources show us the way forward to a viable future. The ocean is our world. With humility and trepidation, let's set out to explore it.

III. Why the Ocean Matters

WHO WE ARE

A Maritime Nation

I have always felt that Americans have no real understanding of our history as a *maritime* nation. The subject is mostly absent from the texts, and the specific maritime histories have been most often enumerations of customs house documents, ship voyages, and the odd naval battle. Only recently has that begun to change as historians from other disciplines have discovered the broad impact and richness of maritime endeavor as a core theme in the American narrative.

Let's take two points of view: internal and external. If you look at the topography of our nation, you see a system of watersheds—great lakes connected to rivers and the sea; streams descending from major mountain systems, east and west; and myriad rivers feeding the Mississippi, a central north–south artery that splits the nation. Those waterways were the paths of early exploration and settlement. Many of our largest inland cities are located on the confluence of navigable rivers. The Erie Canal, an engineering marvel, linked the heartland to East Coast ports and Europe. Lewis and Clark followed the rivers and streams into the west, through the Rockies to the Pacific. Along these waterways passed the grain, cotton, tobacco, and other agricultural products, the iron and steel and coal and timber, and the manufactured goods, distributed internally, to the eastern ports like New York, Boston, Charleston, and Savannah, and around Cape Horn to western ports of San Francisco and Seattle and beyond, as the essence of an emerging American world trade.

The external perspective is also instructive. It reveals trade as more than export—rather, the exchange of goods from Europe and farther east, and, most importantly, the imported return, the arrival of immigrants, refugees from religious tyranny, entre-preneurs, and outlaws, who are our forebears by the thousands. We honor our few remaining indigenous people. But the rest of us came from away, from Ireland, Scotland, and England; from Scandinavia, Germany, and Italy; from Africa; and eventually from all the nations of the world, these diverse ethnicities combining to create the complex nation that we are. Most of these people came free or in chains by ship across oceans, and, today, perhaps by different vessels, they are still coming.

What historians have recognized is that the principal value exchanged by this process was not just the trade goods and financial accountings, but also the ideas and beliefs, the art, the music, and the literature that are the cultural fabric of our moment. We listen to world music and appreciate world art. We are open to multiple religions and spiritual practice. We fuse food traditions, fashion, fads, medical treatments, exercise, sport, and language. We may have new and different portals now, but the process began long ago when the first sailors left shore in search of something beyond their own experience, beyond their limited horizon.

When I look at things now, I wonder where the sailors are. We have become fearful and oppositional and close-minded. We have become complacent within our horizon and hostile to new people and new ideas. We need new leaders to show us the way back to the sea.

Sea Sickness

People often ask me if I am a sailor. I demur, admitting only to owning a boat. I have too much awareness of and respect for real sailors to compare my level of skill. Like many mariners, I get seasick, unless the seas are calm or I am sufficiently infused with mint and ginger. But the susceptibility is always there, the memory of past unpleasant incidents, the anticipation, both physical and psychological, of what is to come, and the thing itself—nauseating, exhausting, humiliating, just plain awful, until it's over and you've found your sea legs again.

Sickness at sea is as old as seafaring itself, sailors subject to wind, sun, heat, cold, dehydration, poor food, and all the rest. We know the tales of scurvy and such. Sometimes when we look more closely, we can sense another disease—that of loneliness, melancholy, depression, the mental illness that can result from extreme physical and psychological circumstance—until it too is over, in the best case with a successful homecoming and revival.

The world ocean is a sick sea. I have never been so definitive before, always the optimist thinking we are not yet there. But the symptoms are no longer deniable: reported spills and leaks, dying reefs, depleted fisheries, hypoxic zones—vast areas so oxygen-deprived that nothing lives. Like mint and ginger, I keep looking for the good news, the growing number of marine protected areas, small victories over the extraction interests, some policy or regulation that draws a line, some triumph by a local coastal community or small island state standing up to protect itself from the sickness.

The thinking once was that the ocean by its vastness would dilute these things. But we are beyond that now, holding on to that homily only as a desperate belief or a cynical justification for permitting the practices that have created the disease itself. What will it take for us to realize that we are the attacking, consuming microbes and that to counter sea sickness we must first heal ourselves?

I read recently the phrase "sea blindness,"[8] referring at some historical moment to public unawareness of the ocean's relevance and relationship to what takes place on land. Yes, there is shipping and trade and warfare, and yes, there is fishing and food production, but true insight and awareness remains dim, clouded by fog on the horizon, or distance from where one lives, or immediacy of these ocean manifestations directly on our daily life. If we can't see it, or feel it, then we can't really do anything about it.

We should be frustrated and furious. We should feel the nauseating, exhausting, humiliating reality of what is happening to our ocean. We should be outraged by governments that delay and prolong any policy, regulation, or action directed toward sustaining this essential natural environment. We should be aware that today in the United States, Europe, the Pacific, the Arctic, indeed everywhere in this ocean world, even the progress we have made is under attack by forces of greed, dilution, revision, and retraction of anything that interferes with the exploitation or corruption of the ocean until we are left with only a toxic sea. What will it take?

There are thousands of ocean advocates, policy-makers, scientists, communicators, organizers, and individuals out there, all over the world, fighting to keep our ocean safe. Hats off! Honor, respect, support, and engage with them wherever you may be. We can all do that. Join them and build their number exponentially.

But my sense is that this medicine is not working, is not yet strategic enough, strong enough, smart enough to do what must be done. We are advocating for the ocean with best intentions and hope. We want to get beyond seasickness to that sustainable place, purged, free, secure. We know what must be done; at every level, locally, regionally, nationally, internationally. We have plans and policies and agreements in place to free us of this disease. We know what must be done, but we are not yet aware enough, mad enough, or desperate enough to do enough about it.

We are talking about survival here. Every human need for the future—fresh water, food, energy, medicine, security, and psychological renewal—is dependent on a healthy, sustainable world ocean. The ocean is our cure. Why would we destroy it?

I submit we are missing the resonating psychological, intellectual, and emotional connection that enables us to understand—and to assert with reason and passion—*why the ocean matters*. We have bits and pieces of the puzzle. We know parts of the whole that convince us. We feel parts of the whole that move us. But it is the union of knowledge and emotion that compels us finally to understand how the ocean affects all things: climate, weather, sea level rise, coastal development, acidification, the polar regions, fresh water, food, health, security, energy, economy, trade, and community.

Consider each of these alone, and then aggregate and relate them into what becomes an integrated system of nature, politics, and social behavior that connects the world through a skein of interwoven cause and effect, the global net in which we swim, trapped perhaps on Earth, surrounded by an ocean of stars. Do we want to save ourselves? Are we not all Citizens of the Ocean? And is not our personal and collective desire for survival and the future enough to move us to the revolutionary action and change required to make it so?

CLIMATE

Everywhere, In Our Backyard

We are all familiar with social and political opposition to change labeled "NIMBY" (not in my backyard.) We believe in wind power, but don't want the turbines in view. We believe in resource management, but not when it limits our livelihood. We want good roads and schools, but not if it means higher taxes. In this context, the influence of climate and ocean may seem very remote, indeed irrelevant. Not so. The ocean *is* our backyard, and its deterioration is connected to consequences that can affect each and every one of us. Power generation and industry, carbon release, increased storms, shoreline inundation, migrating food supplies and disease, loss of cultural traditions: these are not really someone else's problems, are they?

The health of the ocean is a direct reflection of the health of the land. A nuclear accident in Japan allows radioactive material to seep into the sea. A collapse of coastwise fishery regulation enables the final depletion of species for everyone everywhere. Indifference to watershed protection, industrial pollution, waste control, and agricultural runoff poisons the streams and rivers, wetlands, near-shore and deep-ocean, corrupting the water and food chain all along the way. This ignorance, this lack of understanding of evident changing weather, compromises our effective response to storm and drought, inundates our coastal communities, and destroys our businesses, our communities, and our sustenance.

The ocean sits at the epicenter of the climate problem. Paradoxically, it is both the penultimate reservoir of consequence of human intervention into natural systems on land and the embodiment of potential for future solutions from the sea.

Climate has been reduced to numbers, easy to understand, and yet easy to ignore. Until we as ocean advocates can make the case that climate itself is a function of the ocean, along with its impact on fresh water, energy, food, health, and security, the UN and other agents of governance will continue to struggle with the compromised attitudes and actions, or lack thereof, promoted by vested interests.

Ocean and Climate[9]

Debate over the degree and impact of human activity on climate and community continues. While the immediate focus is on CO_2 emissions, the melting of glaciers and the polar ice caps, and estimates of sea level rise, there are further and more complicated linkages between global climate and the world ocean. This is not merely because the ocean's ecosystems, like all others on Earth, are affected by climate changes, but also because it is the oceans that drive planetary climate and weather. Changing climate changes the marine environment, but so too does a changing marine environment contribute to global climate change. It is a closed circle, and that understanding is often overlooked.

The following excerpt from the Mario Soares *The Ocean Our Future* 1998 *Year of the Ocean* report[10] on the impacts of climate change explains the physics governing the behavior of the atmosphere and the ocean:

> *The Earth's weather and climate are the result of the redistribution of heat. The major source of heat to the surface of the Earth is the sun, principally through incoming visible radiation most of which is absorbed by the Earth's surface. This radiation is re-distributed by the ocean and the atmosphere with the excess*

radiated back into space as longer wavelength, infrared radia-
tion. Clouds and other gases, primarily water vapor and carbon
dioxide, absorb the infrared radiation emitted by the Earth's
surface and remit their own heat at much lower temperatures.
This "traps" the Earth's radiation and makes the Earth much
warmer than it would be otherwise.

Most of the incoming solar radiation is received in tropical
regions while very little is received in polar regions especially
during winter months. Over time, energy absorbed near the
equator spreads to the colder regions of the globe, carried
by winds in the atmosphere and by currents in the ocean.
Compared to the atmosphere, the ocean is much denser and has
a much greater ability to store heat. The ocean also moves much
more slowly than the atmosphere. The ocean moderates seasonal
and longer variations by storing and transporting, via ocean
currents, large amounts of heat around the globe, eventually
resulting in changing weather patterns.

In short, without the oceans to "bank" the heat from the sun
and redistribute it globally, the Earth would be freezing by night,
and unbearably hot during the day. The ability of the oceans to
absorb and transfer heat thus moderates the global environment.

As climate change continues to warm the global ocean, it will
change patterns of currents and gyres (and thus heat redistribution) in such a way that there will be a fundamental change in
the climate regime as we know it, and possibly a powerful loss of
global climate stability. The basic changes are an acceleration of
already occurring phenomena: sea level rise, alterations of rainfall
patterns and storm frequency or intensity, and increased siltation.

The key to understanding the loss of global climate stability
is to compare global change to local change. The warming of the

planet appears to be following a pattern that is statistically consistent with the increasing accumulations of CO_2 in the atmosphere. As a result, the warming of the ocean is becoming more measurable and predictable. However, all these heat transfers create local dynamics that are significantly less predictable. At the local and regional scale, due to heat disparities and too numerous points of interaction, the indirect changes in local weather patterns will not be uniform, nor necessarily gradual, nor consistent over time. Rather than taking centuries to change, local weather changes are happening before our eyes. Less snow here, more rain there. Longer periods of drought, later arrival of spring rains. Earlier hurricanes and shorter winters. There will be an accompanying loss of biodiversity as ocean temperatures increase, sea levels rise, and disturbances increase. The day's headlines confirm that these conditions surround us.[11]

Climate Divides

There is a problematic disconnect in our thinking. It is amazing to see how indifferent climate policy has been to ocean issues.

The situation is plagued by political, economic, and social separation between the developed nations and the rest of developing world. The first divide is a function of commitment and degree. In the United States, for example, many individuals and political figures are unwilling to accept the research on global warming and its predictable impacts; oppose legislative actions, treaties, and behavioral change on ideological grounds; and thus inhibit policy and commitment to the type, degree, and cost of necessary action.

The second divide has the developing nations objecting to change required by conditions not of their making and insisting on enormous financial aid to subsidize the cost of imposed new strategies for adaptation and mitigation. The developed countries want to invest in very specific actions with measurable outcomes, while the developing countries want to receive unrestricted compensation. At the various global climate "summits" from which solutions might be expected, these contradicting positions undermine best intentions and effective action and result, sadly, in mostly disappointment and recrimination.

But the dichotomy is false. In fact, the developing world has as much to lose as the developed nations, should the research models prove to be true. But there is no need to await the future when radical change in weather events is already disrupting traditional patterns of settlement, agriculture, and health. The reports of unexpected, extreme weather phenomena are pervasive—hurricanes and cyclones, droughts and wildfires, mudslides and floods—affecting thousands of people around the world. Consequent social disruption, pollution of water supplies, physical and economic collapse, and the outbreak of previously controlled diseases are just some of the outcomes already tragically prevalent in coastal and other communities around the world.

Fifteen of the world's largest cities are located in the coastal zone, including New York, Shanghai, Mumbai, and Cairo. In the United States we know the devastation of storms Katrina, Irene, and Sandy, devastating events from which we seem to have learned very little beyond the cost of reparation. Sea level rise and coastal surge are two of the most obvious indicators of the chain of connection between CO_2 emissions, global warming, and polar and glacial melt. And yet we dither and dispute, day in day out, protecting our narrowest interest and denying both cause and effect, ignoring the research, debating the policy, and doing little in a collective global catharsis of ignorance and selfishness that will do harm to us all and to our children. Social disruption and paralysis are the true climate divides.

Extreme Weather

Today we live with the weather as never before. The news is continuously driven not just by more sophisticated forecast but by the consequences of weather far beyond nearby locale, indeed the world over. We read of and witness the ravages of monsoon and resultant ocean surges, of drought and resultant fire, of ice-frozen fruit, or deluged fields, or displaced refugees with little but their lives to prove their survival. Has weather increased? Well, maybe, but the reporting of weather, the understanding of weather, and the awareness of the impact of weather on our lives have exploded exponentially.

Technology, of course, has made the difference. With the advent of radar and satellite monitoring, weather prediction has become so much more accurate with the ability to track fronts, the elements within, the encircling conditions, and the projected tracks to a degree that we now can receive by radio, mobile phone and other devices, warnings of specific weather dangers in specific areas down to counties and townships. How often do you check the weather? Do you bookmark Internet sites that give you hour-by-hour predictions of temperature and probability of precipitation 10 days out? There are many thousands of weather stations around the world, gathering data and reporting conditions. There are multiple satellites revolving the Earth, taking pictures, measuring temperatures, and recording patterns of wind that, taken into the maw of big data—all the statistics and recordings and pictures previously acquired—are the mix from which we extract predictions and trends.

Extreme weather events show us how water, pushed by wind, amplified by wave, accelerated by current, empowered by a function of 10, can provide important information about the design parameters for rebuilding or future construction of systems required to support an ever-increasing population, moving from the heartland to the coast.

Are we really going to continue to fill the remaining swamps and wetlands that are natural buffers for just such a phenomenon? Will we continue to put oil and chemical storage tanks in the most floodable coastal locations? Must we always rely on fossil fuel or nuclear generating stations alongshore, where they are as devastatingly vulnerable to flood and wave as they are to earthquake or terrorism? Do we have to build our highways and rail lines along the coast? Must we continue to insure private property with public money, provide federal flood insurance on beach houses that will inevitably be damaged or destroyed again soon? Is there any logic to any of this anymore? Can we ever learn from experience?

In the US, Superstorm Sandy called our bluff. She said: Let's see what happens when I become a perfect storm that cannot be isolated in one faraway place, that cannot be denied as an irrelevant, inconsequential event, touching only a few, that cannot be explained as an accidental arrangement of causes for which the victims have no responsibility. She said: Let's show them the true power of Nature, up front and personal, no Hollywood animation, but the real thing, angry and indifferent to who they are or what they own, and see how deep their denial really goes, how bad and how long they really want to mess with me.

The recovery from this storm has now begun the process of building a new relationship with the ocean through new values, new structures, and new solutions for how we live and work along the coast and how we engage and respect the natural world we live in. We must not revert to what was, but build what must be given the realities of changing climate.

Sandy said: Change your ways, people; get smart, take me to heart, think ahead, embrace change, and remember I've got sisters and brothers waiting back home.

But will we really learn from Sandy's instruction? The spirit of rebuilding is welcome, but where, and how, so that when Sandy's threatening siblings do come, they will find us differently arrayed and better prepared to defend ourselves? We can no longer protect ourselves from the cause and effect of climate change through indifference, contrived ignorance, and lack of action. That response is irresponsible to the victims, the coastal communities, and to the rest of the nation who are being asked to finance the reparation this time and next.

We return to the hard questions. If we do nothing now to change, we can foresee the inevitable. If we do something now, we have the knowledge, skill, and time to start. If we do more than nothing, more than something now, we will demonstrate the will and capacity for invention to look beyond the wreckage and dismay and denial to a realizable, habitable future living by and with the sea.

Denial is no solution. These storms will come again. The sea is rising and will rise some more. The edge, the place where sea and land meet, will come under further attack by natural elements the force of which will not always respond to seawall solutions, past politics, patterns of what was, inadequate regulation, or a bankrupt government insurance plan. There will be change. The ocean will make it so.

Climate Impact on Oceans, Coasts, and Small Island States

The Intergovernmental Panel on Climate Change[12] has brought urgent attention to the growing "climate divide" that exists between the developed and developing world where the impacts will be most readily felt. As the IPCC chairman has noted, "It's the poorest of the poor in the world, and this includes the poor people even in prosperous societies who are going to be the worst hit...(as) people who are poor are the least equipped to be able to adapt...this does become a global responsibility."[13]

Developing nations in Africa (which account for less than 3 percent of global carbon emissions) and Asia will be the most affected. Major Asian population centers at low elevations include Mumbai, India; Shanghai, China; Jakarta, Indonesia; Tokyo, Japan; and Dahka, Bangladesh. The five most vulnerable countries are China, India, Bangladesh, Vietnam, and Indonesia. The most vulnerable countries with the largest land area are the Russian Federation, Canada, the United States, China, and Indonesia. The impact of climate will be especially significant in the small island states with sea level rise, beach erosion, coral bleaching, freshwater reduction, and population displacement. Some nations, such as Kiribati, are already at risk to sea level rise with present conditions suggesting total inundation within a generation.

Climate change will also have significant effects on ocean biodiversity, related human health and security issues such as drinking water, coastal agriculture fisheries, and the emergence and spread of disease. Researchers suggest possible extinction of one-quarter of the world's species and the dislocation and death of hundreds of millions of people as a result of these changes. The outcome may be further measured by overwhelmed disaster response and management, weak and fragmented states, collapsed coastal economies, the migration of environmental refugees, human rights violations, local and regional violence and war.

These are extreme circumstances, to be certain. But they are likely, should we not take to steps to analyze the causes, adapt to or mitigate the situation, and define changes in individual, regional, national, and international behaviors to prevent further consequence of failed policy and action.

Facing the prospect of climate change, then, we appear to have three choices: do nothing, change our lives through the exercise of restraint, or change our lives more dramatically in response to environmental and economic challenges. We see these scenarios acted out daily: on the talk shows and blogs, in the press, and in halls of governance. Those that deny or belittle the scientific evidence or have other clearly vested interests in the status quo continue to confuse the debate. Legislation is compromised, diluted, or stalled.

If we look at sea level rise and increasing storm activity and surge as functions of climate change, it is clear that something must be done in the coastal zone to protect life, property, and natural resources.

In 1998, the National Oceanic and Atmospheric Administration summarized our coastal responses as follows[14]:

Accommodate. Under this approach, vulnerable areas continue to be occupied, accepting the greater degree of effects, such as flooding, saltwater intrusion, and erosion; advanced coastal management is used to avoid the worst impacts; improved early-warning systems alert inhabitants of catastrophic events; and building codes are modified to strengthen the most vulnerable structures.

Protect. Under this approach, population centers, high-value economic activities, and critical natural resources, are defended by seawalls, bulkheads, saltwater intrusion barriers; other infrastructure investments are made; and "soft" structural options such as periodic beach re-nourishment, landfill, dune maintenance or restoration, and wetlands creation are carried out.

Retreat. Under this approach, existing structures and infrastructure in vulnerable areas are abandoned, inhabitants are resettled, government insurance subsidies are withdrawn, and new development is required to be set back specific distances from the shore.

What is most revealing about these recommendations is that they offer nothing new by way of systems or values, planning, or financial incentives for alternative development or management. Indeed, retreat may be the only option if, as recently in Bangladesh, an entire region was inundated, with complete destruction of a delta area and massive loss of life.

What might be added to the NOAA summary is a fourth response:

Invent. Reorganize governance boundaries into regional organizations; apply planning concepts that align development with the natural protection features of the environment; provide economic incentives for alternative, survivable residential design and construction; nurture ocean-related industry while locating non-waterfront-dependent business in safer locales; remove exclusive ownership from the coast area and open beaches and natural areas to the public for active and passive recreation.

These are just a few ideas, some radical, some inevitable. We risk much if we do nothing, nor can we expect real change to come through incremental restraint. We can, however, opt for invention, for the application of our imagination and energy, of our science and technology, and of our new understanding of the value of natural systems as constructive contributors to the betterment of our lives, not destructive forces beyond our control, challenging our survival.

Polar Change

Since the 19th century, observers have noted the existence of a layer of haze in the western Arctic that has increased exponentially to the present and may be seen as a significant cause of warming temperatures and loss of sea ice. The source has been attributed to eastern Russia and China, most recently identified as the product of coal-fired generating and manufacturing sites, a phenomenon that will only increase as China and Russia continue to build coal plants and industrial bases at a record rate. Many of us in the eastern United States, of course, think of this polluting process as a west-to-east distribution of poisonous exhaust from similar sources in the American heartland. The point to be made here is that the phenomenon is global, with similar negative outfall and effect downwind from every point of origin.

Rising temperature results not only in ice melt but in the warming of the land-side permafrost layer and the decrease of its ability to sequester massive loads of carbon contained in plant matter frozen therein. Should present parameters increase by just a few degrees, the resultant release of a massive excess of CO_2 into the atmosphere may expand conditions far beyond what we are now experiencing from other sources of greenhouse gas. Some experts warn that such a situation could evolve into a "runaway" scenario that could exceed any possible known mitigation process or estimated sequestration capacity, by land or sea, and permanently shift the climate conditions on Earth.

Climate change impacts the ocean conveyor, the global system of winds and currents that is a powerful component of weather and the distribution of all aspects of the marine food chain. As temperature rises, these patterns may shift with potentially devastating consequences for coastal communities, the fishing industry, and public health. Research has already shown a notable temperature-driven northern migration of certain species of fish moving away from traditional feeding grounds in pursuit of shifting food supply. Public health officials have warned that these species include insects and certain microbes that contain the seeds of infectious diseases that may now newly affect human populations.

We may not fully understand the true cultural impact of all these examples on the indigenous peoples of high-ice environments. There are many consequences beyond environmental change: compromised hunting and fishing, social dislocation and increased poverty, and the destruction of cultural sites and religious traditions that we would find unacceptable in our lives.

These circumstances suggest that we are rapidly coming to understand what is called "the new north." The old north is to be transformed as the glaciers calve, the animal migration routes disappear, and the few native communities are bought out, displaced, and forgotten. The old north is uninterrupted tundra, universal cold, plants that adapt and thrive, hidden in the harshness, complicated, ready to bloom in micro-gardens on one sudden day in the Arctic spring. The new north is port facilities, pipeline routes, service outposts, communications towers and cables, all the systems required to accumulate and move commercial volumes expeditiously for scheduled delivery to consumers below and beyond.

What happens when the systems fail under the force of extreme conditions? What happens when the oil spills and some comes ashore but more, much more, sinks and circulates beneath the ice beyond any futile attempts to clean up or mitigate the damage? What happens when the storms and ice dynamics block narrow navigation channels, or a ship collides with the ice? What happens to the survivors? What happens when the untoward, the unexpected, the unpredictable accident, the inevitable human error occurs and the consequences are beyond rectification? We know what that looks like from example after example in more temperate climes and less exacting conditions. We know the damage to be done.

There are those who argue that we don't need to go there, into the new north. That we should protect this unique and fragile place from our ambitions and endeavors. That we should look to meet our needs for energy or transport in alternative, less invasive ways. That we should let be the far north—and yes, the far south as well—as original, inviolate, pristine, and wild. There are courageous advocates, campaigners, lone sailors, making their voices known in opposition to this corruption of the last pure places on Earth.

Why do we endlessly pursue this behavior? It is surely as old as history itself, but the situation today may be different, first by the number of us on Earth who need equitable distribution of water, food, energy, health, and security; and, second, by our proven capacity to invent our way forward when our conventional knowledge becomes counter-effective, inefficient, uneconomical, and destructive. How do we balance such demand with adequate supply for survival? Is that not the key question for this time?

The attraction of the new north is based on exhausted ideas. Ongoing attempts by Royal Dutch Shell Oil to capture licenses and move drilling rigs to open the area to these dangers were some of the last remnants of such thinking. Shell has just recently closed its Arctic drilling experiment having wasted $9 billion in shareholder value on an ill-conceived, embarrassingly executed exploration failure.

But the real explorers and risk-takers today are the inventors of alternative technologies, the proponents of new systems of governance, and the opportunists who see that we can meet our future needs through imagination and entrepreneurial pursuit of new ideas. Let's incentivize, subsidize, and invest in these, forgo the limited rewards and last vestiges of the old ways, and keep the new north new by leaving it alone forever. We can stand up to Shell, surround the rig with protesting kayaks, but the better defense is to break our oil dependence habit and let the market show them the best strategy is offensive, our collective determination to leave that oil in the ground.

Climate is a global phenomenon. Just as the polar regions are threatened, so too are the mountains and glaciers, sometimes referred to as "the third pole," about which not much thought is given, as least in the context of ocean conservation and sustainability. As temperatures rise, the snow accumulations diminish and the ranges and glacial areas inland are also affected. That change, if only a few degrees, has enormous implication as yet another example of the intricate connections inherent in natural hydraulic systems and of our indifference to and misunderstanding of how these systems work, thereby enabling consequences we cannot control. The Himalayan snowmelt contributes an enormous quantity of fresh water into the intricate river systems of Asia, on which basic sustenance and economic development depends. To diminish the source is to fundamentally inhibit this supply and dependence. The financial and human costs are almost incalculable but are rarely factored into the climate calculation.

Acidification

In my view, the most serious, debilitating circumstance affecting the ocean today is acidification, the changing pH or acid balance in the water column with altogether devastating impact on the marine food chain, species migration and reproduction, and sustainability of habitat. This is a global situation, mostly invisible, and demanding of immediate action.

One of the most unexpected consequences of global climate change may well turn out to be one of the most severe in terms of impacts on life on Earth. As continued carbon emissions accelerate global warming, the carbon dioxide contained in those emissions is able to silently yet dramatically reduce the alkalinity of the oceans. And as the pH drops, marine organisms that produce shells and carbonate skeletons grow weak and die off.

The discovery that carbon dioxide emissions can lower global ocean pH is very recent, even though chemists and biologists have long known that when carbon dioxide dissolves in water, carbonic acid results. However, the sheer volume of water in the oceans has always been assumed to be so vast as to be safe from changes in chemical balance brought about by small-scale inputs. In effect, it is just plain hard to imagine that atmospheric inputs of any kind could significantly alter the chemical composition and nature of over 1.3 trillion cubic kilometers of ocean water. Thus when intrepid oceanographers and marine ecologists set out to address the question of how changing atmospheric conditions that lead to changes in pH could affect marine life, they raised alarms about the possibilities of very large-scale impacts.

The idea is not without controversy. Some scientists still cling to the idea that the buffering capacity of the oceans, by virtue of their sheer size, will counter any acidification effects. Others insist that carbonate inputs from dissolving rocks on land will counteract any reduction in alkalinity in the oceans. Still others argue that a feedback loop between oceans and atmosphere would dampen the effect; others argue that even a significantly lowered pH would not send any marine species to extinction and organisms would adapt to the changes. And even those who are most vocal about the possible effects of ocean acidification acknowledge the uncertainties, and the lack of in situ empirical proof that elevated carbon dioxide in the atmosphere lowers pH and causes significant ecological impact.

The perceived scenario of major biodiversity losses as oceans lose their alkalinity goes like this: carbon dioxide levels double over their pre-industrial values by 2050. The rate of CO_2 occurs on the order of 1.1 ppm/year, two orders of magnitude faster than even the relatively rapid rates seen during glacial—interglacial transitions. Atmospheric exchange with the surface waters of the ocean increases CO_2 concentrations in the oceans, and carbonic acid is formed. Surface pH, having already dropped to an average pH of 8.14 from pH 8.25 since 1751, continues to decline in an accelerated fashion. Calcifiers living on or near the surface or in shallow coastal waters, such as plankton or corals, become unable to form carbonate structures, and some species die out. At sea the phytoplankton community is altered, causing the pelagic marine food web to be disrupted. And inshore, coral reefs lose their reef-building capability, and the entire tropical food web that has reefs at its base shifts to a much less diverse, and possibly less productive, state.

The impact on marine food webs has the possibility of affecting mankind in at least two dramatic ways. First, human populations relying on marine resources will have to adapt their practices to changing conditions, requiring shifts in target resources and fishing practices or other uses. For urban or suburban dwellers in the developing world, there is likely to be little immediate impact except for the loss of favored shellfish from the menu—but for rural dwellers in the developing world that rely on marine ecosystems for income, these changes may well be disastrous. Currently almost 40 percent of the global population lives near and depends on the oceans, and loss of biodiversity and damage to ecosystems will bear social and economic costs.

The other effects may be more insidious and severe. Loss of coral reefs, for instance, means not only changes to treasured ecosystems harboring vast amounts of biodiversity, but also the loss of ecosystem services that serve and protect human communities. Tourism and recreational use of tropical areas will decline as reefs are degraded, as carbonate sands formed by reef ecosystem processes dwindle, and as reefs become less diverse and monochromatic. But we are not talking only of ruining the vacation plans of wealthy tourists. Many coastal economies are wholly dependent on coastal tourism and marine resources. Coral reefs provide a major source of food for a large part of the global population, and they provide coastlines and communities important buffering from storms and tsunamis. If reefs stop growing and cannot keep pace with rising sea levels, these important ecosystem services will be lost.

The public has not responded to the possibility of large-scale changes brought about by this "other CO_2 problem," in part because although the issue has been picked up by the media, the significant uncertainties in terms of how much change will occur and how quickly have also been reported. Scientist investigation of this issue is in its infancy.

Ah, were we only in the position to be able to evaluate ecological risks one at a time, and dismiss those that seemed uncertain. Science, and life, would be so much simpler! But changes in ocean pH are occurring along with large-scale changes in temperature, in nutrient input, in levels of toxic pollution, and in abundance and distribution of organisms caused by extractive use. Coral reefs are but one kind of marine ecosystem already demonstrating the "death of a thousand cuts" phenomenon today—warming is causing widespread bleaching, eutrophication is spurring algal overgrowth, and overfishing is removing grazers that keep algae in check. Add to this morbid scene a significant drop in pH, and it is clear that the tipping point for corals cannot be very far away. Sadly, the fate of other marine ecosystems could follow a similar trajectory.

FRESH WATER

We take fresh water for granted. We use it to sustain our physical health, support our food supply, nurture our landscape, and provide a place for our recreation and pleasure.

As the global population continues to grow, as climate change modifies weather patterns with resultant storm pollution or drought, and as we continue to consume and degrade limited supplies to the point of crisis, the world is forced to explore new technologies and systems to ensure adequate amounts of the one natural resource that each of us needs in equal amount every day to survive: drinking water.

The developed world has taken water for granted. We are profligate water wasters: open taps, swimming pools, endless showers, manufacturing systems, industrial irrigation—the uses are many, and the available resource is consumed without thinking. In most places, water is free or priced far below its true economic human value. The developing world has had the more difficult experience of limited supplies to begin with, carried long distances by women and children for family and livestock consumption, and valued differently as an ever necessary, always compromised source of basic survival.

Why does fresh water matter here? It is perfectly clear that we cannot sustain the ocean without sustaining our freshwater systems. We can no longer tolerate the continuous decline in quality and treatment at the source and expect that the ocean will remain unaffected by the volumes of waste and toxicity that cause red tides and dead seas. There is proof enough. The water cycle, from mountaintop to alluvial plain, is a continuous loop and no part can remain healthy as another part struggles to survive.

Population, Fresh Water, and the Ocean

Estimates of the world population continue to grow. Despite constant discussion, studies and policies, legislation, incentives and disincentives, birth control, even terrorism, war, and enforced sterilization, the statistics keep escalating in inconceivable numbers—so large and ironically abstract that, like national debt, it is very difficult to understand the true meaning, impact, and implication for the future, much less how to deal.

The most recent estimates of global population assert that we will number 9.7 billion people worldwide by 2050, an increase of 2.8 billion in just three decades.[15] Much of this growth will occur in the developing world, but trends in the United States and Europe indicate that recent declines are less evident and are tending flat to a slight increase estimated to follow economic recovery in the industrialized nations.

The correlative requirements to sustain such a population are enormous. According to the 2012 United Nations *World Water Development Report*,[16] freshwater demand will increase 70 percent to satisfy these basic water needs. "People in many parts of the world enjoy improved access to safe drinking water—86% of the population in developing regions will have it by 2015. But there are still nearly one billion people without such access, and in cities the numbers are growing." Add to this the sanitation needs of global urbanization—some 80 percent of wastewater that goes untreated—and you can begin at least to frame the question: where will all this water come from?

At the same time, the Report estimates "that the world will need 70 per cent more food by the middle of the century, with demand increasing especially for livestock products. A surge in food production will lead to an increase of at least 19 per cent in the water required for agriculture, which already accounts for 70 per cent of freshwater use." Add to this the impact of climate change that "alters rainfall patterns, soil humidity, glacier-melt and river-flow and also causes changes to underground water sources. Already, water-related disasters such as floods or droughts are rising in frequency and intensity." The *Report's* authors say that climate change will drastically affect food production in South Asia and Southern Africa between now and 2030, and water stress will spread to central and southern Europe thereafter, with much of the burden falling on the poor, exacerbating tensions and disparities between nations.

The *Report* concludes that this unprecedented growth in water demand threatens all major international development goals and requires a "radical rethink" of the way water is managed, massive new financing for infrastructure, better planning and governance, and innovative adaptations and methods to collect, conserve, recycle, and protect the precious little water we have—all devoutly to be wished.

But a radical rethink? What does that mean? Here's an approach to consider. Fresh water available for human consumption, not locked in the ice caps, amounts to 1 percent of the finite amount of water—fresh and salt—on Earth.[17] Everything discussed above is focused on that small, over-consumed, polluted, and wasted volume. The rest of the world's water—97 percent of it—is available in the ocean to most nations and contributes not just to the freshwater cycle, but also to climate, food, energy, and much more—factors that are seen as threatened by this crisis rather than as an essential elements in its solution: a revised understanding and different engagement with the enormous hydraulic reservoir that is the ocean. Start there, and work backwards. Now that's radical.

From Fresh Water to Oceans

Water makes life possible—no other element is so universally required by living things. Our bodies are comprised largely of water, and all life on Earth depends on it, either for drinking, nurturing eggs and young, or providing living space. Even ocean creatures rely on fresh water; all water is inexorably linked. This essential connection between fresh water and seawater underpins the great array of life in the sea.

Freshwater ecosystems are diverse and valuable in their own right. The number of species supported by freshwater systems far exceeds that which would be expected given the small amount of space they occupy on the planet. For instance, inland wetlands occupy less than 1 percent of the Earth's surface, yet support 40 percent of known fish species. In fact, it has been estimated that a quarter or more of all vertebrate species live in or near inland waters. Endemism—that is, existence of species that exist nowhere else in the world—is generally high in rivers, streams, and lakes, since physical barriers set the stage for speciation.

Rivers and streams deliver fresh water and other nutrients to estuaries, and to all coastal seas. But the link between rivers and oceans also has a cost—whatever degradation is occurring in freshwater ecosystems inevitably impacts marine life as well. As pressures on aquatic systems mount around the world in response to growing needs for drinking water, irrigation, and energy needs, less and less water is able to reach the world's coasts—changing the very nature of marine ecosystems, making estuaries more saline, and diminishing the extent of ecologically important brackish waters. And as poor land use practices lead to pollution and erosion, runoff and other non-point discharges create a toxic brew of coastal seas downstream. Disappearing coastal wetlands only exacerbate the problem, as the ecosystem service of water filtration that these critical habitats provide is being lost.

Thus fresh water has become an issue more and more evident in the press and international awareness. As the impact of degradation becomes apparent—as supplies dwindle, the water table subsides, and rivers run empty into the sea—the public has become more and more directly concerned and affected, leading to many initiatives and policy developments focused on freshwater issues. Indeed, some international conflicts have been reinterpreted as battles for freshwater supplies adequate to protect national interests from upstream degradation and consumption.

What is astonishing, however, is the disconnect between freshwater and ocean issues in the global discussion. For example, the World Water Forum, the major international body for research, the definition of policy, and implementation of freshwater management structures, draws the line of their concern at the salt line. At its international conference in Mexico City in 2006, attended by 10,000 researchers and decision-makers in this field, with hundreds of papers on every aspect of freshwater policy, the ocean was scarcely even mentioned. In reality, the focus of this important body excludes the basic scientific fact of the hydrological cycle, the system of freshwater/saltwater land/sea circulation that is taught to every student in introductory science. To base policy on such flawed science can only lead to flawed policy. And to compound it internationally further denies the incontrovertible impact of bad policy on the coast and beyond—dams, for example, altering the ecosystems of bays and estuaries, or persistent toxic pollutants, circulating worldwide by ocean currents and damaging species and habitats far away.

Some change in this situation is in the air. Some hope lies in the multi-stakeholder and international efforts to better manage watersheds, as is occurring in many of the world's great river systems, and to better understand the downstream coastal and deep ocean consequences of freshwater actions. So, too, does hope lie in the greater awakening of the public to the crucial role that healthy freshwater systems play in supporting the world ocean, and vice versa.

Fresh Water as Resource

Fresh water is one of the most important provisioning services the planet's ecosystems provide mankind. Drinking water is necessary to sustain life, of course, but so too is water needed to provide sanitation, irrigate crops, tend livestock, sustain freshwater aquaculture, support industry, and generate electricity. Contemporary withdrawal uses 25 percent of the continental runoff to which the majority of the population has access each year.[18] However, only 15 percent of the global population lives in relative water abundance, and that figure will drop as population pressures mount and water overuse threatens renewable water sources.[19]

Demand for potable water is on the rise as the world population passes the 7 billion mark; clean and sanitary water supplies are increasingly in short supply and are leading to serious conflict in many parts of the world. The World Bank estimates that one-quarter of the world's low-income population lacks adequate access to fresh water (20 liters of dependable water per day), while 1.1 billion people do not have access to clean drinking water at all.[20] The annual health burden on the global population caused by inadequate water, sanitation, and hygiene is 1.7 million premature deaths per annum and loss of more than 50 million years of life.[21]

Water quality is less important an issue for agriculture, within limits. Contaminated water supplies used to irrigate food crops can cause serious disease outbreaks, and farm animals can fall prey to waterborne diseases. Conversely, water quantity is the main issue for other uses of fresh water, such as for energy generation or transport, although sediment pollution does impact hydropower operations. Some nations have tremendous freshwater reserves—Russia, Canada, and India are among the highest by virtue of their contiguity to Arctic ice or high mountain ranges—but even these supplies can be diminished by the effect of global warming, melting and diluting fresh-water supplies at a measurable rate. Other nations, Norway for example, have been tremendously ingenious in capturing the energy potential in unexpected ways, such as electricity derived from annual glacial melt directed into a vertical mountain tunnel to the sea wherein turbines are driven by the gravitational force that would otherwise run off ineffectively into the fjords.

Freshwater Services

Surprisingly, the extent and distribution of freshwater ecosystems or inland waters is unevenly or even poorly known at the global and regional scales, partly due to difficulties in delineating and mapping habitats with variable boundaries due to fluctuations in water levels. In some cases, such as the extent and location of wetlands, there is no comprehensive documentation, even at the regional or national levels. On the whole, the larger wetlands and lakes and inland seas have been mapped along with the major rivers; however, for many parts of the world the smaller, immensely valuable wetlands are not well mapped or delineated, despite the importance of the services they provide for human well-being.

Freshwater ecosystems provide many services to support mankind and maintain human well-being. In addition to fresh water for drinking, bathing, and cleaning, inland water systems provide provisioning services in the form of food substances, especially fish; materials such as timber, fiber, and fuel, including peat; energy from hydroelectric facilities; and novel products from biodiversity. Within river basins, inland waters provide many hydrological functions and support public good functions that are "free of charge" and extremely expensive to replace. Additional ecosystem services provided by inland waters include: biological regulation; biodiversity habitat; nutrient cycling and soil fertility; local atmospheric and climatic regulation; waste processing and detoxification; bank stabilization; and support vectors of human infectious diseases. In addition, freshwater ecosystems have significant aesthetic, artistic, educational, cultural, and spiritual values, and provide invaluable local opportunities for recreation and, increasingly, tourism.

Biodiversity in freshwater ecosystems is largely unknown and undervalued, much like marine biodiversity. But unlike the patterns of life in the sea, which are widespread, freshwater ecosystems are living labs in speciation, and demonstrate notably high levels of endemism. This means that each freshwater body threatened by overuse, pollution, landscape changes, or removal of water, threatens an uncommon and sometimes unique set of living beings. According to a study done by the World Wildlife Fund and The Nature Conservancy, parts of major rivers such as the Amazon, Congo, Ganges, Yangtze, and the rivers and streams of the south-eastern United States are outstanding for rich fish populations and high numbers of species found nowhere else.[22] In addition, several smaller systems that had not been identified in previous global assessments, such as Congo's Malebo Pool, the Amazon's Western Piedmont, and Cuba and Hispaniola, were determined to have high numbers of fish species unique to those ecosystems.[23]

As water demand is increasing, pollution from industry, urban centers, and agricultural runoff is limiting the amount of water available for domestic use and food production. Water-quality degradation is most severe in areas where water is scarce because the dilution effect is inversely related to the amount of water in circulation. Toxic substances, such as chemical pollution from urban domestic and industrial sources, and from herbicides and pesti-cides, are a serious and increasing threat as land use in watersheds changes. The regulation capacity of inland waters has often been used for waste disposal or remediation, but not always within the capacity of the system to assimilate such materials indefinitely. All these polluting activities have degraded both habitats and services, and contribute to the reduction in human well-being.

Trade-offs and Consequences

Major trade-offs have occurred between various sorts of ecosystem services provided by inland waters, leading to substantial adverse changes in habitats and species, and services such as freshwater and food supply. Such trade-offs occur because utilizing freshwater systems for energy generation, for example, can diminish the ability of these ecosystems to support biodiversity. Such trade-offs are clearly shown in the case of river fragmentation such as modification of a river through dams, reservoirs, inter-basin transfers, and irrigation consumption.

It is true that these changes have improved transportation, provided flood control and hydropower, and boosted agricultural output by making more land and irrigation water available. At the same time, physical changes in the hydrological cycle disconnect rivers from their floodplains and inland water systems and slow water velocity in riverine systems, converting them to a chain of connected reservoirs. This, in turn, impacts the migratory patterns of fish species and the composition of riparian habitat, opens up paths for exotic species, changes coastal ecosystems, and contributes to an overall loss of freshwater biodiversity and inland fishery resources.

Irrigation has similarly led to increased food production in dry lands. In many cases without extensive public capital investment, irrigation is unsustainable, as waterlogging and pollution, especially eutrophication and salinization, degrade the systems and other services. Changes in natural flow regimes have caused a decline in biodiversity and services provided by inland water systems, and those provided by coastal systems.

Threats to freshwater diversity are thus numerous and widespread. In the WWF/TNC study described above, agriculture, industry, human consumption, and livestock watering were found to place freshwater ecosystems in 55 (out of 426) eco-regions under high stress, threatening the species and habitats they support.[24] This represents more than 10 percent of the world's eco-regions, which are defined by a large area encompassing one or more eco-regions that contain a distinct assemblage of natural communities and freshwater species. And, damage is already widespread: more than half the area in another 59 eco-regions has already been converted from natural habitats to cropland and urban areas.

In the United States, news outlets recently reported a looming water supply crisis in the western states, escalated by human-caused climate change that already has altered the region's river flows, snowpack, and air temperatures.[25] Since 1960, thermoelectric, self-supplied industrial, and irrigation water withdrawals increased, reaching a peak in 1980. Demand for municipal and rural use has grown steadily over the past few decades, with municipal demand increasing more rapidly. Total water withdrawals declined about 10 percent between 1980[26] and 1985, and then grew slightly from 1985 to 2000, equaling about 345 billion gallons per day in 2000.[27] Small streams are disappearing not only because of water withdrawals or overdrafts, but also from mining and damming. However, because there is no widely accepted way to classify streams for ecological monitoring, no national dataset exists for reporting on their gains or losses. Thus many freshwater ecosystems in the United States, and the biodiversity and other ecosystem services they provide, are at risk from physical alteration, freshwater overdraft, alien species invasions, chemical pollution, sedimentation, and climate change impacts that affect recharge and source water.

Prospects for the future of freshwater ecosystems and their

noteworthy biodiversity are dim. In the next few decades, some three billion people will live in countries classified as water stressed.[28] As competition for freshwater resources increases around the world, freshwater habitats and species are among the most imperiled.

Upstream Pollution and Ocean Health

Oceans are unfortunate in being downstream of everything. All our chemical inputs, unused fertilizers, debris, eroded silt and topsoil, untreated sewage, medicines—from our farms, our suburbs, our cities, and our factories—eventually make their way to the world ocean. As a result, coastal seas are now described as the most chemically altered environments on Earth; pollutants reach the seas via river inputs, atmospheric deposition, and runoff; expanding dead zones result, endangering fisheries, biodiversity, and human health.

This is a story not easily told, which is why this may be the biggest sleeper issue of all. How much easier to portray the plight of the great whales, or to document the decline in fisheries, or to show a coastline sullied by unsustainable development. Pollution is difficult to see, even harder to trace, sometimes ephemeral, but with long-lasting impacts. Eutrophication—the over-fertilization of nearshore waters caused by too many nutrients from fertilizers, sewage, animal waste, food processing residues—threatens to disrupt the ecological balance of coastal areas around the world. At the same time, toxins enter the marine system and reside there for long periods—until they are actively removed by mitigation or, worse, until they enter the human food chain, leaving the marine environment to reside in our own tissues.

Non-point source pollution underlies ever-expanding "dead

zones"—areas of low or no oxygen, an element needed to support most marine life. In the Gulf of Mexico dead zone, less than a third of the 31 state watersheds in the United States contribute the vast majority of the nitrogen and phosphorus delivered to the Gulf, primarily through non-point source pollution from rural runoff. Corn and soybean cultivation is the largest contributor of nitrogen to the Gulf; while animal waste combined with crop cultivation contribute most of the phosphorus.

Riparian buffers have long mitigated the effects of runoff, preventing polluted fresh water from reaching coastal systems. But as a 2008 study in *Nature* points out, small stream systems may be even more important in removing pollutants and preventing eutrophication of coastal seas. Patrick Mulholland and co-authors found that nitrates were filtered from stream water by tiny organisms such as algae, fungi, and bacteria.[29] This in and of itself was not news; however, the researchers discovered that entire stream networks are important in removing pollution from stream water, not just individual streams. Conversely, the important role that even small streams have in removing and/or transforming nitrates (and therefore preventing eutrophication downstream, and in estuaries and oceans) can quickly be overcome by too many nitrates entering the water. Thus, there are thresholds to the ability of freshwater ecosystems to provide the important ecosystem service of maintaining water quality.

Freshwater ecosystems and marine ecosystems downstream are threatened by both pollutant loading and the loss of stream habitat as development continues to transform the landscape. But the situation is not hopeless. Realization is growing, and market-based mechanisms for better watershed management are being defined and implemented. Perhaps the one bright light in the current worldwide economic downturn is that use of fertilizer is expected to plummet as its cost rises as a result of dramatically increased energy production costs. If the end result is a forced movement to more sustainable agriculture and better opportunities for small-scale growers that practice sustainable methods, this may indeed be both an antidote to an oil-based agricultural economy and to the deteriorating health of the world ocean.

A GLOBAL HYDRAULIC SYSTEM

The Promise of Watershed Management

Marine managers have long recognized that effective conservation of ocean areas and creatures requires delving into watershed management, for all the free-flowing waters of the Earth either find their way into, or dramatically affect, ocean ecosystems. However, achieving this level of ecosystem-based management requires the spanning of disciplines and professions in a way that is not natural to our sectoralized science and management structures, and keeping the big picture, the regional view in mind.

Regional cooperation to address issues of water use and allocation, as well as threats to freshwater systems originating from pollution, overfishing, and changes in riparian landscapes, holds great promise for not only effectively managing river systems and watersheds, but also provides a ray of hope for ocean management through regional ecosystem-based management.

There are good examples of watershed/water basin

management frameworks and institutions already in existence around the world, from the Mekong River Commission (Vietnam, Thailand, Laos, Cambodia), to the International Commission for the Protection of the Danube River (Austria, Bosnia-Hercegovina, Czech Republic, Germany, Hungary, Moldova, Romania, Serbia, Slovakia, and Ukraine), to the drought-parched Murray/Darling Basin in Australia (involving the states of South Australia, New South Wales. However, this large-scale, top-down, command and control form of management has its limitations without effective local involvement at much smaller scales.

A telling example is provided by the Protection of Ecoservices Project undertaken by the City of New York to safeguard the city's drinking water supply. The City made an investment of $300,000 to facilitate sustainable farming practices in the New York City watershed, enlisting the help and entrepreneurial spirit of farmers in the Catskills Mountains to implement measures to preserve water quality. These measures included establishing riparian/stream buffers on private lands, reducing fertilizer/pesticide use, and conserving wetlands that naturally filter water flowing through them. This payment for Ecosystem Services initiative paid off—it saved the City literally billions of dollars in water treatment costs, and it rewarded farmers financially, allowing them to maintain their traditional, small-scale farming livelihoods.

Another example is the Colorado River, long exploited for drinking water diversion to southern California, large-scale irrigation projects along the eastern slope of the Rockies, and water-demanding agriculture like rice and tomatoes in Texas and Mexico. In reality, the annual volume of water from the river in a typical year is effectively "spoken for" as a result of various contracts and obligations. In a drought year, these obligations must be diluted; indeed, some contracts for water to Mexico, to serve large agribusiness interests taking advantage of cheap labor south of the border, cannot be met at all. Thus are diminished snowmelt or drought conditions directly related to economic viability along the river's path; should climate change perpetuate those circumstances, even over the short term, the financial impact on the dependent communities will be immediate and enormous.

Such combinations of public sector management and private sector market mechanisms, however, may still be the best hope we have for conserving freshwater biodiversity and services. The new structures required may be difficult and painful to achieve, but if we are successful in their implementation, we will have come a long way in conserving and using our freshwater resources more efficiently, while also sustaining the marine ecosystems and services that so often lie at the end of the freshwater stream.

Water Efficiency

L isten to the headlines, and you will hear more and more frequent anecdotal evidence of the crisis facing our global freshwater supply. A reminder: only 3 percent of the water on Earth is fresh, and of that some 2 percent is locked in the polar ice caps, thus leaving us with the astonishing conclusion that the entire population on Earth is reliant on 1.2 percent of the available fresh water worldwide to sustain its fundamental need.[30]

That need is universal; each of us—no matter who we are, what we earn, or where we live—should consume at least 2 quarts of water per person per day to sustain basic daily physical health. According to the World Health Organization, an individual requires 18 gallons a day to provide medium-term maintenance to include drinking, cooking, personal hygiene, washing clothes, cleaning homes, growing food, and sanitation and waste disposal.[31]

There is an apocryphal story of a proposed reality television show focusing on the water use of a middle-class American family of two adults and three children. The family of five in suburban New Jersey would be limited to 2 gallons of water per person per day. The value entertainment was to derive from the interpersonal consequences of reliance on the minimal supply to meet the profligate use of water in the United States for domestic uses only. The trial was a disaster and the show cancelled, as the family chosen could not subsist a week in these conditions, deprived of infinite supply of water—for cooking, showers, dishwashers and washing machines, lawn and garden watering—without serious negative psychological effect, inter-family conflict, and rejection of the experiment.

The headlines speak of water shortages everywhere, in large amounts, and in many forms.[32] We read of cities closing down their water systems because of toxic runoff; of the poisoned water from fracking oil wells that leak into watersheds, streams, and rivers; of droughts that evaporate available water and radically decrease supply for irrigation of industrial farms and orchards; of wildfires that cannot be contained because there is no available water to fight them. There are many more examples; add them all up, and you have a water crisis that threatens rich and poor everywhere in the world, has serious financial implications now and for the future, destroys communities, and indeed becomes a context for conflict.

All this threatens total supply and must force us to rethink how we manage the efficiency of our water use. Certain changes seem obvious: become more aware of the problem and modify personal use by turning off faucets, shortening showers, collecting rainwater for gardens, not washing the car, replacing

old appliances with conservation-certified new ones, and understanding that every gallon wasted by indifference is a gallon gone
and irreplaceable for you or anyone else.

Individual actions can of course be scaled up by government
actions and regulations. The Alliance for Water Efficiency,[33]
for example, an authoritative voice for water conservation in
North America, informs and advocates for the development of
state and municipal laws, codes, and standards. It also supports
a national partnership with the United States Environmental
Protection Agency called "WaterSense" that promotes best water
conservation management practices for homes, hotels, factories,
businesses, treatment plants, and water distribution infrastructure, and rewards the best examples of the most efficient water
conservation technologies.[34]

But this is nowhere near enough. Water consciousness must
improve dramatically at all levels of society to enable us to recycle
water effectively, to divert treated water to alternative use, to
channel urban runoff from roofs and storm systems back into the
usable water supply, to revolutionize our agricultural irrigation
practices that today consume a vast majority of water resources
worldwide, and regulate any and all industrial or extraction
behavior that continues to pollute our waterways with harmful
pollutants and poisons with unacceptable local health and downstream consequences.

And yet, in the United States at least, some determined
politicians are attempting to reverse any such intelligent controls
by diluting or overturning clean water laws and regulations
already established in the name of protecting threatened corporate
interests, denying the role of government to regulate destructive
practice, and sustaining the status quo. Wouldn't it be interesting
to put those representative lawmakers in a situation like that

American family? Where they would have to live together—in reality—with their individual hypocrisies, compromised decisions, and destructive political ideologies? I wonder how long they would last having to live together up close and personal in today's global freshwater crisis?

The Global Water Contract[35]

"Water, water everywhere, and not a drop to drink."[36] That familiar Coleridge quotation from *The Rime of the Ancient Mariner* approaches the reality of the world situation, to a point now when an estimated 3 billion people may not have access to clean fresh water to drink, for hygiene, for cooking, for support of necessary economic activity, or for basic survival.[37] What if you were one of these—displaced, disqualified, disenfranchised from this fundamental and irreplaceable source of life?

In 1998, a private commission assembled to address this challenge and to create a Global Water Contract to establish a framework for worldwide understanding, access, distribution, and protection of fresh water as "an inalienable individual and collective human right."[38] Calling itself The Committee for the Global Water Contract, the group was led by former President of Portugal, Mario Soares, who the same year led a similar commission "for the future of the ocean." That the challenge of both fresh and salt water received such intense and productive attention—in the same year and led by the same man—is a tribute to the prescience and leadership of President Soares, his colleagues, and their foundation sponsors.

The Global Water Contract is based on the premise that "water is a vital good, which belongs to all the inhabitants of the Earth in common. None of them, individually or as a group, can be allowed the right to make it private property. Water is the patrimony of mankind. Individual and collective health depends upon it... There is no production of wealth without access to water. Water is not like any other resource; it is not an exchangeable, marketable commodity."[39]

The Committee report continues: "While the sharing of water has often been a major source of social inequality in the past, today's civilizations recognize that access to water is a fundamental, inalienable, individual and collective right. The right to water is a part of the basic ethics of a 'good' society and a 'good' economy. It is up to society as a whole, and at the different levels of social organization, to guarantee the right of access, according to the double principle of co-responsibility and subsidiarity, without discrimination of race, sex, religion, income or social class."[40]

The Committee argues for water as a key contributor to the strengthening of solidarity among people, communities, countries, genders, and generations. Citing pollution, unequal distribution, privatization, geo-economic interests, existing water conflicts, and drought, the Committee asserts that water is "the citizens' business" and that its integrated and responsible protection and management demands democratic governance and choices and practices to ensure environmental, economic, and societal sustainability.

The contract calls for radical change that goes against the consumption and capital-based mindset and conventions of today concerning ownership and valorization of other natural resources. "It is society which must collectively assume all of the costs related to the collection, production, storage, distribution, use, conservation and recycling of water in view of supplying and guaranteeing access to water in the quantities and qualities considered as being the indispensable minimum. The costs (including the negative externalities which are not taken into account by market prices) are common social costs to be borne by the collective as a whole. This principle is even more relevant and significant at the level of a country, a continent, and the world society. The financing must be ensured by collective redistribution. The mechanisms of individual price-fixing, according to progressive pricing, must start from a level of water usage that goes beyond the vital and indispensable minimum. Beyond the vital minimum, progressive pricing must be a function of the quantity used. Finally, at a third layer, all abuses and excesses of usage must be considered illegal."[41]

This is a fundamental, revolutionary change and goes antithetically against the contemporary trends of profligate water use and waste, unregulated, uncontrolled pollution of natural water systems and aquifers, categorization of water as an asset class, private ownership of water resources, distribution, and associated engineering and technology. It would have no chance for success except for the growing reality of water deprivation extending from desert and developing world communities into drought-stricken and over-consumed areas in such affluent places as California where local limitations and emergencies become more frequent and more public. As the Committee concludes: "A partnership predominantly subject, as at present, to the logic and interests of private actors in relentless competition against each other for market conquest could only do harm to the objectives of access to water for all and global integrated sustainability."[42] That is a convoluted way of saying that something very different must be done.

What, then, does the Committee recommend?

First, the citizen must be at the center of decision- making, implying a high degree of democracy at the local, national, continental, and world level. "By definition, water calls for decentralized management and transparency. The existing institutions of representative democracy must be strengthened. When necessary, new forms of democratic government have to be created. Participatory democracy is unavoidable. This is possible, with or without the new information and communication technologies, at the level of local communities, cities, basins, and regions. New coherent regulatory frameworks at international and global level must be designed and implemented, enhancing the visibility of a sustainable water policy at global level by the global community."[43]

Second, success must be founded on co-operation, mutual respect, and effective partnership. "'Partnerships for water' is the inspiring principle behind all the plans (such as 'the river agreements') that have permitted the efficient resolution of conflicts which in certain regions of the world have traditionally poisoned relations between riverside communities who shared the same hydrographic basin. Indeed, we support a real local/national/world and real public/private partnership. A sustainable water management in the general interest cannot but be founded on the respect for cultural diversity and socio-economic pluralism. A partnership predominantly subject, as at present, to the logic and interests of private actors in relentless competition against each other for market conquest could only do harm to the objectives of access to water for all..."[44]

Third, specific steps toward this goal are as follows: the creation of a network of "Parliaments for Water" wherein legislatures create a new legal framework based on these new premises of ownership and management; the creation and validation of a "World Water Treaty," similar in concept to the International Law of the Sea or World Trade Organization agreements; the development or modernization of the systems of water distribution and sanitation for the 600 cities in Russia, Africa, Asia, Latin America, and

European countries that will have more than a million inhabitants by the year 2020 and whose water systems are even today obsolete, inadequate, indeed, nonexistent. Opposition must emerge against new sources of water pollution in the cities of North America, Western Europe, and Japan where contamination of the soil and both surface and deep-ground water is becoming more and more troubling, serious, and in certain cases, irreversible. Irrigation systems in highly intensive industrial agriculture must be structurally reformed. A 10- to 15-year moratorium must be initiated in the construction of new large dams, which have so far created considerable short- and long-term problems for the environment, populations, and integrated, sustainable water management. The Committee also recommended the establishment of a *World Observatory for Water Rights*[45] to collect, produce, distribute, and disseminate the most rigorous and reliable information possible on water access from the point of view of individual and collective rights, water production, its use, its conservation, protection, and democratic sustainable development.

There is no question that public awareness of the world water crisis is growing. Several large organizations and planning endeavors look to water conservation and equitable distribution—the World Health Organization, the World Water Forum, the International Union for the Conservation of Nature, the Millennium Assessment Goals, Pacific Institute, and myriad smaller conservation organizations devoted to preserving lands, river, streams, and wetlands as an integrated watershed system.

Here are seven smaller, unconventional organizations from around the world that you might not have heard of: Charity: Water, Miya, Water.org, Columbia Water Center, Three Avocados, WaterIsLife, Puremadi, and Defending Water for Life.

Our point here is that that fresh water and the ocean are a

single, irreplaceable natural asset that supports the well-being of human endeavor in its every form. It, like the land, is finite. When we destroy it, when we waste it, when we deprive each other of its essential benefit, we are acting so obviously against our true interest and survival that such behavior cannot be condoned or perpetuated. We must hold ourselves accountable. It is our obligation. We are contracted.

FOOD

So often the ocean problems we address are matters of scale. As the world population has grown, as the demand for food has increased, and as science and technology have evolved new and more efficient ways to harvest, our natural ocean systems have been exploited at an ever-increasing scale through industrial agriculture, resource extraction, and fishing. No place is protected from the relentless independent and unregulated consumption of such resources where we can know that soon there will be no more.

The statistics for fishing tell a clear story—the pursuit of individual species almost to extinction, the collapse of vast stocks, the mechanized efficiency of boats and gear that can sweep an ocean floor and water column of all marine life. The taking is so simple, direct, and complete. If only the solutions were as simple, as direct, and as complete.

The collapse or decline of fish species in the ocean has serious implications for a world population heavily dependent on marine life as a primary source of protein. A discussion of policy management systems and regulatory structures notwithstanding, the supply of this invaluable resource in both the developed and developing world is a critical issue for human health and survival.

Historically, the interests of commercial fishermen and conservation organizations have been in conflict, building resentment and misunderstanding between entities that, paradoxically, share very common ground. Fishermen have resisted external intervention, quotas and management practices, and the implication that the theories of research scientists outweigh their experience at sea. Conservation organizations have countered with restrictions, frequent litigation, and the implication that somehow conserving the resource for posterity is more righteous than individual or industrial use. Typically, this conflict becomes the problem, rather than the solution to the underlying challenge to reconcile extremes.

Fish: Endangered Species

We are all aware of the stress on fish species everywhere. There is hardly a coastal community where local fishing has not been impacted by overharvest, unregulated fleets, and an ever-expanding demand for fish products for basic protein and food products, fertilizer, and many other uses in our industrialized world.

The last producing sardine plant in the United States goes out of business. Quota limits reduce the number of inshore vessels and related employment. Persistent organic toxins make some fish unhealthy to eat. Landside conditions create algae blooms that close shellfish beds the length of coastlines. Working waterfronts are abandoned and replaced by industrial or residential developments that only exacerbate the problems. It goes on and on, in every ocean community in the world.

Scientific research informs and complicates the problems. Regulators strive for an improbable consensus framework. Politicians equivocate and policies divide conflicting interests. If you look carefully at the condition of fisheries worldwide you will see more chaos than cooperation, collapsing supply, exponential demand, and traditions that reward independence, indifference to rules and limits, and short-term harvest, to the detriment of any sustainable supply for the future. It is depressing.

Bluefin tuna is the latest example. Fished for more than 7,000 years in the Mediterranean and Atlantic, popular demand has expanded exponentially over the past few decades. More than 80 percent of the catch is consumed in Japan, with the balance allocated to the international appetite for sushi and tuna steak on the grill.[46] Recognizing the problem, the international community invented an intergovernmental agency, ICCAT, the International Commission for the Conservation of the Atlantic Tuna, which, for example, in a recent year, recommended the harvest of 15,000 tons, but set the limit at 30,000 and allowed more than 60,000 to be brought to market.[47] Not very effective, to say the least.

Does this situation sound familiar? Have you heard of similar situations with a fishery of your choosing? Have we not seen before the short-term interest of a vested organization or nation overwhelming science, logic, or even the reality of a policy or structure that has proven successful in the context of realizing sustainability over extinction? At the climate summit in Copenhagen in 2009, the same forces collided: the interests of developed world versus developing, north versus south, rich or poor, have or have not—with no compromise regardless of the emergency state of the problem.

As in so many cases, it may be that the solution lies with our ability to influence in the marketplace. If we boycott plastic bags, the demand declines and the product profit is compromised. If we change bulbs or turn off the lights, our electrical usage goes down and our energy independence increases. If we follow the suggestions of those wallet cards that show which fish are harvested sustainably and safe to eat, we can shift global patterns of consumption. If we buy locally from fishing co-ops holding to responsible limits, we can change the international financial dynamic on which destructive consumption is based. If we exclude tuna from our sushi selection, we take one revolutionary step toward achieving what government cannot. If we can do it here, perhaps we can do it even in Japan.

Industrial Fishing

We are all aware of industrial agriculture, the gradual assimilation of small farms into larger tracts, owned by larger corporations that have consolidated farmland ownership, transformed farmers from proprietors to employees, diminished the cultural viability and values of the family farm, and otherwise applied large-scale technologies to increase efficiency and productivity through capital intensive technology, exponential increase in chemical fertilizers and pesticides, and, in some cases, the introduction of new or genetically modified species that have elicited much controversy. Industrial agriculture is dominated by fewer and fewer corporations, with concentrated and dominating control of supply and distribution of such food basics as wheat, corn, soybeans, rice, and other staples of the global diet.

Historically, fishing has been artisanal and regional, mostly individuals fishing from shore on small craft in localized areas for regional consumption. We are all aware of the decline of such conditions—groundfish in New England, for example—but there are many other instances that have been persuasively documented by studies of the collapse of fish stocks in every ocean. Public awareness of this serious depletion of heretofore abundant protein has resulted in implementation of regulatory structures to control gear and problematic by-catch, define geographic areas for limited permit systems, and establish species quota based on scientific research, administrative oversight and reporting, and independent onboard monitoring of actual harvest. It has become a complex and contentious situation almost everywhere.

In the midst of these developments, fishing too has been industrialized—beyond the number of vessels, each bigger than the one before, expanded by tax incentives and direct subsidies, evident in the ports of every nation. The situation is ever more problematic, especially now as the increased capacity is in critical contradiction to the decreased available supply. But beneath the surface of this circumstance can be found exactly the same elements that changed agriculture. Many of the individual fish boats are now part of corporate fleets with the financial capacity to upgrade technology and to extend range beyond national exclusive economic zones into international unregulated waters. The number of owners of these fleets has also contracted to the point where I believe the public would be astonished to know that a very small number of individuals control the international fishing industry through offshore entities, corporate conglomerates, flags of convenience, interlocking directorates, management contracts, other legal structures and financial instruments, political influence and possible corruption.

A controversial example of this is the supertrawler *Abel Tasman*, formerly the F/V *Margiris*, a recently renamed and reflagged 430-foot, 9,500-gross-ton suction harvest and freezer ship, owned by Seafish Tasmania in partnership with Seafish Tasmania Pelagic, a wholly owned subsidiary of a Dutch company, Parlevliet & Van der Plas BV, itself owned by members of two Dutch families long established in the fishing business. According to its website, that company's fishing fleet consists of 12 freezer-trawlers; it owns and operates multiple cold stores, trading offices, factories, and its own transport; and can "provide service at every point in the process from catch to delivery."[48]

The *Abel Tasman* can be at sea six to eight weeks, fishing, processing, and freezing small pelagic species such as jack mackerel, blue mackerel, redbait, and sardine for ultimate distribution to Africa and elsewhere. It has a special device to prohibit suction of dolphins and seals into its vacuum system. According to a January 2012 article in the *New York Times*, studies of jack mackerel stocks have dropped from 30 million metric tons to less than a tenth of that in two decades, resulting in the South Pacific Fisheries Management Organization to adopt binding quotas.[49] As the proposed agreement is as yet not ratified,[50] companies in Greece, Hong Kong, and the Netherlands have rushed their mega-trawlers to the endangered ground.

The Australian jack mackerel quota, slightly increased even in the face of recent negative estimates, is 36,000 tons; Seafish Tasmania was awarded 17,800 tons, almost 50 percent of the total allocation.[51] As you might imagine, local fishers, marine scientists, environmentalists, sustainability advocates, and Greenpeace were not happy and raised the issue with politicians who, as of now, have legislatively overridden the fisheries authority and the permit is on hold.[52] Seafish is considering its legal options; the Dutch government has raised the issue with the European Union.

The courts will sort this out I suppose. But understand what is evident herein: the ascendency of industrial over artisanal

systems, expensive technology, the effect of offshore capital,
the collision of conservation and consumption interests, marine
species at risk of depletion or extinction, unresolved international
agreements, regulatory standards and enforcement, conflicted
national governance, threatened local jobs and regional economies—all of these explicit within the move to industrialization.

Women in Fisheries

On the water, on the shore, commercial fishing does not
appear to be a widespread occupation for women. This
appearance was recently confirmed by a European Union report
on the perception and involvements of women in fisheries in its
member states.

Here are some of the conclusions:

- The surveys found 70 percent disinterest by women in
  offshore or seagoing fisheries based on such barriers as
  discomfort, danger, lack of facilities, low status, poor
  compensation, and "rough" male company. Disinterest in
  aquaculture, however, was only 35 percent, but similar
  barriers to entry were perceived other than in administrative support functions. Onshore involvement, specifically
  processing and management, revealed equally negative
  circumstances, such as discriminatory pay and poor job
  security as local processing was replaced by machines,
  mergers and consolidation, and foreign competition.

- A key category was women's support of seagoing spouses.
  This function was recognized but under-rewarded, mostly
  unpaid work administering a family business including
  management, communications, bookkeeping, marketing,
  and logistics, not to mention child-care and running of the
  home while husbands are at sea.

- The report affirmed that, despite wide cultural, social,

political, and economic differences, these conclusions were true in both industrial and developing nations worldwide.

- The recommendations were discouraging. Little major improvement in offshore employment was foreseen, primarily a result of choice. Opportunity was seen, however, in inshore small-scale fisheries and aquaculture where capital requirements are less, individuals can enter and participate more freely, and existing interest in the aquaculture as farming can be increased through training in technology and management.

- Little future was seen in processing given larger industry trends, but opportunities were seen in value-added initiatives such as the development of new derivative fish products, marketing and distribution innovation, and as compensated co-managers of family businesses. This was also true in administration where training in environmental and resource management was seen as a path to expanding involvement both in fisheries and in other employment sectors.

- The report's principal recommendation concerned acknowledging, upgrading and expanding women's existing roles in fisheries, through enhanced mutual support networks, improved communication (especially Internet-based), public awareness campaigns to enlist wider community support (especially from fishermen), and training in information technology skills, management, marketing, selling, quality control, modern processing, business planning, accountancy and bookkeeping, employment regulations and taxation, safety at sea, environment and long-term resource management. Such an expanded skill base would encourage women to become better prepared, more effective managers for their family enterprises, to exploit networking capabilities with other shore-based women, and to generate transferable skills in a marketable area should fisheries fail the family or the women require greater independence.

Fisheries Crime

"World fish stocks are being rapidly depleted, and valuable species are nearing extinction. Because fish are a valuable commodity, the last decade has seen an escalation of transnational and organized criminal networks engaged in fisheries crime." So declares the website of a new Environmental Crime Program launched by INTERPOL and funded by the Norwegian Ministry of Foreign Affairs, the Norwegian Agency for Development Cooperation, and the Pew Charitable Trust Environment Group.[53] Called "Project Scale," the initiative is based on the premise that "fisheries crime undermines resource, conservation, threatens food security and livelihoods, destabilizes vulnerable coastal regions such as West Africa due to limited law enforcement capabilities, and is linked to other serious crimes including money laundering, fraud, human trafficking and drug trafficking."[54]

Specifically, objectives are intended to raise awareness of fisheries crime and its consequences, establish National Environmental Security Task Forces to ensure institutionalized cooperation between national agencies and international partners, assess the needs of vulnerable countries, and conduct operations to suppress criminal activity, disrupt trafficking routes and ensure the enforcement of national legislation. In addition to analyzing, planning, training, and generating policy and legal recommendations to address the problem, INTERPOL will actually coordinate and conduct regional or species targeted operations in the most vulnerable regions such as the West African coast. In almost every discussion of illegal, unregulated fishing, enforcement has always seemed the insurmountable issue—the lack of police personnel, customs inspection, forensic and financial expertise, cross-border sharing of information, prosecutorial commitment, and surveillance and arrest capacity on the open ocean and in the off-loading ports and harbors to manage and combat illegal activity that is demonstrably out of control.

The cost to the global economy of this unreported fishing loss has been estimated at $23 billion per year, with the additional un-monetized negative impact on fishing communities, legal commercial fishing interests, species conservation, and the marine environment.[55] So-called "pirate" fishermen, larger flag-of-convenience registered vessels, and multinational corporate interests outside national jurisdictions are responsible for untold hidden profits, evaded taxes and uncollected duties, and other illegal activities as harvesting prohibited species, fishing out of season or without a license, fishing in conservation areas and protected national economic zones, and exceeding national and international quotas established by global management governance associations and bi- and multilateral treaties.

This is an effort long overdue. In conversations with fishermen, government officials, and policy-makers, amplified by news reports and United Nations distress at the level of unregulated fishing worldwide, I have become convinced that the problem, as evidenced by the circumstances described, has at its core a very small group of individuals who through ownership of fishing companies, vessels, interlocking directorates, foreign flag registration, political influence, and assuredly bribes and pay-offs, are responsible for the majority of this illegal activity. I make no specific allegation here, but even the simplest investigative effort on the Internet begins to reveal contracts, relationships, corporate structures, and offshore registrations, frequent ownership/management changes, corporate hiring of former regulators, and other behaviors, surely all legal in the overt appearance of things, that suggest a level of manipulation and control that aggregates the power and return from international commercial fishing to an ever-decreasing circle of players. A forensic investigation of these arrangements, at the level of legal and accounting analysis available only to an international law enforcement agency such as INTERPOL, would be a tremendous step forward in understanding how the system works and thus suggesting specific targets for further discovery, surveillance, indictment, prosecution, and trial for those responsible.

What is additionally disturbing about this challenge is the inevitable integration of these profits into the flow of international financial crimes such as money laundering, drug and human trafficking, arms sales, and terrorism. It is not just about fish as food, or preservation of endangered species; it is about the larger morality play that exposes the continuing theft of natural resources in the form of water, protein, mineral, and DNA, that continues as a dark and corrosive subversion of the ocean as provider, of marine species as food, of fishing as community subsistence, of national confidence and security, and of the sustainability of what we call civilization.

What Does Greed Look Like?

When we speak about the future of the ocean, we use words like "sustainability" and "responsibility." We also lament the actions by oil and gas interests that declare their indifference to sustainability by word and irresponsibility by deed. Again and again, we identify instances when total consumption overwhelms any alternative approach. The conflict is between human need and greed.

What does greed look like? Shannon Service, a journalist,

in an article published by *The Guardian* newspaper in October 2014, provides insight into how greed works in a description of China Tuna Industry Group, from 2011 to 2013 the largest Chinese supplier of premium tuna to the Japanese market, a product considered by various international conservation organizations as "seriously overfished" or "near endangered."[56] China Tuna had applied for an initial public stock offering on the Hong Kong Stock Exchange, and Service found in the draft IPO submission documents revelations about how the illegal fishing industry works. In her article, Service discovered the company stating "that it intended to circumvent international conservation limits by simply ignoring them. A series of circular documents stated that China, which presides over the world's largest long-distance fishing fleet, would not crack down on companies engaged in illegal fishing because it had never done so in the past; that the catch limits set by Regional Fisheries Management Organizations apply only to China the country, not to actual Chinese fishing boats; and that even if the catch limits did apply, the regional fisheries organizations would not honor them because 'there is no sanction for non-compliance with Big Eye catch limits.'"[57]

Service attempted to follow up. She found that the company was owned by a 24-year-old Chinese woman with a St. Kitt's passport, and her father. The company had no office, an unlisted telephone number, an accommodation address with another Chinese company that at first denied any connection, and a subsidiary company that finally admitted that China Tuna was indeed its parent while refusing to identify or connect with any company officers or directors.

In her article, Service writes, "I have yet to speak with anyone who admits working directly for China Tuna. But the firm's combination of bravado and impenetrable corporate structure offers clues as to why the health of the oceans is in free-fall. China has told the world that from 2000 to 2011 it caught 368,000 tons of fish annually in international waters. But as the *Wall Street Journal* reported in 2012, the European Commission estimated the catch as closer to 4.6 million tons, or 12 times greater."

In this, and in so many other instances, China defends its environmental practices by citing its status as "a developing country" with weak and unsophisticated management practices over which central government agencies have no control. Anyone with any awareness of Chinese finance, government structures, and regulatory powers will only laugh at such assertions.

But there is more. Service quotes a China expert, Tabitha Mallory, who told her that "fishing lies at the intersection of Chinese ambitions for military expansion and food security. While the many political analysts refer to the 21st century as 'the China century,' Mallory told the US-China Economic and Security Review Commission in 2012, China also calls it 'the ocean century.' She points to a 2010 Chinese task force report stating that 'marine biological resources are seen as the largest store of protein, therefore owning and mastering the ocean means owning and mastering the future.'"[58]

So, what we have here is fishing as an exercise of international power, the implementation of which needs be indifferent to treaty, law, international policy, or limiting regulation. Those Chinese fishing boats, sometimes accompanied by military vessels, may be more than the actions of rogue fishermen, but rather carefully applied tools of territorial aspiration and nationalistic political action. In such a case, rule of or by law does not pertain. Everything is a lie. Everything is possible to meet any objective regardless of impact on anyone else. Such an attitude and such action is a depressing portrayal of greed.

Failing Down the Food Chain

I live on the Gulf of Maine in the northeastern corner of the United States. This coast is characterized by hard granite edges and islands that have supported communities first based on fishing and farming, later with the arrival of summer visitors and tourists, and now with retired or urban-flight year-round residents. The heart and soul of Maine is its relationship with the ocean, and surely that is the reason that I too came aground here.

Artists have rendered our shoreline for centuries—the gray, grained walls against which the sea breaks constantly, the edge with its occasional gravel beaches, pools filled with marine life, and dark forms of seaweed, mostly rockweed, seen moving below the high water, then revealed as the tide recedes to a clinging mass of varied greens and yellow strands of glistening plant life teeming with small marine species, seen and unseen. This weed constitutes shelter for such species, an incubation place for plankton, sea urchins, periwinkles, and other shellfish, young adult lobsters, and other coastal animals, above and below the waterline, that forage there for nutrition.

That nutritional value extends of course to us, and there is a small but long-lived harvest of seaweed in Maine, mostly by a small group of seasonal workers who live alongshore. The market has been for lobster packing and locally produced health products. But that is changing, and today even the lowly rockweed has its corporate, big-money attraction. Over the past few years, demand has grown for seaweed for fertilizer, health products, and additives to processed foods. And typically, as a small place, independent-minded and without many regulatory resources, Maine has become vulnerable to larger interests, the increased need and cost of processing, and foreign corporations coming into the area because they have exhausted their own supply or have been regulated against by their own governments. What we have here is another classic example of unrestricted harvest, with no interest in sustainability of the resources or the local community. Fish, oil, gas, minerals, water, we see the same phenomenon worldwide.

Consider the history of fishing in Maine. In the 19th century, cod-fishing was at the center of our economy. In the 20th century, due to unrestrained overfishing, the supply and the monetary return collapsed. Whole communities were abandoned. What has followed? Exactly the same thing with groundfish; taken until less than a handful of boats are operating today from Maine ports. In 2015 the scallop season was shortened, the shrimp season closed completely, and the opening for lucrative elvers was delayed until quotas and regulations could be finalized. The Maine lobster industry, a huge contributor to the state economy and to its cultural identity, is regulated, sometimes to the dismay of the lobstermen. But recently the presence of mercury, purportedly from an upriver chemical manufacturing enterprise, forced the closing of an area at the mouth of the Penobscot River because of contamination in the lobster meat—an example of a sudden possible shift in the ecology as evinced by temperature change, algae bloom, or another toxic release resulting from ecological damage already done, that might threaten the lobster fishery elsewhere with dreadful, devastating financial and community consequences.

Processing is another problem. For years, Maine shipped most of its lobster harvest to Canada where it was processed, packaged, and distributed not as a product of Maine. The increase in rockweed harvest has produced a similar situation, where the state has one private, inadequate processing entity and the rest is exported north to be transformed into a Canadian product, circumventing the local harvest limits, and allocating the real profit from this endeavor to others. Even the harvesters are affected, with some locals still at work, while some of the companies look to employ temporary migrant workers from away to harvest the weed at less than competitive wages. In the Maine legislature, measures to control rockweed harvest areas, regulate for short-term plant regeneration, protect the associated habitat and fisheries, establish certain no-cut zones, and create a management plan are stalled in the usual debate between environmentalists and vested economic or political interests. In the meantime, without guidelines and controls, the rocky coast is being stripped bare, southward one cove at a time.

What are we doing? Rockweed is just another example of "failing down the food chain." Again and again, we affirm short-term profit over long-term sustainability, governance fails us, and we lose an irreplaceable asset. Why? Will we ever learn? Will we ever understand how we damage ourselves with this consistent illogic and narrow thinking? This is not just an embarrassment and loss for Maine, it is emblematic of comparable losses we are facing all round this world, and we should know better.

Trophic Cascade

A trophic cascade is an ecological phenomenon triggered by the addition or removal of top predators and involving reciprocal changes in the relative populations of predator and prey through a food chain that often results in dramatic changes in ecosystem structure and nutrient cycling. A recent article by Gwynn Guilford in the April 2013 issue of *The Atlantic* points to fishing practices in China as examples of trophic cascade resulting from the extreme overharvest of sharks for shark-fin soup, several other species with high value as components in various Chinese elixirs and remedies, and the manta ray, also known for its medicinal qualities.[59]

Shark-finning is of course a well-known practice, the cutting of the fin and discarding of the rest, as the key ingredient in a recipe for soup that is especially prized by Chinese gourmets and those wishing to demonstrate their financial standing and success through the consumption of a very expensive (and not particularly tasty) status dish. There are have been several major public campaigns against shark-finning, promoted by active non-governmental organizations that have had some success in limiting the harvest, exposing the harvesters, and shaming the consumers. The *Atlantic* article points to two other examples: the bladders of totoaba fish found in California waters and a similar fish, the bahaba, native to Chinese waters, both believed to promote fertility. A bahaba is reported to have fetched almost $500,000 on the black market, this for a species listed by the Chinese government as "protected" and thought by others to be nearly extinct. "Like the totoaba bladder and shark fins, gill rakers of manta rays—cartilage that filters the ray's food—are prized for their supposed medicinal properties," states *The Atlantic*, "so much so that they fetch about $251 per kilogram. The $5 million trade in manta ray gill rakers—almost all of which occurs in Guangzhou, in southern China—has depleted manta populations so severely that they were classified as endangered."[60]

So what about this trophic cascade? What is happening here is that the dramatic removal of large predators at the top of the ocean food chain will have additional impact on the species below. As sharks are killed, their predators flourish and increase, with consequences that change the interaction between lesser species, and that alters the predation pattern and thus the relative population numbers, food chain structure, and ecosystem balance. The change at the top, the sudden disappearance of a major determining force, then results in changes below that further disrupt the existing order of the marine system.

Let's see if I have got this right. It seems silly to say so, but is it not true that this entire process is justified to provide virility/fertility medicines or status symbols to consumers most probably ignorant of or indifferent to the consequences of their desires? Isn't it ironic that we can harvest one species to extinction in order to foster procreation in another? The Chinese can kill fish, deplete their own waters, waste an astonishing volume of protein, intrude on other nations' sovereignty, destroy coastal livelihoods on distant shores, deprive local tourism and economic development in struggling countries, lie, under-report, or otherwise game the system, ignore international quotas and agreements with impunity, and defy the concept of sustainability as a strategy for the future—all in the name of pleasure. Talk about your trophic cascade!

So who's the top predator here? In this case, it's the Chinese. But there are other examples, other responsible parties; it's any of us who sit at the top of the food chain and are able—intellectually, financially or morally—to support a system as absurd as this one. Where is the meaningful social value in this situation? If fish bladders, fins, and gill cartilage really do contain a cure for cancer, are there not other ways to meet the demand without decimating the supply?

By-catch to By-product

The crisis in fisheries is primarily the result of too many vessels chasing too few fish. We are all aware of declining supplies, threatened extinction of many species, and critical impacts on the developing nations where impoverished populations rely heavily on fish as their primary source of protein. Overfishing, unregulated, illegal fishing, industrial fishing—these are the problems that we hear constantly in the news, research reports, policy studies, and regulatory initiatives.

In this context, what has always been most frustrating to me has been those images of ton after ton of fish discarded from the harvest, an enormous amount of marine life washed overboard, dead and wasted. We have all seen it: the dramatic haul of the dragged net or purse seine, the flood of fish on the rolling deck, the separation of the most desirable product into the holds for icing or freezing and the next steps en route to market and plate. We have all seen what follows: the seawater hoses washing over-board a slurry of so-called junk fish—juveniles, undesirables, unrecognizables—of no apparent value.

A 2009 op-ed contribution by Paul Greenberg in the *New York Times* brought this issue again to mind. Greenberg commented on the use of wild fish to produce fish meal, fish fertilizer, and fish oil, about a third of the total harvest used to feed aqua- and agricultural use, to enrich our soil, and to infuse our bodies with purported anti-cholesterol properties.[61] Environmentalists have long opposed this as an inefficient harvest of one biomass to feed another, as the transfer of PCBs in fish to humans through the other food we eat, and as an intervention in the food chain that deprives other marine species such as whales and seals of their main source of sustenance.

Greenberg pointed specifically to the pet food industry. Think about that wall at the pet food store or supermarket—the creative mixtures of tuna, mackerel, anchovy, and herring with chicken or pig or vegetable, all fed or fertilized with fish, as if our house pets were actually able to discern the subtleties of such a refined menu. Of course, all this adds up to an enormous commercial enterprise, a conflict compromised by millions of dollars in pursuit of an already diminished resource.

But how comprised is it when all that by-catch is wasted? Why is it that we cannot relate the value lost overboard with value to be gained by using this product to meet or supplant the established use? Surely that slurry swept overboard has value as fish oil or fish pellets or food for felines? Why is it just thrown away?

I wish I had the answer. When I ask, I get predictable replies: not as lucrative as tuna for sushi, or no ships or shore facilities set up to harvest and process, no market, or, worst of all, that ever-depressing response of "that's the way we've always done it before."

But these arguments don't match up with reality. Soon, there will be no tuna. We have abandoned ships, piers, and factories that could be adapted to a new use. We have an already proven market and increasing demand for product that this supply could meet. And we have a workforce of fishers and processors who by not doing things differently found themselves with nothing left to do.

If we were to capture all that waste and transform it into value, wouldn't that allow us to manage other fisheries in crisis in a more sustainable manner? Wouldn't we be able to use product already harvested to meet an existing demand, to promote economic development, and to the unemployed back to work on the sea?

From by-catch to by-product: it sounds like an opportunity to me.

Ocean and Human Health

We all know that the ocean is a valuable source of protein. We all know that the ocean is an increasingly valuable source of minerals and metals. But we don't all know the true value of the ocean as a pharmacological source with deep implication for the development of new medicines for present and future diseases, indeed for enormous contribution to global public health.

Healthy, vibrant oceans are essential for human health and well-being. A surprising statement? It shouldn't be.

The world ocean provides important health benefits to humans, ranging from food, nutritional, and other resources, to recreational opportunities, to support for industries, to better understanding of human physiology, and to new treatments for human disease. However, as oceans become more degraded, human health effects from exposure to dangerous substances, including synthetic organic chemicals, polycyclic aromatic hydrocarbons, heavy metals, marine toxins, and pathogens have been increasingly recorded and are now of great concern. Coastal and marine habitats that have been impacted negatively by human use and development are unable to provide goods and services, and add to the human health risks posed by degraded oceans. Degraded seas thus move from being great providers to becoming threatening to human health. The result: increased rates of starvation and poverty, diminished sanitation and hygiene, accelerated spread of disease and poisoning, beach closures and reduced access to ocean areas, and ever-increasing public health costs and societal conflict.

The indirect degradation of oceans is an increasing problem, despite government regulations on pollutants. This is partly due to the fact that the ocean system's most vital organs: the coastal wetlands, sea-grass beds, and mangrove forests that are its lungs, liver and kidneys, filtering out toxins before they reach the open sea, continue to be destroyed through coastal development.

The story of how human health and ocean health are related is not one easily told. How much easier to portray the plight of the great whales, or to document the decline in fisheries, or to show a coastline sullied by unsustainable development. But make no mistake, the ocean contributes to almost every health aspect of our lives, and thus as it deteriorates so too, inevitably, will the quality of those lives be comprised.

The Ocean as Frontier for New Medicines

Many of us are more aware of the health benefits of fish, rich in protein and omega-3 fatty acids. A majority of the world's population derives its primary food supply from ocean products, a source that is diminishing dramatically through overfishing and other impacts on ocean sustainability.

According to a 2007 report by The National Academies of Science, Engineering, and Medicine, the ocean also supports human health in new and surprising ways.[62] For example, the discovery in 1945 of a marine organism derived from a Caribbean sponge, later named *Cryptotethya crypta*, eventually led to the development of a whole class of drugs that treat cancer and viral diseases—for example, AZT that fights the AIDS virus, HIV; Ara-C that is used in the treatment of leukemias and lymphomas; and acyclovir that speeds the healing of eczema and some herpes viruses.

Historically, the development of new drugs has focused on land-based natural resources—terrestrial plants, animals and microorganisms—with more than 120 drugs available today. But scientists are finding that source close to exhaustion—relegated primarily to the refining of existing medicines, treatment of side effects, or countering resistance. Thus, the potential of marine organisms is not just an exciting alternative, but also rather an entirely new and open path to novel microbes with enormous implication for the future of human health.

That simple sponge, for example, represents a natural system that protects itself from an animal invading its space, comparable to the human immune system trying to kill foreign cancer cells. Bathed in seawater containing millions of bacteria, viruses, and fungi, that sponge had developed antibiotics to control pathogens that can be used to treat human infections. Sponges are in fact among the most prolific sources of such diverse chemical compounds; an estimated 30 percent of all marine-derived medications currently under development—and about three-quarters of recently patented marine-derived anti-cancer compounds—come from sponges.[63]

The Census of Marine Life, a global endeavor to catalogue all species existing in the marine environment, has discovered literally millions of new organisms, any one of which could hold an important treatment for a heretofore-untreatable disease.[64] Prialt, for example, an effective neuromuscular block for individuals with chronic pain, stroke, or epilepsy, has been derived from the powerful neurotoxic venom used by a type of cone snail to paralyze and kill prey for food.[65] Other marine-derived drugs are being tested against asthma, breast cancer, and cystic fibrosis.

What is clear is that the ocean represents a unique opening to a vast new pharmacopeia still mostly unknown. It must be both protected and explored if this potential is to be sustained. If we continue to pollute and degrade the oceans, and to ignore this powerful opportunity, it will certainly be lost, and with it an infinite benefit for human health and survival.

The Mercury Cycle

Mercury is a documented poison, affecting our bodies with symptoms from rapid heartbeat, high blood pressure, bleeding from mouth and ears, to blindness, loss of hearing, impaired memory, disturbed speech, birth defects, and more. It is no wonder that the US Food and Drug Administration recommends that pregnant or nursing women, women who may become pregnant, and young children completely avoid eating swordfish, shark, king mackerel, and tilefish, eat no more than 6 ounces per week of albacore tuna and 12 ounces per week of shellfish, and otherwise avoid seafood consumption of predator species that have revealed dangerously high levels of mercury in their flesh.[66]

How has this situation come to pass? Carl Lamborg and his fellow scientists at the Woods Hole Oceanographic Institution in Massachusetts have undertaken serious research in pursuit of an explanation. In a recent report in the Woods Hole publication, *Oceanus*, the mercury cycle is described as an interconnected exchange from earth to atmosphere to ocean and back to earth through a system of biomagnification up through the food chain from micro-organisms to ourselves and our patterns of living.[67]

Mercury enters the atmosphere in part from volcanic eruptions, earthquake, and other natural phenomena, but the largest single contribution is through human activity, about 160 tons a year in the US alone from the burning of high-sulfur coal and other fossil fuels, and the dumping of industrial waste carried by rainwater into the sea. Perhaps the most dramatic historical example of such mercury poisoning was the revelation in the 1970s through the disturbing photographs by W. Eugene Smith published in *Life* magazine of the deformed children of Minamata Bay, Japan, the site of an unregulated mercury-producing chemical plant. Those photographs were so powerful and emotionally compelling that they were removed from public display in deference to the subjects and their families.

The Woods Hole scientists are working hard to understand the process, investigating the air—sea exchange, the process of toxic mixing, the concentration in low-oxygen areas in coastal sediments, and in a layer between 100 and 1000 meters in the water column. The research suggests that the conversion of mercury into the more toxic, concentrated mono-methyl mercury is ingested by phytoplankton at the base of the food chain and thereafter amplified upward as it is further consumed by zooplankton, small fish, and larger species where it arrives finally on our table, the ultimate predator. The phytoplankton have 10,000 times more toxin than the surrounding seawater; the biomagnifications then amplify to measured concentrations in the meat of shark and tuna of 10 million times, enough to pose health risks to people.

Waiting in my doctor's office last week, I noticed a wall poster confirming the FDA cautionary notice. In my wallet was one of those "what fish are safe to eat" cards that carries the same admonition. This is serious business, not something to be denied and dismissed as alarmist or unsubstantiated. Clearly there is consensus among public health officials that we must pay real attention to these warnings, even if we don't yet fully understand how the system works.

Eventually we will, however, and we will have another example of how seemingly esoteric science and research can lead to our better understanding of how our ocean world works and how we might modify our behavior to protect ourselves and our children from ignorance and its tragic consequence.

The Ocean Genome Legacy

The genome is the sum of all DNA within a living cell or organism. It is the blueprint upon which a species is built and a record of its physiology, ecology, history, and evolution. Genome resources are defined as materials from which genetic information may be obtained, including tissues, cells, cultured strains, nucleic acids, nucleic acid libraries and amplification products, information that is not only invaluable for protecting species from extinction but can also help to cure disease and improve the sustainability of global food production, energy supplies, and new contributions to medical therapies and human health.

The Ocean Genome Legacy is a nonprofit marine research institute and genome bank, based in Ipswich, Massachusetts, in the United States, dedicated to exploring and preserving the threatened biological diversity of the sea. According to executive director Dr. Dan Distel, the purpose of the collection is to provide a central physical repository, secure storage, and appropriate public access to genomic materials from endangered, rare, and unusual marine species and ecologically critical environments, to create a forum for sharing samples, data and ideas among a global community of scientists and non-commercial research institutions, and to serve as a catalyst for the development of new science and educational opportunities that can help to understand and protect marine ecosystems and improve the human condition. The project is funded in part by the US National Institutes of Health, the National Science Foundation, and private foundations. Its board is comprised of marine scientists, microbiologists, conservationists, and two Nobel Laureates. The Ocean Genome Legacy also undertakes its own research projects; in the Philippines for example, studying the capacity of marine worms to convert cellulose to sugar as a means to develop scaled processes to produce ethanol as a possible alternative energy source for the future.[68]

All this may seem far too esoteric and incomprehensible, but it is of course what scientists do. And the task is enormous. Of the approximately 200,000 named marine species, the project has collected some 10,000 in its short history and is working with a growing network of research organizations and vessels to augment this inventory as feasible according to a strict collections policy and procedure. A satellite repository with the Australian Institute of Marine Science is planned.

This approach to the understanding of ocean systems is not so new as to raise concerns about intellectual property and commercial development, about the protection of such marine resources within national boundaries, and even about the threat of "biopiracy," the theft of such resources for unauthorized, uncontrolled exploitation. The Ocean Genome Legacy is but one means to address these issues and to protect the extraordinary potential of marine species and systems, and it is not too early to do so given known "bio-prospecting" in the ocean which is well underway outside general public view.

Waterborne Diseases

Some viruses, bacteria, and parasites that occur in ocean waters can be harmful agents for humans. Degraded coastal waters can spur the growth of pathogens, and marine ecosystems with altered biodiversity quickly lose the ability to keep harmful populations of microbes in check. Marine pathogens have been responsible for some large epidemic events, such as the cholera outbreak in the Western Hemisphere that resulted in over 1 million cases and over 11,000 deaths between 1991 and 1995.[69]

Around the world, it is estimated that marine contamination—related diseases from swimming in polluted seawater and eating contaminated seafood are responsible for more than 3 million disability-adjusted years (based on premature death and years of loss of health life) per year, with an estimated economic impact of US$13 billion.[70]

Warmer oceans associated with a changing global climate increase the potential for humans to be affected by waterborne diseases. The best-documented case is cholera, whose causative agent, *Vibrio cholerae*, can be transported in seawater. Researchers have found links between pollution-driven algal blooms (population explosions that are enhanced by warmer surface waters) and incidence of cholera outbreaks.[71] Such outbreaks are not only a public health issue but a human well-being issue as well: epidemics extract huge financial costs via lost profits in fisheries and tourism, for instance. Because many other human pathogens can be found in seawater, there is good reason to fear that warmer seas will result in a sicker world, as pathogen development rates and geographic ranges increase.

Filter-feeding animals, such as oysters and clams, can concentrate pathogens, such as hepatitis A and Norwalk virus, found in sewage.[72] The pathogens then can be transmitted to people when shellfish, especially if uncooked, are eaten. Shellfish beds downstream from sewage treatment plants often are closed after storms until pathogens are naturally released from the shellfish. Viruses can be so lethal that ingesting a single virus can cause infection. Rotaviruses, for example, are extremely robust in seawater and cause diarrhea and death, killing an estimated 870,000 children around the world each year.[73] In a more straightforward route of infection, illness can also occur by direct contact with contaminated water containing viral, bacterial, or protozoan pathogens.

These are certainly brutal statistics to hear. And the estimates of financial losses, the monetization of such devastating human loss, seem disrespectful and irrelevant in the face of a single death. But it is critical to understand the speed and degree of impacts resulting from indifference to these conditions and the need to correct them. The newspapers and television report such stories as single events, but they are occurring frequently and everywhere, from the closed beaches along the Atlantic coast, to the shores of east Africa, to the Amazon delta in South America. The statistics and linkages must be persuasive enough to convince policy-makers and politicians to confront these conditions and implement the changes required to protect human life.

Megacities by the Sea[74]

When we are threatened, our natural instinct is to protect ourselves. That truism applies to our bodies, our homes and families, indeed to all the things we hold essential and sacred. So, too, with the ocean, this vast nurturing global resource that is being affected and altered in real and critical ways that threaten our lives in an ever-expanding catalogue of negative impacts and consequences.

How, then, do we protect the ocean? First, we look to the most obvious threats—the circumstances and conditions that offer the best evidence of the challenges we face. We argue about climate change, CO_2 emissions, acidification, fisheries collapse, extreme weather, sea level rise—all of which are evident in continuing research, real-time and real-world conditions, and personal experience. The counterarguments, however, enable procrastination, divert us from modifications and changes that do not require huge investments, dilute and distract political will, and otherwise sustain the problems with little progress toward solutions. The process is entropic, and we can feel and measure the decline a little bit each day.

Perhaps the most popular tactic present in play for ocean conservation is the "marine protected area," a growing number of places around the world designated and structured to shelter pristine ocean space from intrusive activities. Fair enough, but hardly substantial in the great scheme of things. If we are to invent a new primary strategy for ocean protection, we must look elsewhere beyond these distance places, and move, without question, closer to home to the megacities and associated urban agglomeration that are the true point source, in extreme variety and magnitude of scale, of the most dangerous and deadly contributors to the ongoing pollution of the world ocean.

The 26 largest megacities—urban centers with more than 10 million residents—are populated by almost 500 million people, growing at a rate of 2–4 percent annually.[75] Of these, 20 are coastal, three are located on major rivers leading to the ocean, and three—Mexico City, Moscow, and Tehran—are inland albeit still a factor in the surrounding watershed and atmosphere. Many are also national capitals, and, as such, centers of policy and governance determining political response to the larger environmental conversation. And, by the way, new such cities like Johannesburg at 9 million inhabitants are coming along strong. These numbers will only continue to grow. It is in these places that we find the extreme concentration of development, industry and manufacturing, toxic waste, untreated chemicals, air pollutants, sewage, and all the rest that mixed with groundwater runoff and extreme weather events turns the quality of air, local rivers, adjacent wetlands, and alongshore areas into zones where sickness incubates or, worse, little or nothing can survive.

The smog brings tears, coughs, and allergies; mangrove swamps are filled; the reefs are killed; the fresh water is undrinkable; the beaches are un-swimmable; the fisheries are gone, at such a mammoth scale of effect that it can never be mitigated by this protected area far away or that point-source improvement even nearby. It is an enormous, ever-escalating, mutually degrading process of destruction, much of which is invisible or otherwise lost in a fog of indifference, inaction, or deliberate avoidance. It is not that we don't know what's happening; it is that we don't have the determination to save ourselves.

Histrionic? Alarmist? Maybe so. But what will it take for the reality to sink in? Mass infections and diseases? Rivers spontaneously on fire? Air so dirty and un-breathable that the residents can no longer function? Water so vile and undrinkable that the essential daily supply cannot meet the insatiable daily demand? And what happens to those millions if the city becomes unlivable? Where do they go? What do they do? What happens next?

Environmental groups must stop fiddling around the edges where the victories are easy. I believe that these organizations should find the energy and imagination to modify or change their strategies to turn their focus on the megacities, not the empty spaces, to transform those "urban agglomerations" into visionary laboratories for change, to transcend the global perspective and look to home where even the smallest improvement will touch millions of people for the better. I believe they should apply their conservation values and financial resources to a new, integrated strategy that attacks multiple problems at multiple levels within the local community, re-allocating existing intellectual, political, and financial capital from within to design and implement the technologies and systems without, many of which are within our grasp, that will advance a different, coherent, community-based response that will challenge conventional situations, processes, and social behaviors now and set them on end. Let's take those cities by the sea and turn them into exemplary marine protected areas.

SECURITY

Water Security

There are interesting signs that the public is awakening to the urgency of ocean and fresh water issues, to understanding the crisis of supply, degradation, and governance.

One such sign is the more and more frequent use of the word "security" in the context of water and ocean, a term adding a particular emphasis, putting the issue to the front of the line, asserting a gravitas that must be addressed, and implying consequence more threatening and real than reports of climate change, glacier melt, sea level rise, acidification, depletion of fish stocks, indifference to extant policy, failed enforcement of legislated regulation, and confused or insufficient governance. While environmental advocates have been talking about these conditions for years, it has been difficult to penetrate public awareness in any meaningful dimension, the message lost in the cacophony of contradiction, disaster, and diverting entertainment.

From the beginning, the World Ocean Observatory has declared its primary mission "to expand public awareness of the implication of the ocean for the future of human survival." Survival—a stark term, a precise term, an urgent word that states the truth as life or death. On many occasions, that mission statement has been challenged as too extreme, too dire, too alarmist, less a fact than a cynical means to capture public attention, build public awareness, or affect political change. I have always rebutted those comments as purposeful denial of overwhelming incidence and evidence, naïve response to the depth of crises known, unrealistic understanding of the extent and consequence of our indifference, and fearful unwillingness to accept and implement the change required to sustain the Earth and to survive.

A stunning example may be found in a 2012 article generated by ClimateWire and re-posted by *Scientific American* that points to the area around Lijiang, Yunnan Province, China, typically a heavy rainfall district, but where over the past four years precipitation has dropped by 70 percent to drought conditions that have already critically diminished agricultural and hydroelectric production, the productivity of local wells and aquifer, and, yes, the survivability of a provincial population of some 45 million that has grown 12 percent and quadrupled economic output per capita since 2000.[76] In the face of that growth, according to the article, available water resources per capita have dropped by half.

According to the *Scientific American* article, "Yunnan is known as Asia's water tower because many important domestic and international rivers start from here," explains Duan Changqun, an ecologist at Yunnan University. "Drought means less water flows in the downstream, sending a blow to the ecosystem of other parts of China as well as South Asian countries."

It is a vicious cycle: atmospheric circulation change affects rainfall, creates drought, denies tobacco, herb, rubber plant, and agricultural irrigation requirements, reduces hydroelectrical distribution locally and regionally, collapses the freshwater fish stocks, negates the $1.8 billion tourist industry—dried-up lakes, dry streams, and no snow-capped mountain vistas—and limits household water supply in the capital, Kunming, to four hours a day. Local media have estimated the economic loss at $4.2 billon since the drought began in 2009. Add to that the retreat of the local glaciers, 70 percent of which are predicted to disappear by 2050 due to increased average temperature, and the extreme pollution of the remaining water by unregulated waste disposal, sewage, and fertilizer and manufacturing runoff, and you have a truly toxic recipe that does not bode well for security or survival.

To solve the problem, the article suggests the Yunnan government is introducing water-saving technologies and proposes to construct "new water reserves" of 3 billion cubic meters, a 30 percent increase in capacity, at untold cost, but it does not indicate from where that water will come.

So, this is an example of the water cycle interrupted at every turn: reduced glacial supply, no regenerating rain, diminished aquifer, dry rivers, polluted reserves, collapsed economy, and catastrophic local and downstream consequences beyond provincial borders to other regions, other nations, to the coast and, finally, the ocean. It is a case of "hydraulic society" destroyed at every level by a conspiracy of human causes, all the essential value of water and its distributive, generative power dried up, poisoned, insufficient—depriving individuals, businesses, communities, regions, nations, inter-nations of water, the most essential element of human life. And Lijiang is not the only example. When you consider all this, add it all up and confront the integrated reality, insecurity is the word that comes to mind, and that does not bode well for anyone.

War and Water

Our time is fraught with war and water. The headlines confirm that for what seems like forever there has been conflict in the Middle East where sectarian and religious rivalries, the pursuit of oil, and the geopolitical collision between economic aspirations and impassioned ideologies continue unabated. Many thousands have died—children, women, men as combatants or collateral damage in an endless time and place of conflict.

The most recent manifestation, following a brief hopeful moment when it seemed that there was some respite to be found in elections, new political faces, and the withdrawal of American and western coalition troops, is the so-called Islamic State or ISIL, a particularly feral group of Muslim militants with the intent to re-establish the historical caliphate that once extended from the Mediterranean Sea to the Persian Gulf. Suddenly, everything reverts to air strikes, international outrage, and the possible return of "boots on the ground."

I have been looking at the maps indicating where so quickly the ISIL forces seem to have taken control, and wondering at their length and direction that extends from the northern border between Turkey and Syria southeasterly almost to the limits of Baghdad. The obvious explanation is that the extent of their success mimics the main highway than runs from Aleppo through Raqua, Qaim, Haditha, and Fallujah to the capital city. A larger segment of controlled territory is enclosed to the east by a similar route that connects Mosul south to Tikrit, Samarra, and Baghdad where the situation deteriorates into the ambiguity of warfare and shifting political ambitions.

But if you look closely at your atlas map of Syria and Iraq, you discover an underlying revelation: that those cities are placed and those highways run exactly along the course of several major rivers—the Euphrates, Tigris, and their tributaries—that originate in the mountains of eastern Turkey, bifurcate the empty desert, and descend to and past Baghdad where they empty at Basra into what ultimately becomes the Arabian Sea. In the vast, dry, unpopulated expanse of the region, this war is being fought down a watershed.

My map is also marked by numerous three-dot symbols that are used by cartographers to designate significant historical cultural resources—indeed locating places called Zenobia, Dura Europus, Nimrud, and Nineveh, names that speak to the earliest human settlements in what the history books call "the cradle of civilization."

Those rivers nurtured our beginnings, before Islam and Christianity, before conquest from elsewhere by imperialists, then and now, following the trade routes to resources and connections beyond. There are other such symbols on my map—miniature drilling rigs signifying the major oil fields that fuel this war and all others, cultural icons of our modern time.

The irony here is that after all the tumult and shouting, after all the air strikes and beheadings, all the assertions of conflicting systems of law, all the moral justifications, the only thing that matters is the water—to drink, to secure hygiene and health, to irrigate crops, and to sustain the communities regardless of sect or religious belief, to allow the descendants of those who lived in these places centuries before to continue and thrive.

The location of these cities and the caravan or highway routes between them are all testimony to the fact that for all time water has enabled the true security of the region. Take away the slogans and guns from these people, whoever they may be, let the people live there and the water will sustain them.

We speak often of the healing and unifying nature of water. Below Baghdad, along this same riverine watershed, there lies an

enormous lake and swamp system into which all these waters
flow, an area that has been home to so-called "marsh Arabs" who
had thrived there for a very long time in what were very fertile
conditions. In the 1990s, as a strategic part of an earlier iteration of
this present war, the area was drained by canals and dikes to isolate
and destroy the residents by removing their shelter and livelihood.
It became a desert like elsewhere, devoid of plant life and birds,
of shelter and safety, until recently, through the efforts of a small
activist group, the dikes were broken, the waters returned, the
marshes filled, and life began there anew. It is a cautionary tale of
how we might, through the free and unencumbered flow of water,
build a home without terror and its collateral damage.

Climate Refugees

In June 2015, the resolution of a legal case in New Zealand
captured world media attention.[77] Ioane Teitiota, facing
deportation to his home in Kiribati, claimed refugee status
resulting from the impact of climate change, sea level rise, and
extreme weather on his small island nation which some have
predicted will be inundated within decades forcing the entire
national population, some 50,000 people, now inhabiting a narrow
island of just six square miles, to seek a new homeland.

The High Court Judge denied his claim, dismissing it as
"unconvincing" and "novel." Well, legally unconvincing maybe,
the government defenders easily able to find legalistic reasons to
discredit the argument. But novel? That is a different matter. The
judge should not have been afraid of precedent; after all, lawyers
seek and cite precedent all the time. But the implication of a novel
standing as a refugee from climate change, the result of deliberate
national policies and private actions over which a single citizen

or even small undeveloped country has no control—now, that is another matter, indeed that is terrifying by its implication.

Beneath any vindication of Mr. Teitiota's claim lies another acceptance: that of responsibility for the contribution by the developed economies and multi-national corporations to environmental conditions resulting in storm surges, flooding and water contamination, community dislocation, and, in such cases as Kiribati, the probable collapse of a nation. It is facile to deny the link between certain human behaviors, economic policies, and corporate actions and changing climate, to ignore the arguments and evidence of responsible science, and to argue that the energy demands of the larger world and its growth and consumption-based economies are far more important than the life of one man, or even one insignificant country. Tell that to the residents of New Orleans post-Katrina or the devastated homeowners along the New Jersey and New York shoreline post-Sandy, and you may find angry pushback from those citizens of the developed world seeking compensation for the destruction not just of property but also of their lives.

These events are not going away. In 2013, the super-typhoon Haiyan struck the central Philippines with unprecedented strength, leaving almost 6,000 dead and millions displaced. Entire villages were destroyed, entire livelihoods, entire families—a tragedy that joins other perhaps lesser events with equal, terminal impact on those affected. But think also what this leaves behind, what faces the survivors in the form of reconstruction of buildings, infrastructure, occupation, food supply, local and regional economy, and the critical water and health needs of the area. Millions are left behind, and why would we not expect them to move to higher ground, safer communities, new opportunities for themselves and their families? Many of these will become refugees, not from war and politics, but from the consequence of climate change.

The New Zealand judge cited the United Nations Refugee Convention in his decision, stating that Mr. Teitiota did not meet the "fear of persecution" criterion that is central to the UN definition. But is not fear of persecution by circumstances already demonstrated, or by a high probability of similar destruction, reason for seeking an alternative status in a safer place? Especially when the situation is known for both its cause and its inevitable effect and the victims have no defense against the indifference of the perpetrators? And is it only the numbers that matter? Must the destruction be measured only in massive political disruption? Or gross national product? Or vast economic loss? Or untenable cost of reconstruction? Or numbers of people killed or driven from their homes, never to return? Must it be millions?

In "Unsafe Climates," a recent 2015 article in *The New Yorker*,[78] Elizabeth Kolbert writes:

> *In Syria, the rainy season begins in November and ends in April. Only a third of the country's farms have irrigation systems; the rest depend on what the season supplies them with, which, even in good years, isn't all that much. The northeastern most province of Al Hasakah, where much of Syria's wheat is grown, receives an average of about eleven inches of rain a year, which is what New York is likely to get between Labor Day and Thanksgiving.*
>
> *In the winter of 2007, the rainy season never really began. The next year was worse; the country experienced its driest winter on record. Wheat production failed, many small farmers lost their herds, and prices of basic commodities more than doubled. In the summer of 2008, according to a leaked diplomatic cable, Syria's minister of agriculture told officials from the United Nations that the consequences of the drought, both economic and social, were "beyond our capacity as a country to deal with." Meanwhile, Syria's representative to the U.N.'s Food*

and Agriculture Organization warned American officials
that the situation was contributing to "a perfect storm" that
could undermine the country's stability, and asked for aid.
(The Americans, the leaked cable shows, were unmoved by this
appeal.) The drought persisted through the following winter and
the winter after. Hundreds of thousands of people abandoned
the countryside and moved to cities like Homs, Damascus,
and Aleppo. There they joined more than a million similarly
desperate Iraqi refugees.

On the list of horrors that led to Syria's civil war, it's hard to
know how high to place the drought or its destabilizing conse-
quences—the spike in food prices, the internal displacement,
the further crowding of already overcrowded cities. Certainly, it
ranks below the repressive brutality of Bashar al-Assad's regime.
Still, as Secretary of State John Kerry put it recently, in a speech
about climate change and national security, it's probably "not a
coincidence" that the war was preceded by four years of failed
rains. Kerry also observed, "Because the world is so extraor-
dinarily interconnected today—economically, technologically,
militarily, in every way imaginable—instability anywhere can be
a threat to stability everywhere." This was, explicitly, an allu-
sion to ISIS, which arose out of the civil war's chaos.

Ioane Teitiota lost his case and was deported. Thousands
of those Syrians eventually fled, by boat, to Greece and Europe
beyond where they, among others similarly displaced, have
become a controversial presence, a social, economic, and political
issue, that is affecting those countries and the rest of the world
where they, and many thousands, perhaps millions more to come,
seek *refuge*, a place where to find a new, stable, sustainable life.

Cause: climate change, rising seas, extreme weather, global
warming, drought, dislocation. Effect: social collapse, failed sustenance, unemployment, civil conflict, emigration, relocation. The

consequences now transcend distant conflicts to disrupt patterns closer to our homes. How ironic and tragic was the juxtaposition in Paris of delimited climate negotiations and anarchist violence, the sudden resultant disintegration of trust and tolerance, and the shift in international perspective and politics that has ensued. The challenge becomes global. No one is immune, thereby making climate refugees of us all.

Environmental Justice

Justice may be defined as fair or moral conduct, the exercise of authority in the maintenance of right. The United States Environmental Protection Agency defines *environmental* justice as "the fair treatment and meaningful involvement of all people regardless of race, color, national origin, or income with respect to the development, implementation, and enforcement of environmental laws, regulations, and policies. EPA has this goal for all communities and persons across this Nation. It will be achieved when everyone enjoys the same degree of protection from environmental and health hazards and equal access to the decision-making process to have a healthy environment in which to live, learn, and work," all of which makes sense given our Constitutional guarantee of "equal protection under the law."[79]

Of course, in reality, it does not always work that way, and there are many examples when the equitable distribution of environmental risks and benefits, fair and meaningful participation in environmental decision-making, recognition of community ways of life, local knowledge, and cultural difference, and the capability of communities and individuals to function and flourish in society have not been respected and implemented. Many examples can be found along the coasts: the location of incinerators and landfills, sewerage treatment plants, nuclear installations, large

landscape-altering infrastructure projects, chemical and manufacturing facilities, and other uses with known hazardous and
unhealthy environmental impacts that affect the local communities, typically inhabited by indigenous peoples, minorities, and the
poor who do not have easy access to defense. It is no wonder that
more affluent areas can resist such impacts through legal challenges and well-financed campaigns "not in my backyard."

The situation is by no means limited to the United States.
There are innumerable similar situations in other countries
and at sea where waste and persistent organic pollutants are
exported and deposited in the deep ocean away from scrutiny
and national regulation.

Atmosphere

Air is a fluid. The science of fluid dynamics is complicated
and well beyond my understanding, but a simple definition
might suffice for discussion today, accepting that air is a fluid in
that it can be formed, reformed, and compressed to fit the shape
of its container. We take a glass or a tank or even an embayment
where the confining shape is determined by topographical
circumstance and into which the fluid, the air, the water, is
confined. External forces can be brought to bear—gravity, physical
energy, compression, among others—that can push or pull the
fluid within its confines, and even, if the force is great enough,
break the constraints with undesirable results.

I don't want to belabor this definition. But I do want to
discuss the value of clean air, comparable to clean water, in its
essential requirement for human health and survival. We tend to
forget this fact—unless, like my son, you have just returned from
two years of residence in Beijing, China, where the air is dark and

heavy with dust, sand, and pollution; an extreme that requires air
filters in offices and homes, air masks for walking or exercising,
and staying within these unnatural confinements in order to
protect body and mind from the detrimental effect of cough and
sinus infection, serious respiratory disease, and other harmful
consequence of constantly inhaling unhealthy, unbreathable air.

As long ago as the 1997 Kyoto Agreement regarding climate
protection, the problem has focused on the rising rate of greenhouse
gas emissions resulting primarily from the burning of fossil fuels to
meet our increasing demand for energy. The 2014 People's Climate
March in New York City and around the world was an expression
of pent-up anger and resistance to the inability or unwillingness
of governments to regulate, restrict, legislate, and enforce behaviors that continue to add to this serious worldwide health threat.
According to CorpWatch.org, a watchdog organization, only 122
companies generate 80 percent of greenhouse gas emissions, 10
percent caused by just four of the largest energy corporations worldwide.[80] This is not new news, and we have spent too many years
debating the question and postponing the answer.

The solution typically offered is "cap and trade," a system
by which one nation, heavily reliant on polluting technology, can
buy a quota from another nation that has reduced its output or
switched to alternative technologies. Germany and Denmark,
for example, which have initiated accelerated change away from
coal- and oil-fired energy generation, would have a massive
credit to sell to China or the United States, for example, nations
that for various reasons can't or won't respond internally to their
conventional production and deleterious effect. There have been
experiments to create markets for such transactions, none yet
particularly successful.

What underlies this approach, of course, is what underlies the

critical consequence of the continuing commodification/monetiza-
tion of natural resources—forests, minerals, fossil fuels, and water,
along with all the associated activities thereupon based. Ironically,
the solution is based on the continuity of the problem. While the
so-called assets are traded to the advantage of some, the results
are not necessarily modified globally to the advantage of all.

Certainly air, like water, must be free, untainted by destructive anthropogenic behavior, and available to everyone to breathe
and drink freely, breath by breath, swallow by swallow, day by
day, in the name of individual and world health and security. But
that is not the case, especially if you examine the essential premise
inside the present dialogue that would seem to continue to
enable private interests to usurp the essential value of the world's
natural resources, to control and trade them in a closed, exclusive,
self-beneficial market, and to debase and exhaust, however illog-
ically, the very asset base on which their profit, as well as their
own survival as citizens of the Earth, must depend.

What is missing is a sense of climate justice, of the understanding that we have moved beyond any rationale argument
against the transformation of our historical assumptions,
methods, financial structures, and patterns of governance, that
by perpetuating these we act against our universal best interests,
and that by failing to invent and accept alternatives to our ways
of governing and living together we are taking an irresponsible
risk for our collective future. The situation must now be politically unacceptable.

People will march in the streets. People will change their
individual patterns of consumption. People will act locally to
limit the market and restrict the availability of products that rely
on unsustainable ways. People will fight in favor of land conservation and forest protection; people will protect aquifers and

public water supplies, waterways, wetlands, coastal and marine resources. People will demand clean air. People will band together to assert their justifiable demand for equitable and universal access to what Nature provides for human subsistence, health, and growth. People will stand up for the land, the air, and the ocean as an integrated and enduring global social system, indeed they will stand up for a world community.

ENERGY

Our collective reliance on energy to support our lives and our industries has driven an unending search for new, lost-cost, and accessible sources of energy across the entire planet. The vast oceans of the world hold great potential to meet our energy needs, especially as land-based fossil fuels become harder to find and exploit, and as concern for global warming begins to drive more forceful movement toward renewable energy use.

We are locked today in a political debate over energy— between those who wish to extract as much oil, gas, and minerals from the earth as fast as possible and convert it to profit, and those who wish to sustain such resources, develop and transition to less-polluting alternatives, and invent more efficient processes and products that will enable equal, more equitable growth worldwide. Everywhere you look, there is a battle engaged over our energy future, near and long term, with interests vested in the status quo up against interests vested in change and a sustainable future.

The debate pits those benefiting most from the present system and its profits against those who assess the ecological and political damage from such reliance and the future implications of resultant climate change, diminished resources, and capacity to meet the predictable demands of the growing world population. It is a battle for gratification now or survival then.

The news continues to report one oil drilling or refining mishap after another. BP is fined billions for the Deepwater Horizon spill. Transocean, the actual operator of that platform, is fined millions for its responsibility in that disaster. BP and Chevron are in lawsuits over refinery explosions and leaks in Texas and California. And, most recently, Shell has withdrawn from the Arctic, having wasted some US$9 billion of shareholder value in the name of unrealistic expectation, of market demand, and technological possibility. Statoil, the Norwegian energy giant, has followed suit.

Gazprom, Russia's state oil company, however, has continued its Arctic activities in the Pechora Sea off the island of Novaya Zemlya, an unprecedented incursion with unproven technology, and a construction cost of $800 million.[81] *Marine Technology News* (MTN), an industry news service, describes the project as follows: "Drilling plans envisage up to 40 directional wells (19 producing, 16 injection and five reserve). All wells will be drilled from the single rig on the platform, with simultaneous drilling and production. Perimeter water flooding of horizontal injection wells will occur at near-fracturing injection pressures. Production is expected to last for 25 years."[82]

The MTN article continues: "Gazprom maintains that the... platform was designed to exclude the possibility of discharging oil, formation fluid, contaminated industrial and storm waters as well as other harmful substances into the sea. Obviously, how robust and safe the rig really is, only time will tell." All oversight will be

Russian with no independent audit of the project's safety standards.[83]

These are just the largest and most publicized incidents, only a few among other smaller, reported and unreported incidents of failed management, failed operations, and failed technology. But this risk is huge: unproven technology, extreme dynamic forces of persistent extreme weather, wave, wind, current, and earthquake, subzero temperature and high ice loads, complicated oil storage systems to prevent corrosion, leaks in and out, and consequent explosions, unprecedented off-loading demands, disposal of drilling and production waste, severe working/living/rescue conditions, fire protection, spill prevention, cleanup and mitigation challenges never before required in never-before-known environmental conditions.

The oil companies counter with statistics citing all the successful rigs and the world's compulsive need for more oil and gas, even as the United States, for example, reports supply surpluses and moves to lift the long-standing export ban. To sustain this behavior, and especially to protect supporting subsidies and exemptions, the US Congress is besieged by oil lobbyists and political donations, just as the public via television advertising is inundated with self-justifying assertions of the oil companies' contributions to education and culture, jobs and taxes. These arguments, while transparent, are nonetheless effective, at least perhaps until now, a moment when continuing spills and accidents, increasing transparency and revelation of hypocritical behaviors, and the contradictions of their own arguments and actions are increasing political aware- ness of the companies' collective fecklessness and hostility to the public interest and the environment. Add to that ever-increasing understanding of the damage of fracking to the land and social fabric, and you have a time when the industry, defending itself by doubling down on its bankrupt arguments, may be vulnerable to changing politics and courageous leadership.

The ability of the vested energy interests to maintain, even accelerate, the consumption agenda is evident in the political stalemate in legislatures, the lobbying and advertising, the denial of any science that challenges the conventional assumptions, and the pressure to discover more and extract it quick regardless of consequence. And the area of interest where the greatest potential, and the greatest danger, lies, is, of course, the ocean.

The energy industry has transformed the American landscape: removed mountaintops, scarred vast areas of open pits, destroyed agricultural lands, poisoned aquifers, lakes, streams, rivers, and coastal wetlands, produced emissions that contaminate our air and acidify our waters, fought emission controls and environmental regulations every step of the way, justified wars, and otherwise promoted behavior indifferent to human and community health. Why would we even think of permitting them to despoil anything more? Why would we trust them with the ocean?

Strategic Oil

The post–World War II global industrial expansion has been based primarily on technology and the extraction and consumption of fossil fuels and other natural resources. These two forces have driven our consumption-based growth, measured as gross domestic production, expanded our ability to fertilize and protect our crops from disease, and created new products and processes that have transformed our traditional occupations.

Expanded oil and gas extraction, exponential increase in demand, and worldwide distribution systems and controls have been at the center of global economics and geopolitical cooperation and conflict. Behind market fluctuations, nationalistic aspirations, territorial occupations, and war lies the apparently insatiable need to discover, recover, and expend the Earth's natural resources—its fossil remains, rare earths, forests, and water—in an unsustainable, worldwide collaboration, indeed conspiracy, to grow at an ever-increasing rate in the name of progress.

Nowhere is immune from strategic oil—the desert, coastal waters, the deep sea, the rain forests, and the polar regions. Despite the appearance of environmental concern, action, regulation, and treaty, this imperative to grow has defined our national interests, our economies, and our strategic objectives. Technology has enhanced this phenomenon through new engineering, capacity for globalized trade, speed and extent of financial transaction, worldwide communications, and much more. Thus, the extraction required to feed this exponential consumption has led us beyond a manageable condition to where now we approach the limits of supply, of unsustainable demand, of corruption, of continuing disparity between rich and poor, and of uncertain security for nations, tribes, and communities.

The ocean is unfortunately a key element in this situation. As the United States has consumed much of its conventionally recovered oil and gas, it has turned to fracking as a technology to extract every last bit of these resources from its still finite supply, miraculously transforming us from a import nation to an export nation with no market, a delusionary short-term tactic that postpones the inevitable and, without care and concern, leaves behind further devastated land, water, and community. Not too long ago, we looked to the Gulf of Mexico, the North Sea, and other ocean places around the world for the same reasons, and now too, those supplies diminished, we will begin to frack those deposits below the ocean floor, extending the consequences with no apparent will to look beyond the end of fossil fuel as the organizing paradigm for value and social behavior in the future.

What are the odds in this desperate gamble in the name of strategic oil? What price growth?

Offshore Oil

An editorial in the *Ocean News and Technology* October 2014 issue describes the status of the offshore oil exploration and licensing in the United States as follows:

> *A routine call for public comment on the next 5-year offshore oil-leasing plan has provided industry with a rare opportunity to expand the federal program beyond the measly 13 percent of the US offshore region currently open to drilling.*
>
> *Influential industry groups like the American Petroleum Institute have been after politicians, spanning numerous election cycles, to allow companies more access to federal waters through leasing. These efforts have largely failed.*
>
> *But the stars are aligned this time around. Backed by reputable opinion polls reflecting overwhelming support for more offshore exploration and development, industry advocates now have the public's backing as they do battle against the environmental community as well as President Obama's so-called "all of the above" energy policy, which on the oil and gas side has thus far produced nothing but declining production of federal acreage, offshore and onshore.[84]*

The map illustrating the present situation shows the remaining 87 percent of the area along the Atlantic and Pacific coasts, the eastern Gulf of Mexico, and western Alaska. The two areas presently open are the central area of the Gulf, where drilling has been fully developed for many years and which includes the site of the massive Deepwater Horizon spill, and off the most northern coast of Alaska in the Beaufort Sea—areas of high urban density or endangered ecological resources.

To be expected, the industry argument neglects to include the fact that in recent years, through increased production on land by means of hydraulic fracturing, overall United States energy production has been transformed dramatically. That, along with alternative energy supply, meets the national requirement without any additional capacity from any new license areas. World oil prices are significantly decreased and the market disrupted by this new supply.[85] Opinion polls exist that certainly counter the editorial assertion of majority public support.[86] In 2014 at the Peoples' Climate March, 400,000 people walked the streets of New York to protest the industry contribution to climate change and its ever more revealed consequences. Claims of improved safety are excerpted almost daily by reports of additional polluting accidents and spills.[87] Certain states have succeeded in incentivizing alternative energy technology and production, capturing market share.[88] All of these factors argue *against* any compelling need to open new areas for development other than narrow corporate interest. It is as if the industry has a deaf ear not just to changing public opinion but also to the rapidly deteriorating realities of the world market.

What Price Extra Oil?

It has been very interesting to watch over the past few years this shift in public understanding of international oil and gas supply for the future. Not too long ago, the rush to renewable and alternative energy sources was strong, with public subsidies and private funds in full support of solar, wind, biofuels, and other new technologies and approaches. There was much talk of "peak oil," the tipping point when future supply cannot meet future demand. There was talk of carbon taxes, offsets, and trading as viable means to nurture what would be a painful but necessary shift in consumption and response.

But suddenly all that went away. Climate change, as a reflection of the emission consequence of fossil fuels dependence, was aggressively denied by companies, lobbyists, politicians, and investors. New oil deposits, from the tar sands in Canada for example, were suddenly available, extending the perceived viability of established supply and existing corporate agendas. In addition, natural gas became the new source, a revision that changed the United States from a natural gas importer to an exporter, the result of new and dramatic supplies accumulated through a rapid expansion of fracking technology. Hydraulic fracturing, a process to extract natural gas from heretofore inaccessible reserves in shale deposits mostly inland, is the energy industry's newest technology for augmenting fossil fuel reserves to meet national and international demand. Reportedly developed by Halliburton and promoted by the predictable corporations and their lobbyists, fracking is seen by some as the financial salvation of the industry and its future supply and by others as yet another egregious, short-term assault on the nation's environment with serious detrimental consequences for human health and the support of developing energy alternatives. Fracking is in use in over 30 states in the United States and is also being investigated for use in Africa and elsewhere.[89] It has been utilized for almost 10 years in some areas, and the outcomes beyond gas collected have become better known to neighbors, communities, and in the press, fueling what is now a fervid debate about its practice. It was recently banned in New York State with local bans in Maryland, Pennsylvania, California, North Carolina, Texas, New

Mexico, Colorado, Ohio, Indiana, Illinois, and Michigan.

Focused particularly in historically agricultural areas, fracking caused farmers to sell their mineral rights for high prices, abandoning their farms, many leaving their traditional homeland. The result of this fracking technology is much debated: on one side the energy companies and their supporters, on the other environmentalists and community activists radicalized by the obvious degradation to their towns and surrounding environment. While the estimates of resultant future supply are seductive and diverting, they mask the serious questions about the true nature of this technology and its impact on land and sea.

One major question is the chemical composition of the water used in the process. The companies refuse to reveal the actual recipe; the water left behind, however, shows serious toxic effect, so much so that it must be stored, isolated, and restricted from entering the healthy water cycle around it. The usual cautions and disclaimers are given the public, but the devastation to the landscape, the ever-increasing reports of toxic water and waste from the process, and the ever-expanding health impacts on the people nearby are truly disturbing counters to corporate blandishments and apologists. Why can't we know the chemical mix used? Is proprietary exclusivity so important that it can excuse such physical and financial destruction? Do we have to poison our already limited water supply, and our neighbors, and do it in secret?

A 2015 Reuters article[90] points to another, depressingly familiar, equally dangerous situation—an offshore well in the North Sea, one of many operated by Total, the French energy company, that had to be shut down due to the corrosive effect of a chemically enhanced drilling fluid that under pressure, and heated to over 280 degrees Fahrenheit, had weakened and cracked the piping. Leaking for over a month, it produced a cloud of flammable gas, and the platform was evacuated from the area lest a spark ignite a devastating explosion and fire. The corrosive chemical is reported to be calcium bromide, one of a number of halide fluids known as "brines" that, as discovered after the fact, are corrosive to steel. After an internal investigation, still not officially concluded, Total closed "a minimum" of 10 such wells in operation and felt compelled to notify Shell with its neighboring field off the Scotland coast, using a similar method to extend the productivity of wells thought exhausted. According to the news report, this technology is being used extensively in wells off the coast of Brazil and the Gulf of Mexico.

What are we doing here? What are we doing to ourselves? To the ocean and earth? Why are we standing by and letting this travesty continue? When even the beneficiary company admits the problem and warns its competitor of the danger, why cannot the regulators and authorities put an end to the foolishness once and for all? According to the Reuters article, the process of abandonment will take three years and cost the company Total over $200 million, as if this loss matters at all when compared to the loss already inflicted on the environment, not to mention the future loss implicit in any failure to restrict this dangerous technology, not to mention the loss of time and investment in the alternatives. There is nothing, absolutely nothing, to be gained from this short-term avoidance and denial of the terminal reality of reliance on fossil fuels. There is nothing, absolutely nothing, to be gained.

Fracking the Ocean

What does fracking have to do with the ocean?
First, studies have estimated that some 4 to 7 percent of the gas that flows up the wells escapes as methane into the

atmosphere.[91] Multiply that by thousands of projects, and you
have yet another measurable negative contribution of toxic
emissions to deteriorating air quality with further impact
as increased acidification, diminished ozone protection,
global warming, and changing climate conditions, the very
same factors that were are trying to identify to relieve us of
the consequence of our dependence on oil. The water cycle
guarantees that much of that consequence finds its way directly
and indirectly to the ocean, the marine food chain, the depleted
reefs, the red tides, the closed beaches. It is only a matter of time
and concentration before those consequences find their way into
our drinking water, our food, and our bodies.

Further, fracking uses enormous amounts of fresh water,
some 6 to 8 million gallons per well, water that is mixed with
chemical additives including diesel fuel, biocides, industrial
solvents, hydrochloric acid, and radioactive elements that are
intensely harmful to humans at very low levels of exposure.[92]
That toxicity is injected into the water table, must be extracted and
stored either deep underground or in effluent evaporation pits,
and cannot be further leaked lest it contaminate the soil, groundwater, and water supply in the surrounding areas. The companies
are reluctant to reveal either the nature or amounts of these
chemicals in detail, certainly not reassuring to those who already
experience the results. There are documented examples of violations of the Clean Water Act, EPA regulations, corrupted aquifers,
polluted ponds and streams, tap water ignitable at the spigot,
localized health problems, and underground reservoirs (where the
companies have stored the untreatable waste water) broken open
by natural tremors and minor quakes.[93]

What is most important to understand here is that all that
poisoned water is removed from the finite supply on Earth that is

already at the limits of consumption and sustainability.

It becomes stunningly clear when the impacts are scaled up to the reality of demand. Researchers have found that between 2005 and 2009 over 866 million gallons of fresh water were mixed with some 750 chemicals, including lead and benzene, the full inventory of which is undisclosed by the companies to protect proprietary or trade secrets.[94] Moreover, the present fracking push in Pennsylvania, New Jersey, and New York is focused on the nation's largest unfiltered freshwater supply, the Delaware River Watershed, serving more than 15 million people in that East Coast megalopolis.[95] Remember: that watershed, if poisoned, leads directly to the sea.

What astonishes me about this is that we have done it all before. The past 50 years have revealed where the trade-offs lie. We have polluted the earth; we have polluted the air; and now, we are repeating exactly the same rationale to justify this initiative and polluting our water, fresh and salt. It makes no sense. But the farmers continue to sell their land to the highest bidder, moving on to somewhere. The politicians continue to sell our resources to the largest contributor, unaccountable, and caring less, and we just let it happen, helpless, disinterested, accepting the consequence.

I think again of Rachel Carson's *Silent Spring* and *The Sea Around Us*. She sounded the clarion call for earth and ocean decades ago. We listened but we did not hear. And so it goes, beyond pathos.

Oil Pollution

The threat of oil spills at sea is well known. The grounding of the tankers *Torrey Canyon* off the coast of France and the *Exxon Valdez* in Alaska are notorious; images of oil sludge, bedraggled birds, and blackened beaches appalled television audiences worldwide. Heightened public awareness, legal proceedings, and insurance issues stimulated a global review of the oil and chemical transport business and resulted in new construction standards for tankers, particularly the design of double bottoms, navigation procedures, and loading practices.

In many cases, spills are the result of human error. The challenging conditions of storm and fog can force ships ashore or disorient their operators, just as fatigue, drugs, alcohol, and indifference can cause disastrous errors in judgment. And yet despite increased training, technology, and awareness, these accidents continue to occur. Recent spills in the Black Sea and San Francisco Bay are tragic examples.

But oil pollution is not limited to the most highly publicized examples. Spills occur every day as tankers and smaller barges offload and transfer liquid cargo, as ships and yachts are fueled, or as accidents occur on oil platforms at sea.[96] Many leaks and smaller spills occur on land, from pipelines and storage facilities and industries in the coastal zone. Another, increasingly familiar source of ocean pollution results from diluted oil mixed with water as a result of tank cleaning, both on ship and on shore. Indeed, even the smallest oil leaks from automobiles and trucks eventually seep into our waterways through roadside runoff into storm drains leading to the ocean. And it is not just oil, but a vast inventory of chemicals, toxic and nontoxic, that are moved worldwide on the ocean.

The impact on our environment is universal and ongoing. Industry and government have both responded. The entire global tanker fleet, for example, will be replaced over the next decade in a wave of newly constructed double-bottomed ships, separate ballast systems, shore-based holding tanks and treatment for oil mixtures, more secure loading equipment, and rapid response and containment procedures.[97] In addition, environmental groups have organized cleanup networks for natural resources and treatment centers for birds and other animals trapped by spills. Despite all this, the damage will last for decades, sometimes forever.

Who pays? Well, of course, we do—in many ways. First, we must accommodate the cost of the event itself—what to do with the ship, how to minimize further damage, how to mitigate damage done. Second, we must assimilate the loss not just of the product, ship, or human injury, but also the loss of related revenues from fishing, tourism, and other dependent businesses. And third, we must absorb the future loss of compromised natural systems, degraded species, and irrevocable impact on human health and enterprise in the area. Some of this cost is measurable; some is not.

The international community has responded, particularly in terms of the definition and assignment of civil liability for such events. Early agreements enabled the right of nations to intervene in incidents on the high seas resulting in oil pollution and dealt with the obligations of both ship owners and cargo interests to cover incident costs and to compensate victims. For more than 20 years now, a series of agreements have evolved to increase liability limits, improve design and operating standards, define safe practices, and increase inspection, licensing, training, and enforcement.[98]

Is it better? Yes. Is it perfect? No. The number of incidents continues to grow, in part the result of increased surveillance and reporting, but primarily the result of the growing demand for oil and chemicals by both the developed and developing nations, bulk cargoes that can only be transported by sea and upon which their economies depend.

What about the future? The record orders for new tankers and transports would argue against any short-term change.

Alternatively, improved ship design, containment and mitigation technologies would argue for better response and diminished impact of many incidents. But as long as the world depends on oil and chemicals to sustain their economies and quality of life, the probability of accident and its consequence will remain.

The Dark Side of Oil

The catastrophic accident at the Deepwater Horizon rig in the Gulf of Mexico presented us with the pure consequence of actions taken and untaken. Explanations and responsibilities aside, we are faced with cruel evidence of precautions avoided, short-term economies, and conflicting responsibilities. But what is more evident is the devastating results of decisions made indifferent to the complexity and dangers inherent in exploitation of an environment as challenging as the ocean.

The situation is fraught with pain and irony. There is the memory of Hurricane Katrina that attacked that same shore. There is the memory of the *Exxon Valdez*, heretofore the most destructive oil-related environmental event in our history. The remnants of both phenomena are still with us—in the Alaskan habitat as well as the social fabric of New Orleans and alongshore. How much damage will this incessant bleeding of oil do to the species and habitat of the area and to the communities that have made much of their living from its exploitation—be it fishing or servicing the rigs? How long will it take for them to recover, regenerate, renew?

What has now taken place in Louisiana and her Gulf neighbors, beyond exposing the inherent risks of drilling offshore at great depth, is the creation of a wave of "environmental refugees" displaced from their occupations and homes by an anthropogenic event, our intrusion into an environment where it is very, very dangerous to go. We are seeing it in the impact on local fishing, tourism, and associated services. We will be seeing those businesses fail, those communities and families disrupted, those coastal citizens forced to move inland and elsewhere, hoping, like Katrina refugees, to be assimilated into some new life. That this is happening in the most developed nation of the world is the most terrible irony of all.[99]

Ocean experts have been studying these issues for decades. They have warned of indiscriminate exploitation, pursued the explanatory science, defined baselines, developed alternatives, and initiated novel protection and management structures to defend some of the most valuable marine resources in the world. Much of what they have recommended has been implemented by local, regional, and international policy, legislation, and treaty. But most of it has not. If there is a single inhibition to this work it has been the perceived contradiction between conservation and sustainable practice, and economic value and financial return. That argument has persuaded politicians for years, and so we are left with the resultant offset between our need for energy and the true cost thereof. At a time when peak oil is predicted and alternative technology is in accelerated development, the Deepwater Horizon disaster is both reality and symbol of a mismanaged political process dominated by the oil companies, their lobbyists, the financial markets, and the shareholders. We have had the knowledge and the technology in place to avoid such catastrophe, but we have not had the political will.

But now it is too late to avoid a predictable future. Will we learn anything from this to inform our actions on additional offshore drilling, coastal management, fish stock sustainability, and climate? Will we see anything with new clarity beyond Deepwater Horizon?

The environmental movement has mobilized around the

offshore drilling issue, finding new vigor and outrage, perhaps new sympathizers, members, and donors, among those affected directly and indirectly by the inexorable, undeniable evidence of ecological catastrophe. There is anger, opportunism, and a strong sense of "we told you so" in the air, something similar to the emotion surrounding the consequences of Hurricane Katrina where, too, the inadequacy of engineered safeguards was demonstrated by inundated wetlands, breached levees, a flooded city, and closed coastal refineries and power plants fueled by offshore oil, possibly from Deepwater Horizon. At the time, the thought was that we would learn our lesson, modify our ways, and revivify the city and coast through the application of values and technologies shaped to the new opportunity. We would understand that our management of ocean forces and ecological systems would change for the protection and future benefit of the local community.

Now here we are again—a different manifestation of the same causes and failed effects. We are dealing with the consequences of our intrusion upon Nature—the placement of a city in a vulnerable low place, under-protected by insufficient engineering—the failure of technology to deal with the complexities and risks of drilling and responding to the challenging conditions of failure a mile down in the deep ocean. And that same Nature complicates even our near-term responses: recurring storms to assault the improved levees, or currents that take the oil ashore and circulate it powerfully in a loop that extends the disaster exponentially. Even in the statements by those charged with response and cleanup we hear the assertion that in the end the oil will disperse, the coastal consequence will be local and limited and heal itself, and the ocean in its enormity will dissolve the problem away.

This is simply not true, and we know it. What amazes me is the fact that nothing has been mentioned of the insult-to-injury aspect of Deepwater Horizon, the addition of its devastation to a region already severely impacted by the distribution of nitrates from fertilizers in the heartland descending through the water-sheds and rivers to create a massive hypoxic zone where already most, if not all marine life, is starved of oxygen, dying or dead. Several hundred thousand gallons of oil does not create a problem, rather extends it probably to a point of no return across a larger arc of coastwise geography.

Take a good look at the pictures of Deepwater Horizon—the fire, black smoke, gushing oil, globs of it on the surface and in the water column, the dead fish, fouled birds, despoiled beaches. Take a look at the pathetic fireboats, containment booms, toxic dispersants, the hapless human response, the destroyed lives and communities, the hypocritical politics, the lack of accountability, the finger-pointing, the responsibility denied, the time energy and money wasted, the Nature destroyed. When you look at the climate issue, you don't see those things on the surface—but they are ALL there, scaled up and more deadly and even more impossible to fix.

As we watch the climate debate, we hear the same old denials, the ideological divides, the subversive financial arguments, the political games, and the paralytic inaction. How many times can we fool ourselves? How many signals can we ignore? How many disasters will it take for us to see beyond the deep-water horizon?

Oil to Plastic

Plastic, plastic, plastic, everywhere along our roads, in our streams, in our ponds and lakes, in our coastal wetlands, along our beaches, in vast gyres of accumulated plastic debris as large as islands in the ocean, and finally up and down the ocean in the water column. We have read about this, seen the photographs, and raised our concerns about the impact of plastic on natural ecosystems everywhere. We have recycled certain kinds of plastic packaging; we have boycotted and banned plastic bags; and we have organized community cleanups, passed ordinances and legislation, made informational films, sailed voyages to attract public attention, and otherwise shouted the evils of non-biodegradable plastic far and wide across the planet.

Plastic lasts forever. If we could recycle all the plastic extant in the world today we would never have to manufacture another bit of plastic ever to meet demand, thereby leaving all the future requisite fossil fuels in the ground, preventing all the consequential emissions from the atmosphere, and perhaps taking a serious step toward real mitigation of temperature rise, changing weather patterns, ocean acidification, and all the further negative manifestations embodied in plastic that affect our world today. Think about it: a plastic cycle, an independent revolving system of utility re-utilized through reduced demand, product reformation, and alternative behaviors. What a good idea.

To understand just how pervasive plastic is in our lives—and just how difficult it will be to implement this good idea—consider the microbead: a tiny polyethylene and polypropylene particle, about one half of one millimeter in diameter. These beads exist by the millions in consumer products such as skin creams and toothpaste that find their way by the millions down drains and into the sewage systems of our towns and cities where they eventually find their way to the ocean. Microbeads work as exfoliators in deep-cleansing beauty creams or in those teeth-whitening pastes that suggest a bright white smile. 5 Gyres, an organization dedicated to informing the public about the dangers of plastic pollution, has asserted some products contain between 1 percent and 5 percent microbeads and that one tube of Neutrogena's "Deep Clean" product contains an estimated 360,000 such particles ultimately loosed into circulation in the name of beauty.[100]

The beads float through the wastewater network, frequently unfiltered by sewage treatment plants, finding their way into storm drains and runoff, and eventually becoming an invisible manifestation, infestation if you will, of plastic into our natural world. A 5 Gyres 2012 study in the Great Lakes, for example, found evidence of more than 600,000 beads per square kilometer. In effect, the beads are a pervasive host for other pollutants like DDT, PCBs, flame-retardants, and other industrial chemicals, become suspended in the water column, and are ingested by various marine species along the food chain, some of which are harvested and consumed by our families. Little good can come of any of this.[101]

There are alternatives. Ground apricot shells and cocoa beans are proposed as substitute natural exfoliates for the various products. But if the industry ignores the argument and resists product modification, there is as always the option to legislate a solution. California and Maine have banned microbeads and bills are under consideration in New York and Illinois; in December 2015 the United States Congress banned microbeads at the federal level. And, as with plastic bags and plastic packaging, those concerned with such detrimental effect can intervene in the market by refusing to purchase these products, advocating to retailers to take the products off the shelves, letting the manufacturers know, testifying in opposition to the inevitable industry lobby in the state legislatures, and joining groups like 5 Gyres to spread the word.

In the 1967 classic American film *The Graduate*, the character portrayed by Dustin Hoffman was given one word of certain advice on which to base his future: plastics. It seemed funny, even absurd at the time, but it proved prescient, and almost 50 years later we can now see what that future has become, encased in plastic.

The Plastisphere

Recent articles in *The Economist* and multiple press releases worldwide recently reported "the discovery of a new ecological habitat in the ocean, a diverse multitude of microbes colonizing and thriving on flecks of plastic that have polluted the oceans—a vast new human-made flotilla of microbial communities that they have dubbed the 'plastisphere.'"[102] In a study recently published online in *Environmental Science & Technology*, the scientists suggest that "the plastisphere represents a novel ecological habitat in the ocean and raises a host of questions: How will it change environmental conditions for marine microbes, favoring some that compete with others? How will it change the overall ocean ecosystem and affect larger organisms? How will it change where microbes, including pathogens, will be transported in the ocean?"[103]

> *The collaborative team of scientists—Erik Zettler from Sea Education Association, Tracy Mincer from Woods Hole Oceanographic Institution, and Linda Amaral-Zettler from the Marine Biological Laboratory, all in Woods Hole, Mass.—analyzed marine plastic debris that was skimmed with fine-scale nets from the sea surface at several locations in the North Atlantic Ocean during SEA research cruises. Most were millimeter-sized fragments.*
>
> *"We're not just interested in who's there. We're interested in their function, how they're functioning in this ecosystem, how they're altering this ecosystem, and what's the ultimate fate of*

these particles in the ocean," says Amaral-Zettler. "Are they sinking to the bottom of the ocean? Are they being ingested? If they're being ingested, what impact does that have?"[104]

Using scanning electron microscopy and gene sequencing techniques, they found at least 1000 different types of bacterial cells on the plastic samples, including many individual species yet to be identified. They included plants, algae, and bacteria that manufacture their own food (autotrophs), animals and bacteria that feed on them (heterotrophs), predators that feed on these, and other organisms that establish synergistic relationships (symbionts). These complex communities exist on plastic bits hardly bigger than the head of a pin, and they have arisen with the explosion of plastics in the oceans in the last 60 years.

"The organisms inhabiting the plastisphere were different from those in surrounding seawater, indicating that plastic debris acts as artificial 'microbial reefs,'" says Mincer. "They supply a place that selects for and supports distinct microbes to settle and succeed."

These communities are likely different from those that settle on naturally occurring floating material such as feathers, wood, and microalgae, because plastics offer different conditions, including the capacity to last much longer without degrading.

On the other hand, the scientists also found evidence that microbes may play a role in degrading plastics. They saw microscopic cracks and pits in the plastic surfaces that they suspect were made by microbes embedded in them, as well as microbes possibly capable of degrading hydrocarbons.

"When we first saw the 'pit formers' we were very excited, especially when they showed up on multiple pieces of plastic of

different types of resins," said Zettler, who added that under-graduate students participating in SEA Semester cruises collected and processed the samples. "Now we have to figure out what they are by [genetically] sequencing them and hopefully getting them into culture so we can do experiments."

The plastic debris also represents a new mode of transportation, acting as rafts that can convey harmful microbes, including disease-causing pathogens and harmful algal species. One plastic sampled they analyzed was dominated by members of the genus Vibrio, *which includes bacteria that cause cholera and gastrointestinal maladies.*

The project was conducted aboard one of two Sea Education Association traditional sailing vessels that have offered college level semesters at sea since 1971. The research was conducted on a 2010 Atlantic voyage; a second expedition begun in 2012 has been completed in search of comparable data and information on a Pacific voyage between California and Hawaii aboard a second SEA vessel. This joint expedition is an excellent example of collaboration between scientists with common interests pooling their financial and physical resources, using a sailing vessel as an unexpected plat-form for ocean science, and generating fascinating new information regarding the impact of the accumulation and deterioration of vast amounts of discarded plastic in the ocean.

So begins a new exploration of the "plastisphere," earth and ocean so saturated by disintegrating plastic and associated chem-icals that the ecological consequences will determine the fate of novel microbes, myriad marine organisms, and humans for years, perhaps centuries, to come.

It may be apt to name this new historical period beginning from the second half of the 20th century, The Plastiscene.

Ocean-Based Renewable Energy: Wind, Solar, OTEC, Tidal

A ttempts have been made to harness the enormous energy potential of moving ocean water for decades. As far back as the mid-11th century, people were making the logical extension from exploiting energy in running rivers, streams, and canals.[105] Early attempts to harness the kinetic energy contained in moving seawater were focused on estuaries, where both river hydrology and tides influence the water movement. But wave energy can be harnessed, in theory, anywhere where there are predictable waves, including in areas far offshore. The first commercial-scale wave energy plant was commissioned for the Isle of Islay, Scotland, in 2000.[106] But ocean energy technology has been historically hindered by the engineering and operational challenges, the availability and low cost of oil and gas, and the resultant low purchase rates and lack of government and public interest. With oil supplies at or near peak, and the price at record highs, renewable energy from ocean-based systems has seen new interest and new investment.

When considering alternatives to non-renewable fossil fuels, we are all aware of the potential for wind and solar energy generation. We have seen the many large windmills in the hills of Europe and the United States. And yet the oceans provide not only vast amounts of space and sufficient sunlight and wind, but also provide these as a commons property that can in theory be more easily accessed than private property to meet the public good. Of all the energy alternatives, these are the most advanced.

Offshore wind farms are common in some parts of the world, such as Northern Europe.[107] Oceanic wind is a preferred alternative to other forms of energy generation in areas where land is in short supply, and where coastal winds are sustained and strong.[108] Denmark has led the effort in harnessing sea wind, and constructed the first offshore wind farm in 1991 off the Port of Vineby.[109] According to the *Financial Times*, wind farms are expected to supply 8 percent of Denmark's electricity by 2008.[110] The Netherlands have constructed many alongshore projects, and the United Kingdom opened its first offshore wind farm in 2000 in Northumberland, and is following Denmark's lead with expanded wind farms and feasibility studies for siting in many new areas.

The oceans are also the world's largest solar collector: 1 square mile contains more energy potential than 7,000 barrels of oil.[111] Solar arrays with unfettered access to sunlight can be installed in virtually any coastal area sheltered from excessive wind or waves. Currently most offshore solar plants are used to power oil platforms and in situ research equipment, but new visionary options are under development.

The oceans can also be harnessed for energy by using the temperature differential of surface and deep waters to drive energy, a process called ocean thermal energy conversion or OTEC. The differential exists because the sun warms the surface layers of the ocean, especially in the tropics, while deep waters stay cool. In order for the technology to be able to capture the thermal energy, this temperature differential must be more than 25 degrees Centigrade.

Using the temperature of water to make energy actually dates back to 1881, when a French engineer by the name of Jacques D'Arsonval first thought of using ocean thermal energy gradients. His student, Georges Claude, built the first OTEC plant in Cuba in 1930, producing 22 kilowatts of electricity with a low-pressure turbine. The best-known and largest-scale pilot effort to harness ocean thermal energy was constructed in Hawaii in 1974; it was a technological success but the cost was non-competitive when compared to the very inexpensive price of oil at the time. As a result, enthusiasm for the technology waned.[112]

Although the temperature differential between surface waters and the deep ocean is significant in almost all parts of the globe, there are constraints to being able to harness this potential energy. Main among them is having deep cold water in close proximity to warm surface waters. Tropical island nations in the Pacific Ocean that have narrow continental shelves are particularly suited. According to NASA, some 98 tropical countries could benefit from the technology.[113]

OTEC also has spinoff benefits, including air conditioning, chilled-soil agriculture, aquaculture, and desalination. And OTEC also may one day provide a means to mine ocean water for 57 trace elements, many of which are very valuable. Thermal energy conversion has great potential, but enormous challenges remain. The technology is still very inefficient, and piping large volumes across great depths of ocean (a kilometer or more) is a major engineering feat. Yet some energy experts believe OTEC could produce billions of watts of electrical power, and, with oil today dramatically fluctuating, it may soon be cost-competitive with conventional power technologies.[114]

Finally, tidal generation has long been an alternative energy opportunity with high expectation. But unlike wind, and even wave technology, tidal has been inhibited by engineering challenges, projected high cost, and environmental issues in the areas where tidal flow is most advantageous for maximum return. According to William Kingston, a professor at Trinity College Dublin in a recent article in *Marine Technology Reporter*, tidal energy can succeed only when there is no interference to navigation, invisible installation, a large swept area to exploit slower flows, safety from storm wave damage, minimal drilling cost and rock for anchoring, and no special tender needed to position, install, and maintain. The challenges of gathering generated power, transferring it ashore, and distributing it into the grid are a constant in all ocean energy applications.[115]

There are three factors that currently constrain us from using ocean energy to meet our needs. First is the lack of investment in researching new energy sources and technologies. Costs of developing and then utilizing these new technologies are prohibitive; investors cannot be assured of returns on investment for small-scale experimental projects, but larger-scale economically viable projects cannot be developed without the small-scale prototypes. Few governments are progressive enough to sufficiently subsidize research and development in ocean energy technologies. And the few stalwart private sector companies who have embarked on the exploratory trail are understandably not willing to share their trade secrets with other companies or with government energy agencies. The solution thus lies in strong public-private partnerships.

The second obstacle is insufficient education of the public at large. For too long the people of the developed world have taken energy for granted; it is only in times of high energy costs (particularly rising costs at the fuel pump or on home heating bills) that the public is even conscious of the fact that supplying energy is a costly, and sometimes unpredictable, endeavor. The sudden surge of interest in the effects of global warming, and increasing geopolitical tensions between oil-supplying and oil-consuming countries, has opened many people's minds to considerations of new sources of energy, as well as to issues of energy conservation. But even those open minds have had difficulty accessing good information about the costs and benefits of ocean energy. Public education and outreach that is based on the best available science, and uninfluenced by vested economic interests or political ones, is a top priority.

The last constraint is related to the first two. The public sector must find ways to increase incentives for the private sector to research and develop cost-effective and environmentally sensitive ocean energy ventures. And in order for that to happen, there needs to be political will—political will built on the realization of ocean energy potential, and political will driven by the demands of an increasingly educated and informed public. Such political will cannot blossom if politicians continue to yield to the enormous political pressure being brought down upon them by the lobbyists and spokespeople of conventional energy corporations. Indeed, those very corporations must go beyond lip service and facile advertising to serious development of alternatives as a function of good business and financial sustainability.

ECONOMY

Most of us probably have some sense of the economic value of the ocean as a function of local fisheries, certain food products, and shipping. But very few of us have the broader perspective of the total contribution of maritime enterprise to global finance or to our national gross domestic product.

In many regions of the world, the nations depend greatly on the sea to facilitate trade and development and sustain their communities, both inland and coastal, through port operations, vessel construction, and repair, transportation, food production, offshore oil and gas, and coastal tourism. The rich maritime history of the Andaman and South China Seas, for example, reveal an astonishing record of exchange through Arab traders and other seafarers who introduced different technologies, European markets, and the influential spiritual ideas of Islam, Buddhism, and Christianity. That history takes modern form in a full range of maritime activities, in 2006 accounting for $352.8 billion.

Maritime industry is also both a signifier and contributor to our understanding and solution of the problem of worldwide unemployment. Consider the extent of its reach as a global employer in such areas as shipbuilding, ocean transportation, port operations, shipping and cruise lines, offshore energy rigs and platforms for oil, gas, wind, and tidal, underwater pipelines and communications cables, associated construction and support services, coastwise transport, ferries, salvage operators, insurance companies, admiralty lawyers, exploration activities, and all the other endeavors at sea that, not always known, encompass the vast ocean contribution to the world economy and employment.

Recently, the Global Environment Facility (GEF) and the United Nations Development Programme (UNDP) combined their talents and experience to address ocean solutions on the scale required to make a difference. As we always tend to measure value in dollars, they predicated their recommendations on the following analysis:[116]

> *Marine and coastal resources directly provide at least $3 tril-*
> *lion annually in economic goods and services plus an estimated*
> *$20.9 trillion per year in non-market ecosystem services.*
> *Unfortunately, coasts and oceans are exposed to increasing*
> *threats such as pollution, overfishing, introduced species, habitat*
> *and species loss, and poorly planned and managed coastal infra-*
> *structure development. The cumulative economic impact of poor*
> *ocean management practices is at least $200 billion per year. In*
> *the absence of proactive mitigation measures, climate change will*

increase the cost of damage to the ocean by an additional $322
billion per year by 2050. The ocean is estimated to have absorbed
25–30% of anthropogenic carbon dioxide emissions. While this
has served to mitigate atmospheric warming to a sizable extent,
it has increased the acidity of the ocean by 30%, with significant
threats to calcium carbonate fixing organisms that serve as the
foundation for many ocean food chains upon which hundreds
of millions depend for food protein and livelihoods. Climate
change is already affecting surface ocean temperatures, driving
fish stocks to migrate to more favorable waters and reducing
upwelling of vital nutrients to key fisheries areas, further
threatening fisheries yields. In addition, sea level rise, due to the
thermal expansion of seawater, glacial melt, and groundwater
extraction, endangers millions living in the coastal zone and
island states, mostly in the world's least-developed countries.

Measuring Ocean Value

When I ask people how and why the ocean is important,
their responses typically point as a measure of value to a
personal, spiritual connection based on the beauty, energy, and
bounty of the sea and coastal environment. The ocean retains
in their minds an idea of purity, of the wilderness, and freedom
once associated with the land, now erased by the reality of cities
and population, and consumption of the elements—real and
mythic—which comprise the idea of nature.

Another way to measure value, of course, is by the numbers.
We distribute voting rights by population density; we seek certainty
and indices, gross national product, or the Dow Jones average, that
give precise indication of our national health and market well-
being. We calculate employment, construction starts, commodity
prices, mortgage rates, and much more, all in an attempt to measure

and manage the statistical profile of our actions and their contribution to our personal and institutional vitality.

Such a study has indeed been begun for the ocean: the National Ocean Economics Program,[117] led by Dr. Charles S. Colgan, University of Southern Maine, has been assembling and interpreting the contribution of ocean-related enterprise to the larger economy of the United States. In the study, the ocean economy is defined to include living resources, marine construction, marine transportation, offshore mineral resources, ship and boat building, tourism and recreation, and alongshore development. The statistics include the coastal zone, the Great Lakes, large embayments, and the major river systems that find their way to the sea. In 2001 the ocean GDP was reported in excess of $123 billion; today, more than a decade and a half later, certainly substantially more. In 2004, total ocean-related employment was estimated at 2.3 million jobs versus 1.1 million estimated for agriculture, forestry, and fisheries, the latter ironically classified outside the ocean calculation. The study was a first attempt to measure ocean economics.

The Ocean Health Index, a new project led by Dr. Steve Katona, former president of the College of the Atlantic in Bar Harbor, Maine, is a larger, more inclusive definition of ocean-related economic and social inputs designed to create "a baseline index that will enable more comprehensive and precise indications of the full value of the ocean that can be tracked and compared from year to year."[118] The Index has been updated with new statistics and new criteria. It is an excellent measure and indicator of the full breadth and reality of ocean health worldwide.

Which way should we have it? Why not both? For those who think literally, the numbers may be more effective, and it is up to the ocean community to communicate those facts to the decision

makers: the administrators and politicians who control the regulatory and legislative processes that enable or disable any inclusion of
this value into the legal and appropriation actions required. Logic
does not always prevail here, with the intrusion of ideologies or
lobbyists' agendas having no bearing on the facts. This does not
mean we should stop trying, because it is possible that eventually
the persuasive reality of financial decline and unemployment in the
ocean economy will reach policy makers and lobbyists' ears and
motivate some kind of responsive action. An ocean GDP of $123
billion providing 2.3 million jobs seems like a lot to lose.

And what about the spiritual value? In his compelling book,
The View from Lazy Point, journalist and ocean advocate Carl
Safina writes, "The moral must guide the technical."[119] He goes on
to argue for an ocean ethic that demands that we not compromise
and corrupt the beauty, energy, and bounty of the sea by our
short-term, consumption-based, market-driven measurements of
value. He suggests a spiritual alternative, a challenge to "advance
compassion and yet survive in a world of appetites. The compass
of compassion asks not what is good for me but what is good. Not
what is best for me, but what is best. Not what is right for me, but
what is right. Not how much can we take, but how much ought we
to leave. Not what is practical, but what is moral. The loss here is
measured in our souls."

Either way, or both. Whichever, we must choose.

Maritime Contribution to Gross Domestic Product

A group of Southeast Asian nations has undertaken an
assessment of ocean industry, for the first time defining and
including all aspects, calculating economic value, and measuring
offsetting effects of environmental degradation. The methodology

defined five types of value: direct use, value, indirect use value, optional value of goods and services for future use, existence value or what people will pay to sustain the environment without use, and bequest value or the benefits from ensuring that certain resources will be preserved for future generations.

The studies defined the maritime sector into categories that included living resources like coral reefs, mangroves, sea grass, fish and other marine species; non-living resources like oil, gas, salt, and energy; marine support activities like shipyards, fish processing for export, and insurance; tourism; defense; surveys; and pharmaceutical products derived from the sea. Against this total was deducted an estimated annual cost of environmental degradation such as coastal erosion, oil spills, and tsunami impacts. This complicated calculation represents a model and first attempt to understand the full range of a national maritime enterprise that can then be included as a realistic, meaningful part of gross domestic product that can serve as a true baseline for growth, for comparison with other economies in the region, and for a better understanding of the nation's correlative place in the global economy.

The ocean percentage of national GDP of the industrialized nations—Australia, New Zealand, Canada, France, United Kingdom, and the United States—falls between 1 percent and 4 percent. By contrast, in China it represents 10 percent, and in Indonesia and Vietnam 20 percent or more. Employment in the ocean economy runs at roughly parallel figures.[120]

These results are not so surprising when the diversity of the industrialized economies is taken into account. But the numbers are nonetheless significant and when added together into regional totals indicate that the developing countries play a disproportionate role in maritime industry worldwide and the global economy.

These analyses are useful in many ways. They provide a full catalogue of services associated with marine endeavor. They provide insight into future development and investment as populations worldwide continue to grow and locate along the coasts. They provide guidelines for policy and regulations to sustain these benefits and to protect them from indifference, financial uncertainty, and natural disaster. And they show how the developing and industrialized world interrelates as competitors, partners, and managers for the sustainable ocean.

RENEWAL

The Rejuvenative Power of the Ocean

In the summer of 2014 I was able to get away for three weeks at sea, not a bold deep-water crossing but that wonderful cruising, mostly coastal Maine, that is such a rejuvenative part of living here. With wife and dog, we gunkholed from cove to cove, occasionally rafting up with friends, mostly going it alone, guided by wind and weather. Two storms passed through—one had us on a mooring in the Benjamin River, the other had us cozy for two days in the Mud Hole at Great Wass Island.

It was a strange summer for us all, and instructive in how weather can affect not only our gardens, but also our psyches. The constant rain of June and July, and the unavailability of the boat, taken to Nova Scotia by our partners, made for an odd compensatory mixture of compulsive work and introspection, a different way of being, provocative, frustrating, sometimes depressing. It was typical to hear grousing and complaint, dour thoughts and dire opinions, from friends and neighbors.

I spent more time reading, for me always a diversion, a dive into the calming waters of narrative, a good story, the odd poem. I had been recommended an ocean book, *The Sea Can Wash Away All Evils*, by Kimberly C. Patton, a professor of comparative and historical study of religion at the Harvard Divinity School. I was unsure about an academic text with titles like *Ocean as Divinity and Scapegoat*, or *The Crisis of Modern Pollution*, or *The Purifying Sea in the Religious Imagination*. But Professor Patton surprised me with her observations about the sea and the supernatural, the marine rituals of ancient Greece, Hindu submarine fire, and Sedna, the Inuit indwelling spiritual force, or Sea Mother. Part historian, part theologian, part folklorist, part cultural anthropologist, Patton made me think about the ocean again differently, to pause the pursuit of the science or economics or governance of the marine ecosystem, and immerse myself in the psychological swim, the realization and understanding of value in the ocean that is aesthetic, moral, perhaps divine, that has been known, articulated, and expressed ceremonially for all time.

Her text explores the idea of pollution as both the unreflective dumping of waste into the ocean, a kind of senseless vandalism, and as a rejuvenative element that can cleanse us of despair. "In tons of water," she writes, "in saltiness, in bottomless depth and endless horizon, and, above all, in the many forms of ceaseless motion, human populations, especially those who live along the littoral, see—and have always seen—in the world's oceans a mighty, efficacious means of 'cleansing' our habitat and making it safe, clean, and viable."[121]

The sea, she suggests, is both familiar and strange, and

represents a place of reunion, of heart and mind, body and soul, past and future, abandonment and dedication to the meaningful things in our lives. In 1921, after a long separation from the ocean, William Faulkner wrote to his mother:

> *Then suddenly, you see it, a blue hill going up and up, beyond the borders of the world, to the salt colored sky, and white whirling necklaces of gulls, and, if you look long enough, a great vague ship, solemnly going somewhere. I can't express how it makes me feel to see it again, there is a feeling of the utmost inner relief, as if I could close my eyes, knowing that I had found again someone who loved me years and years ago.*[122]

Sacred Places

As each year turns, we think of renewal, beginnings rather than ends, hopes instead of fears. For many, the traditions of formal religions provide the words and order of these preoccupations; for others, private thoughts and special places provide. In each of these, nature plays some part, as allegory, animation of the divine, or sacred spaces wherein we find the source and strength for the future.

Many such spaces exist alongshore throughout the world, as both symbol and reality of the complex, intangible relationship between us and our originating web of life. The ocean itself is frequently invoked for its emotional depth and dynamic breadth as a metaphor for freedom from life's burdens and tyrannies and for opportunity for passage into the future.

In a recent collection of essays, *Sacred Natural Sites, Conserving Nature & Culture,*[123] the editors discuss this phenomenon worldwide. Among many examples, islands hold special meaning—Lindisfarne Island, for instance, that since 635 AD has been a holy site for Christian pilgrimage linking nature and spirituality. Located on the northeast coast of England at the Scottish border, Lindisfarne is surrounded by rich wetlands, and is accessible only at low tide, across sand and mud flats marked by an ancient pilgrim's path and a modern causeway, today home to a resident community of 150 and to half a million visitors per year who come a place that housed for centuries Christian monastic communities and nurtured the lives of saints. Primary among them is St. Cuthbert, described as "one of the most important saints of Medieval England and Europe," whose affinity for nature, seabirds, and the protection of wildlife and wild places foreshadowed the modern conservation movement.

There are many other examples, in Ireland, France, the South Pacific region, Africa, India, Japan, and elsewhere. In the Philippines, on Coron Island, off Palawan, the indigenous Calamian Tagbanwa people have defined 10 sacred areas in the sea where they believe divine spirits dwell and which must be protected as sanctuaries from which fishing, dropping of anchors, or culturing seaweed are prohibited. These sites can only be entered by shamans, elders, and worshippers whose prayers name and invoke the wide variety of marine species and natural physical characteristics of the areas, thereby connecting spiritual beliefs with natural phenomena through unique personal and community religious practice.

Amazingly, such places have found allies in the biodiversity protection movement and associated governance designed to conserve the fulsome catalogue of species and habitat typically coexisting with sacred spaces. Research studies, management practices, legal instruments, education and training projects abound, justifying protections, providing models and international conventions, and establishing communications and enforcement methods that meet the goals of both religionist and conservationist.

What are the premises on which this unexpected coalition is based? First, there is a real and widespread interconnection between sacred spaces and biodiverse areas around the world. Second, the degradation of one threatens the integrity of the other, and these degradations are accelerating and destructive to the value of both. Third, faith, spirituality, and science are different but complementary ways of understanding human-nature relationships, and the protection of places where all three intersect can be seen as a means to sustain ecologically sound ways of life. And fifth, by virtue of these premises, a strategy to build public awareness, supportive policies and laws, and other local, national, and international actions is worthwhile and urgently needed.

Should we not all have such places—a river or lake to sit by, a beach to walk, a space in which to reflect and renew?

Intangible Cultural Heritage

"Heritage" refers to practices or characteristics that are passed down from one generation to the next. I may have long misunderstood the definition, conditioned to think that heritage is embodied only in places and things—in castles, chateaux, churches, and monuments, in paintings, drawings, objects, and other physical remnants associated with the great events, institutions, and movements in our history. Frequently, we lament the loss of such last great places, or endangered spaces wherein took place defining elements of our civilization.

The United Nations Educational, Scientific, and Cultural Organization, known as UNESCO, is the international agency charged with identification and protection of such places. Many of you will be aware of the *World Heritage Site* designation, a list of the most monuments and cultural remnants considered the most important worldwide; to see all these places in a lifetime would be an education worthy of the time, energy, and cost of getting there.

There is also a second designation of "intangible cultural heritage," defined by the UNESCO Convention as "the practices, representations, expressions, knowledge, skills—as well as the instruments, objects, artifacts and cultural spaces associated therewith—that communities, groups and, in some cases, individuals recognize as part of their cultural heritage. This intangible cultural heritage, transmitted from generation to generation, is constantly recreated by communities and groups in response to their environment, their interaction with nature and their history... (in the form of) oral traditions and expressions; performing arts; social practices, rituals and festive events; knowledge and practices concerning nature and the universe; and traditional craftsmanship."[124]

Here are the four *ocean-related* practices paraphrased from their UNESCO descriptions:

In Belgium,

Twelve households in Oostduinkerke actively engage in shrimp fishing, using Brabant draft horses, walking breast-deep in the surf, parallel to the coastline, pulling hand-woven funnel-shaped nets held open by two wooden boards, with an attached chain dragged over the sand to create vibrations, causing the shrimp to jump into the net to be emptied into baskets hanging at the horses' sides. The event takes place twice a week, except in the winter months, and culminates in a two-day Shrimp Festival for which the local community spends months building floats, making costumes, preparing street theatre, and introducing shrimp catching to over 10,000 visitors every year.

In Iran,

Lenj vessels are traditionally hand-built and are used by inhabitants of the northern coast of the Persian Gulf for sea journeys, trading, fishing and pearl diving. The traditional knowledge surrounding Lenjes includes oral literature, performing arts and festivals, sailing and navigation techniques and terminology, weather forecasting, and wooden boatbuilding. Iranian navigators could locate the ship according to the positions of the sun, moon and stars, using special formulae to calculate latitudes and longitudes, and special vocabulary to estimate water depth, type of wind, and the characteristics of approaching weather.

In Mali,

The Sanké mon collective fishing rite takes place in San in the Ségou region every second Thursday of the seventh lunar month to commemorate the founding of the town. The rite begins with the sacrifice of roosters, goats and offerings made by village residents to the water spirits of the Sanké pond. The collective fishing then takes place over fifteen hours using large and small mesh fishing nets, followed by a masked dance on the public square featuring Buwa dancers from San and neighboring villages who wear traditional costumes and hats decorated with cowrie shells and feathers and perform specific choreography to the rhythms of a variety of drums.

In China,

Beginning on the fifth day of the fifth lunar month, people of several ethnic groups throughout China and the world celebrate the Dragon Boat festival. The festivities vary from region to region, but they usually include a memorial ceremony offering sacrifices to a local hero combined with such sporting events as dragon races, dragon boating and willow shooting; feasts of rice dumplings, eggs and ruby sulfur wine; and folk entertainments including opera, song and unicorn dances.[125]

Each one of these events, and more than 200 more on the list, strengthens the *tangible* bonds between the participants, families, neighbors, and visitors. Each is based on the harmonious relationship between humanity and nature, individual imagination and collective creativity, identity and continuity, community and cultural diversity—revealing, conserving, and communicating a vivid sense of cultural identity that we can see, touch, feel, and celebrate.

Oceans of Faith

Despite the premise of separation of church and state on which our governance is based, religious principles and beliefs today are frequently mentioned and brought to bear on social issues, legislative initiatives, and other actions of governance that impact us all. We hear analysis of the political influence of the so-called religious right; we hear religious principles applied to arguments for or against proposed laws, regulations, and even appointments of individuals to key posts in government; we hear individual politicians declare their religious beliefs in speeches as the basis for a position or vote, sometimes in opposition to polls indicating differing beliefs of their constituents. We hear GOP candidates, mostly from the religious right, shrilly pledging, if elected, to abolish the Environmental Protection Agency and everything it stands for.

Their opposition extends to almost every environmental issue: the Clean Air Act, the Clean Water Act, climate change legislation, alternative energy, watershed protection, coastal management, fisheries regulation, endangered species protection, national ocean policy, and much more. I have never quite understood this, from my own limited religious understanding and knowledge of the Bible, sensing an inherent, inexplicable, irreconcilable contradiction therein.

To explore this further, I recently visited the website of the Religious Partnership for the Environment, founded in 1993 between the US Conference of Catholic Bishops, the National Council of Churches, the Coalition on the Environment and Jewish Life, and the Evangelical Environmental Network. Here are quotations from that site on water, climate, and ocean.

First, on water:

> Throughout the Jewish and Christian scriptures, water is perhaps the pre-eminent symbol of life, both spiritual and physical. Abundant, pure water, so necessary for human survival and comfort, manifests divine mercy and healing and occasions gratitude and rejoicing.

> The lack of clean water is one of the most serious health issues for the poor around the world. Ensuring an adequate supply is an important goal for economic development, and preventing some from contaminating others' drinking water is certainly a demand of environmental justice.

And then this, on climate:

> Although it seems vast, comparatively speaking the atmosphere forms only the thinnest envelope around the mass of the earth. By introducing a few novel gases into the air, we have thinned the ozone layer that protects life on earth from deadly ultraviolet radiation. By burning fossil fuels such as coal, oil and gas, we have injected harmful pollutants and particles into the air we breathe. Moreover, we have increased the atmosphere's heat-trapping properties, potentially altering earth's climate for generations to come.

And then this, on oceans, specifically from the Evangelical perspective:

God's oceans may indeed be vast, but they are not invincible to our behavior. For instance, populations of large predatory fish have been reduced to 10% of pre-industrial levels. Nearly one third of the world's fisheries are being fished at their maximum level.

Current estimates are that 10% of all coral reefs are degraded beyond recovery. Thirty percent are in critical condition and may die within 10 to 20 years. Sixty percent of the world's coral reefs may die completely by 2050. The destruction of coral reefs is indeed unfortunate, because they harbor more than 25% of all known marine fish, as well as a total species diversity containing more phyla than rainforests.

There is much more. But here is their conclusion:

While the current state of God's oceans could tempt us to despair, as Christians we must remember that the One who walked upon the water is ultimately the Lord of Lords, and He has empowered us to care for His waters. As followers of Christ, the protector and Sustainer of all life, we cannot forget His oceans, nor can we think of them as invincible and not in need of our care and protection. That He has reconciled all things is our hope—and what we are called to participate in.[126]

So, if indeed we are called to participate, to care for and protect water and climate and all living things as God's will, why then do we obfuscate and deny the research and science affirming positions quoted here? Why do we act against the interest of human health, economic necessity, and social justice? Why do we invoke scripture and religious belief to act against the very lessons of that scripture and the very essence of those beliefs?

Given this terrible irony, is it not fair to ask those who stand against these interpretations of divine will, who it is in reality that they serve?

IV. Why We Need a New Way of Thinking

IN PURSUIT OF CHANGE

Beyond Hope

No day goes by when I do not have multiple conversations about the ocean. Whether it's face-to-face, telephone, email, or social media, the discussion continues to grow among people all over the world, most of them strangers, who connect with the World Ocean Observatory and its mission to promote public awareness and political will toward actions, policies, and behaviors that address the challenge to conserve and sustain the world ocean as a natural system, political system, and social system for the benefit of all mankind. Big job, seemingly impossible, but these connections, however remote or abbreviated, are the indicators that people out there are listening, believing, and acting as best they can to meet the challenge.

There are many negatives—the continuous litany of oil spills, fish kills, and marginalized communities, once secure in their relationship with the ocean, now threatened by climate change, extreme weather, depleted fisheries, toxins and pollutants, industrial incursion, and disrupted patterns of life—all the resultant insecurities from which no ocean dweller, rich or poor, today can hide. Thus, frequently in these conversations I hear expressions of hopelessness. What can I do? What can I do to combat these forces, distant and powerful, that seem indifferent not just to the natural environment, but also to the values and traditions that have been part of our engagement with the ocean forever? The situation is hopeless. I am paralyzed by the overwhelming vastness of the challenge. It is beyond hope.

To counter this despair, indeed to transform it into some kind of solace, renewed optimism, and engagement, ocean advocates actually use the language of hope. Sylvia Earle, the American oceanographer and tireless proselytizer for the world ocean cause, points to "hope spots," a network of pristine places around the world, some protected by conservation structures and agreements, some not, still vulnerable, but momentarily still pure and needful of protection.[127] Through her tireless calendar of speech and promotion, Sylvia embodies and advances the definition of hope: the feeling that what is desired is possible, the message that things will turn out for the best if only we believe and work to make it so. Don't lose hope, be hopeful, and the best of the ocean will be recognized, sustained, and endure beyond the threats into the future.

Personally, I too am an optimist. But I struggle with this emotional approach, based on profound empathetic identification with the beauty of marine animals and nature in that it omits the awful counter-force of human activity that does not respect these things or share the emotion, indeed dismisses it as naïve and ineffective. That is the quandary that all ocean advocates face—the reality of the dark side of ourselves, our inability to coalesce around specific actions to combat the power of excess and pollution, and the sense that, optimism notwithstanding, we are not winning the argument against the degradation of the ocean worldwide.

So, is hope enough? What lies beyond hope; isn't that the fundamental question? What do we do next? How do we apply our optimism and to what end? How do we as individuals, groups, associations, movements, focus the force of hope against the oppositional force of irresponsibility and excess, unsustainable consumption, profit at any cost, and delusionary justification for behaviors that even the perpetrators know will not end well? What about the inadvertent victims of such behavior—those poor and displaced by coastal inundation and rising sea level, those whose livelihood depends on a healthy ocean, those who follow and will need what the ocean provides to survive? Where is their hope? Where is their justice?

Thinking about this makes me angry. And that frustration often finds its way into my personal encounters. A friend counseled me recently: Peter, rage is not effective; it is too easily dismissed as shrill invective and works against the positive engagement communicated by the quieter language of hopeful belief. But aren't we, as advocates, meant to advance the cause, to plead in favor, to urge by argument, to recommend aggressively and publically the counter-strategy, to promote specific solutions, to share commitment far and wide, and to reach for a just outcome? Are we not obligated to channel our anger forcefully for the fundamental, indeed revolutionary change required to meet our most hopeful aspirations for the health and welfare of the ocean and for all of us who live by and around it? "Hope springs eternal," writes the poet. Eternity? No time for that.

The Ocean Commons

Most of us are familiar from our colonial history lessons with the idea of the commons, that central portion of land around which a settlement was built that was shared by all for pasturage of animals, agriculture, and general well-being.[128] We may also be aware of the influential essay, *Tragedy of the Commons*, by ecologist Garrett Hardin, first published in the journal *Science* in 1968, which describes a dilemma arising from a situation in which multiple individuals, acting independently and rationally consulting their own self-interest, will ultimately deplete a shared limited resource, even when it is clear that it is not in anyone's long-term interest for this to happen.

The ocean is the greatest commons of them all. International law delimits national interest in ocean resources to an "exclusive economic zone" up to 200 miles offshore. The balance—that is, 64 percent of the ocean surface and 90 percent of its volume[129]—lies outside such governance and includes the high seas, the ocean floor and subsoil, an enormous compendium of natural resources to include all marine species, minerals, chemicals, and genetic resources of incalculable value to humankind.

It is a vast challenge to protect, manage, and sustain such a resource, especially when agreement involves multiple levels of governance and a broad spectrum of public and private enterprise. The tragedy of the ocean commons is evinced by the intrusion of polluting elements from the nations and their self-interests that invade and destroy the shared value without constraint, without question.

It may be the most important geopolitical question we now face. How do we govern, how do we manage, the ocean outside national jurisdiction to use it responsibly, to sustain its value near and long-term, and to assure its potential forever for the benefit of all mankind?

The situation has been the focus of innumerable conferences, declarations, multilateral agreements, and treaties. At Rio+20, the 2012 international summit on sustainability involving hundreds of national leaders and thousands of policy-makers and activists,

that question was asked on a global scale. At the first such conference 20 years ago, the ocean was hardly mentioned. The present
situation is improved in that ocean issues are included, hopefully
for the better, but the outcome of the entire exercise remains to be
seen. Did the conference make a difference?

The truth is that we have many tools now in place that have
addressed, and can continue to address the issue aggressively:
local management plans, marine protected areas, spatial planning,
pilot zoning projects, environmental assessments, management
training, and transfer of an ever-expanding reservoir of ocean
information and technology. We also have many organizations:
the United Nations General Assembly, the UN Intergovernmental
Oceanographic Commission, the UN Food and Agriculture
Organization, the UN International Maritime Organization, the
International Seabed Authority, the Convention on Biological
Diversity, the Conference on Sustainable Development, various
fisheries agreements, the Antarctic treaties, the UN Law of the Sea,
and many more—a skein of overlapping policy-making and regulatory structures that account for what progress has been made over
the last few decades.

Some would argue that that progress has been very little.
Serious problems do remain: data gaps, irregular process, limited
coordination, inequitable geographic coverage, lack of time
and financial resources, regulatory failures, legal limitations,
outdated laws, and inadequate compliance and enforcement. But
let's not rush to the cynical conclusion. The irony is that despite
these inhibitions, we do have the knowledge, the principles, and
organizations in place to be successful. If we could address these
existing issues, invigorate these existing organizations, we could,
by just applying the tools already in hand, make a powerful
difference in our ability to address the deteriorating condition of

the ocean commons.

The attendees at Rio+20 opted for another noble declaration of principles. Some policy issues were promoted, and the ocean was included in the final recommendations. No serious resources were committed. Unfortunately, we need willpower and action, not ideals and intentions. In the end, it must come down to agreement on what is our ultimate self-interest. Do we care enough? Do we understand the ocean's capacity to provide the nurturing imperatives for our future lives? Do we want to live in a world where everyone, not just a few, has access to the common wealth of the ocean for generations to come? Can it be that simple?

Failed Governance

In the headlines, we read of international meetings to address the continuing degradation of the environment, both land and sea. Kyoto, Copenhagen, Mexico City, Rio de Janeiro, and now Paris (COP-21) where the world community gathered to address global climate policy and conservation goals for the 21st century. Many heads of state and prime ministers attended; papers, presentations, and plans were abundant; goals and resolutions were proposed, discussed, and declared. Funding commitments were made. But to what avail? I have attended these meetings, but no longer. I cannot bear the disappointment, the optimism betrayed so quickly thereafter when the triumphant announcements become hollow echoes, the specifics compromised, or, worse, deliberately ignored by national and private interests vested in no change, no sustainability, seemingly no future.

I have great admiration for the policy-makers and activists from the United Nations, certain nations, and the large community of non-governmental organizations that are the originators and perpetuators of progressive concepts, structures, and proposals to demonstrate best practices built on conservation principles and values. They are, of course, paid to persevere, but, nonetheless, without them there would be no successes to point to, nothing but a continuing consumption-based reality careening toward implosion and indifferent to the Earth's capacity to support its equally accelerating population growth and demand. This is beyond entropy, in that it is a deliberately chosen strategy for immediate gratification selfishly motivated and dismissive of ensuing generations.

Protecting the Marine Environment in Areas beyond National Jurisdiction, an excellent report by one such NGO, the Foundation for International Environmental Law and Development based in London, was prepared in anticipation of the Rio+20 global meeting in 2013. The report analyzes the challenges for conservation and management of biodiversity in marine areas outside the exclusive economic zones of nations, an extremely important area of interest under severe pressure by the fishing and extraction industries, among others. The report is comprehensive, instructive, well organized and reasoned; it outlines the essential principles for protection and management; it concludes with recommendations that reflect the best thinking of the international conservation interests and with this final note:

> But while the international community debates ways forward, and negotiations around a new international agreement may begin, meaningful marine protection efforts need to be taken by all stakeholders within the existing legal framework as a matter of urgency. With a view to the rapid creation of a system that will ensure the effective use of area-based management strategies...and thus contribute to the conservation and sustainable use of the world's oceans as a whole, action needs to be taken now—before it is too late.[130]

If the global community is unable to respond in time, perhaps we can look to more local governance, national ocean policies that will put in place structures and approaches that will at least mitigate local contribution to the larger international challenges. Australia, New Zealand, and the European Union have established such plans and are addressing the problem in the context of national or regional management and regulation. The United States seemed to be heading in that direction when President Obama created a National Ocean Policy by Executive Order in 2010. Recently, however, as Congress addressed funding for these activities, 23 Republican representatives sent a letter to the House Appropriations Committee objecting not just to increased funding for the plan, but also to any redirection of existing funds toward these new progressive objectives. Their letter concluded, "We urge you to impose a 'time out' so that these questions can be answered before more federal funds are reprogrammed towards the implementation of the National Ocean Policy. We request that language be included in all relevant appropriations legislation for FY 2013 that would prohibit the use of funds for implementing the National Ocean Policy." And so it goes in what passes for governance in the United States.

There are too many such examples. The point here is that international and national governance of ocean issues has mostly failed, either directly or by inadequacy of urgency and action. We need to tell ourselves so. We need to stop clinging to shreds of false optimism that somehow it will all change just in time. We need to understand that hope now lies only in ourselves, in the power of "citizens of the ocean" who are prepared to act individually and collectively to demonstrate by our example and insist by community action that we will no longer accept behavior as usual and will withhold the consent of the governed.

Hard Edges

Our traditional approach to potential inundation by water has been the hard edge. It represents our cultural assumption that Nature is there to serve our needs and, when necessary, to be engineered to that advantage. You see hard edges everywhere: seawalls, dikes, and levees. Riprap erosion controls. Dams. Canals that artificially connect water bodies for transport by ship, for hydropower, or for redirection away from alternative, seemingly more economically desirable development.

Indeed, we have created large bureaucracies—the Army Corps of Engineers in the United States, for example—with the mission to protect us from the encroachment of water, to shield ports and harbors against storm and surge, to facilitate the most efficient marine transportation, and to otherwise manage the environment—lakes, inland waterways, and coastwise—to human advantage as defined by the financial exigencies of the time.

The fate of coastal wetlands is another blatant example of hard over soft. Once massive buffers against storm incursion, wetlands served human needs additionally through complementary cultivation of hay for fodder for saltwater farms. But as those farms gave way to more concentrated settlement and sprawl, the marshes were first ditched to control pesky mosquitoes that annoyed suburban residents, a disruption of the natural arrangement that increased erosion and drained the buffer zone, followed thereafter by hard edges behind which could be deposited dredge spoils, construction debris, and other unnatural material that transformed the soft soil into hard ground on which could be constructed more housing, parking lots, shopping malls, and manufacturing plants—all uses antithetical to Nature's original intent. You could describe a similar history for the destruction of coastal mangroves in other areas around the world.

Highways are hard edges. In southern New England where I once lived, the major north–south interstate highway that extends from Florida to Maine was built to follow a coastal route that created a concrete wall between the shore and the entire land mass and marine system upstream, to the point that the entire natural watershed was blocked and redirected to three cement conduits beneath the highway, not only interrupting and concentrating the natural drainage, but also the animal migration and surface-water distribution that sustained the historical ecosystem, resulting in all sorts of changes, disruptions, and negative environmental consequences to the region.

More modern examples of hard-edge thinking also include such things as the Thames Barrier designed to protect London, England, from flooding. According to the Royal Borough of Greenwich, the structure is built across a 1,710-foot-wide stretch of the Thames, dividing the river into four 200-foot and two 100-foot navigable spans. There are also four smaller non-navigable channels between nine concrete piers and two abutments. The floodgates across the openings are circular segments in cross section that operate by rotating, raised to allow "under spill" for operators to control upstream levels and a complete 180-degree rotation for maintenance. All the gates are hollow and made of steel up to 1.6 inches thick. The gates fill with water when submerged and empty as they emerge from the river. The four large central gates are 66 feet high and weigh 3,700 tons. Four radial gates by the riverbanks, also about 100 feet wide, can be lowered. These gate openings, unlike the main six, are non-navigable.[131] In January 2013, in a letter to the *London Times* newspaper, a former member of the Thames Barrier Project Management Team, Dr. Richard Bloore, stated that the flood barrier was not designed with increased storm and sea level rise in mind, and called for a new barrier to be looked into immediately.

Finally, the Netherlands has long used the hard-edge concept to protect the almost two-thirds of its national territory that is at or below sea level and otherwise susceptible to flooding by three major rivers, the Rhine, Meuse, and Scheldt. Before 1000 AD, the Dutch began to protect their coastal areas with earthen dikes, followed through the centuries by timber walls, followed by higher structures reinforced by crushed rock and cement, covered over by earth on which sheep continue to graze. But flood-control engineering was soon augmented necessarily by the need for increased protection, and the Dutch innovated radically with the construction of an enormous barrier system that closed the natural opening to the ocean and transformed the Zuiderzee into the IJsselmeer, literally "from a sea to an inland lake." This was followed in the 1990s by the Delta Works, an even larger storm surge protection system that today, in the face of projected sea level rise, is nonetheless considered inadequate for the future and has sent the Dutch engineers back to the drawing board.

Hard problems, hard thinking, hard edges: might there be another way?

Soft Edges

Some years ago, a museum exhibit comparing American and Norwegian maritime culture provided an understanding of how one can respond successfully to the challenges of the ocean with two very different solutions. In this case, it was boat construction, the traditional Norwegian boats made with light ribs and planks that flexed and conformed visibly to the shifts in wave and water condition. By contrast, the American boats were built plank-on-rigid-frames and, while these vessels were no less adaptive, or even beautiful, they confronted the ocean differently—rode *on* the wave, not *in*, pushing over or through the water rather than adapting to the forces in play.

The obvious alternative is "soft edges," more amorphous and flexible ways to absorb rather than divert the ocean's powerful incursions, indeed to let the water in. This of course has been the argument made often by environmentalists when opposing the filling-in of wetlands, the destruction of marshes and coastal waterways, and the eradication of mangrove forests that for centuries provided natural protection by embracing the water and its destructive power and keeping it from the higher land beyond. We have seen the failure of the hard-edge way, as storms overwhelm the barriers, destroy the resorts and beachfront homes, and otherwise demonstrate the hydraulic power of the ocean twice: once on the way inland, the other as the water withdraws, doubles down on the destruction, and draws the detritus in the sea. We had only to look at the devastation at Fukushima, the tsunami inundation of a coastal nuclear power installation in Japan, to witness this two-part threat.

There are slowly emerging examples of soft-edge response, exacerbated now by the undeniable rise in sea level in many places, the consequent frequent flooding, and the unmitigated and very expensive destruction caused by ever-increasing incidence of more powerful storms like Superstorm Sandy in the United States. How can we turn these new circumstances to advantage?

In the Netherlands, long the most highly successful practitioners of hard-edge strategy, government is now evicting farmers from polders or marshes enclosed by dikes and converted to agriculture, to restore those areas as control and containment areas when the other defenses are overwhelmed. According to a recent

New York Times report, the Dutch have expanded this concept to a $3 billion integrated plan to construct and connect flood controls, spillways, polders, smaller dikes, and pumping stations, into a kind of engineered capillary system that can accommodate vast increases in flooding volume as a serious alternative in public investment in additional and very expensive hard-edge security.

There are other examples of this evolving thinking. Andrew Cuomo, the Governor of New York State in the United States, has proposed post-Sandy that coastal properties, susceptible to continuous flooding, be purchased by government, that the owners be compensated and relocated, and that the land be designated for public recreation and as natural barriers to future storm events. The cost-benefit analysis of the purchase and redefinition of the coastal lands compares advantageously with the financial requirements of just a single storm, not to mention the more to come, as a practical and economical allocation of taxpayer funding. It was ironic to note that recently while a US Congressional debate was ongoing regarding public monies to reimburse Sandy-devastated coastal dwellers and businesses through reparation payments and a subsidized national insurance scheme that enables owners to rebuild where-is, and sometimes as-was, that very same federal program was advertising on television to recruit new clients for more coverage in those marginal areas. It made no sense. The cancellation of that ill-advised insurance program would no doubt begin to disable coastal development substantially in the United States, a radical and very controversial policy shift.

In other countries, private groups, supported by international NGOs, are initiating the restoration and replanting of extensive mangrove forests in coastal areas, again for the same reason, to rebuild a natural, relatively inexpensive system that has proven its effectiveness as both storm and habitat protection, a very different double-down based on knowledge and experience of Nature. In Arcata, California, the city managers have created a wastewater treatment plant that passes effluent through a primary clarifier that separates suspended solids (using a digester to transform into methane and compost for sale), passes the resultant fluids to oxidation ponds and treatment wetlands for additional settling, and then to enhancement and treatment marshes (which also serve as recreation areas), and, ultimately, as clean water into Humboldt Bay—a natural hydraulic progress that mimics the natural cycle with effective result.[132] It is this wisdom that we must look to for instruction lest we drown in our conventional thinking. It is through this learning that we will find our way to new ideas for ocean solutions.

V. Toward Solutions

THE RIGHT OF PASSAGE

Thinking Like an Island

Discussing solutions to challenges on land and sea, we speak often of patterns of consumption. We are a society organized around apparently insatiable consumption—of our natural resources, of the products derived from those resources, even of our heroes who we use up and discard with abandon equal to changing fashion—and it is this drive that has created such stress on our terrestrial and marine environments. Our social needs and financial system enable the extremes, for example, fishing tuna to exhaustion to meet immediate lucrative demand with no concern for limits or the inevitability of extinction.

Some argue this is the result of evil capitalism. I will leave that discussion for another time, another place. But think of it this way: We approve investment in research and development of pharmaceutical products that treat disease; we disapprove of similar investment in such products that compromise the health of our children. It seems to me that the problem lies not so much in the financial system itself, but rather in the investment and consumer decisions and their consequences that either heal our sick or poison our fields, streams, and ocean. It's all about values. How, then, do we shift our priorities, change our behaviors, alter our patterns of consumption, make different decisions so as to sustain the resources that remain and assure our future survival?

I suggest that we start thinking like an island.

Assume the satellite perspective and look down upon the Earth to view an ocean world in which float islands, be they atolls, nations, or continents. If you now descend and join those island communities, you will discover people whose lives are defined by different limits, different needs, different utilities. Islanders are by definition more reliant on things to hand: water locally drawn, food locally raised or harvested from the sea, local skills required to make and fix things for themselves. They are more or less connected to a mainland that may provide fuel, additional supplies, even law enforcement, doctors, and priests, but they know that fog or storm may cancel that connection at any moment and they will be required to fend for themselves. I have no interest in romanticizing island life; it is hard, challenging, often lonely, not always united in politics and beliefs, and forever formed by natural forces that are omnipresent in changing weather and wave.

Nonetheless, these circumstances demand different standards for living. Islanders must focus first on first things, on utilitarian needs not frivolities, on the essential requirements of individuals, families, and neighbors. Islanders reuse and recycle things; they run machines longer on precious little fuel. They invent and create; islands are good places for artists and makers. They police and govern themselves. They teach and coach children they know. Islanders choose to limit themselves to the circumference of the land and to the quality of the life so defined by the omnipresent maritime beauty and enduring community they have found and built there. Many times, islanders choose to stay because they reject the way of living known on another shore. They are not ocean-bound; indeed, now, given the Internet, they can communicate and exchange goods, services, and ideas worldwide.

What are the characteristic values evident in such places? Independence, self-reliance, practicality, frugality, ingenuity, respect for work, success within limits, cooperation, and community. What if we suddenly drew invisible lines in urban places and applied these same values there? What if we looked at our cities, our regions, even our nations as islands? What if, as citizens, we all start acting like islanders, applying such values individually, locally, and nationally in our purchases, our institutions, our expectations of governance, our life choices? What if we abandon the rigid, mis-valued ideologies that paralyze us and engage instead in a fulsome exercise of island living? Do we have to wait for our leaders to tell us what to do? Why can't we do this for ourselves? And do it now?

The global recession has brought home to nations and individuals alike the painful bankruptcy of systemic overconsumption, driven by credit, as an unsustainable model for the future. Only the most vested interests hold on to the delusion that all will be as it once was. There are signs among some countries and some executives that the application of such values to governance and business development can be a successful, competitive, and profitable way to behave in the world marketplace.

There are signs that citizens of nations whose resources have been exploited and consumed, whose destroyed environments can no longer sustain water and food supplies, are demanding, sometimes violently, the attention or replacement of politicians complicit in the old model. There are signs that we are beginning to think and act as if we understand that Earth, too, is an island. Such signs are not enough. We must do more, quickly. Fellow islanders, unite!

Policy, Planning, and Governance

If I had my way, what would I do to change the causes and effects of our actions that amplify with such portent around us? The question is complicated, thus so too must be the answer. Here are a few actions, however improbable each might sound, to outline changes in policy, planning, and governance that just might make a difference.

First, remove pro-consumption subsidies, public support of private efforts to exploit natural resources of every kind. As enterprise does respond to incentives, redefine and reward behaviors through public finance directed toward the implementation of new land use planning, development in the coastal zone, and relocation of nonessential, non-marine-related functions inland.

Second, base evaluation, permitting, and regulatory oversight on a new system of economic analysis that calculates and integrates into budgets and prices the true cost of protection or loss of non-renewable resources, of potential damage and financial consequence of failed design or natural disasters, and of the downstream impact of localized implementation indifferent to the larger region and beyond.

Third, declare the coastal zone to be a laboratory for such innovation, the place where the growing majority of the people of the world choose to live, where new planning technologies, management structures, and political coalitions will thrive. Indeed, focus on the coastal megacities, the epicenters of population, consumption, poverty, risk, and opportunity. Put everything up for review: water, wastewater and solid waste systems, industrial placement and pollution control, urban energy and food production, building and appliance codes, tax policy, and job creation linked to the socioeconomic changes that, taken together, are essential to a successful alternative to the status quo.

Fourth, enforce the regulations and treaties that exist, voted and ratified, to confront the abuses already known. Identify and reject the vested interests, individual and corporate, that work incessantly to undermine or corrode these structural deterrents to antisocial behavior.

Fifth, build public awareness and political will at every level through research, education, leadership development, accessibility, transparency, and governance.

Some argue these are impossible ideas. But if you take them apart, you can find in each the seeds of change that are the agendas of small, local, issue-based constituencies and political entities, non-governmental organizations, research institutions, and educational groups that, galvanized around a single issue or strategy shift, are working now for incremental change. It is that effort that matters, the focus on one this, one that, that can make the difference. There is perhaps no readily apparent over-arching vision that unites it all, but there is a dynamic force for change in these myriad revolutionary facets and pieces, and there, in that collectivized action, lies hope for the future.

VALUE SHIFTS AND NEW PREMISES

Toward New Definitions of Value

If we are convinced that we must look to the ocean for solutions to our most pressing future challenges—for fresh water, food, energy, health, and security—then we must declare these goals as essential "values," that is of the highest worth as measured monetarily, socially, and morally, and therefore act to affirm and sustain them even if it means that previously valued systems and approaches be modified or abandoned. The irony here is that none of these things are new to our pursuit of life, liberty, or happiness, but the circumstances have changed and we must now perforce redefine our actions and behaviors in a new global context of critical supply and demand. If fresh water has been historically valueless due to its previous accessibility and surfeit, then it now becomes invaluable as a commodity threatened by overconsumption, pollution, and drought. To accommodate that change requires revolutionary assessment, the abandonment of past assumptions, and the creation and adoption of new systems, organizations, and political and social decisions for success.

For example, we may choose to price things differently, to value fresh water as the one resource we all need in equal amount daily to survive and therefore infinitely more important than gold or pork bellies or financial instruments for the economic estimation of things. We may choose to tax things differently, a carbon tax for example, that limits consumption and creates a revenue stream with which to deal with the negative impact of the polluting consequence of fossil fuels. We may choose to create exchanges or systems of barter or offsets that allow companies to trade adaptations over time to improved or new technologies that balance and decrease negative contribution to environmental decline. We may choose to make changes in our personal lifestyle to conserve energy in our homes, decrease our contribution to the market for polluting products, and advocate for different patterns of utility and social organization that affirm our new value definitions over old. We may engage with our neighbors and communities in setting revised priorities for planning, economic development, and governance that implement new values where we live.

Changed premises will determine changed outcomes whether for individuals, families, social structures, regional organizations, or nation states. Does it require a revolution? It should not if reason and openness to change can prevail. But if resistance based on vested interest in the status quo or fear of change denies the evolutionary nature of this process, then, with our very survival at stake, more dramatic political action may be certainly justified.

What form might this newly valued world take? We might not have to look too far into the past, actually, to find a new model for the future. And we might take note of the long-lived value systems of indigenous peoples based on close observation of Nature, preservation of biological diversity, understanding of the inter-related worth of natural process, and the integration of living successfully in the landscape with community and cultural identity. We have relegated these people to the margins, placed them on official and unofficial "reservations," and too often relegated their ideas to superstition and ignorance in the face of our science and technology, source of much present good, but yes, as much present evil when their measure is taken in the resultant condition of the Earth today.

In Hawaii, at least until the mid-1900s, there existed a system of resource management known as "Ahupuau'a," designed to support a growing population with limited resources. The islands were similar topographically, with a central volcano or mountainous region as a highest point from there descending to the sea. Communities were organized into comparably sized, wedge-shaped geographies aligned to the descent of fresh water from high springs and runoff into streams, rivers, and the ocean. Thus, the land nurturing the sustaining natural growth and agriculture, even to include a riparian area near shore, was allocated, exploited, and managed to provide fresh water for drink and irrigation, terrestrial and marine food, shelter and well-being, community and governance—in effect a needs-based, maximized, and sustainable system of living organized along the natural flow of water—yet another example of hydraulic society. Could such a concept inform the solution to the challenges we face today? Could we not apply our new 21st-century values to the organization of a similar structure, certainly more complex, but equally useful, productive, and successful? Just how might we do this?

Beyond Denial

Recently, a group of 26 Senators from the US Congress held an all-night vigil speak-out about climate change and the imperative for some kind of legislative response by the American government. It was mostly a symbolic event in that the group, all members of the Democratic party, led by Rhode Island Senator Sheldon Whitehouse, did not have a majority to pass any such legislation and that the House of Representatives, dominated by the most conservative Republicans, would never touch the issue at all.[133]

Thus, does one of the most pressing issues for the future of our national security, our public health, our financial viability over time, and our standing as a world leader get left unaddressed, premeditatedly ignored, by some of those elected to be most responsible for those very things for all of us?

This failure to govern is the most egregious and depressing aspect of American life today. It is driven by short-term thinking, blatant self-interest, indifference to science, and ideological principles that are at best contradictory, exclusionary, and regressive. Communication, compromise, and consensus—three pillars of practical and successful governance—have been abandoned and relegated to the memory of a time when civil discourse and legislative innovation recognized and addressed the most pressing problems of the day. Not so now; our legislators filibuster, read fairy tales to empty halls, and stand through all-night vigils as symbolic gestures against agendas bereft of intelligence or action.

Much has been made for and against the overwhelming evidence that anthropogenic behaviors have created demonstrable changes to our land, waterways, and ocean; have made debilitating changes in the air we breathe, the food we eat, and the rapidly depleting supply of natural resources on which our consumption-driven lifestyle depends, at least until there is nothing left. We ignore the results; we deny the evidence; we ridicule the proposed solutions; and we obfuscate any ideas and subvert any individuals that argue otherwise.

We are exhausting the land, the atmosphere, the ocean, and ourselves. We deny the obvious; we deny any suggestion of change; and we deny by the inevitable outcome of our paralysis any counter to the equally inevitable decline of our ability to act, even for our children.

Denial is just the front for something far worse. Denial asserts that there is no problem, and therefore there is no need for solution. There is no need for research. There is no need for education. There is no need to even discuss an issue that, denied, does not exist. Thus, any correlation between fossil fuels and energy consumption, automobile and generation emissions, air and water quality, acidification and the marine food chain, short-term return and long-term sustainability are not even to be discussed. The word "climate" is to be expunged from every official document, regulation, or future statute because it means nothing. It is Orwellian; words legislated to silence.

What lies beyond denial is what concerns me most. If we

choose to deny looking beyond, toward the reality, the consequence, even the hypothetical probabilities, of our failure to act, we are abrogating the very idea of responsible governance, exemplifying one of the defining characteristics of a failed state. In the words of Senator Whitehouse, "It's Time to Wake Up."

Millions of people the world over know this. They are engaged every day as individuals, organizations, educators, and activists in our towns, our capitols, and our international collaborations, in an effort to counter the force of denial, to define alternatives, and to promote solutions. From our ocean perspective, we see volunteers cleaning beaches of post-consumption litter, environmental groups advocating for marine protected areas, fisheries policies, waste management schemes, water quality controls, air quality standards, alternative energy systems, and so much more. I am in awe, not just of their efforts, but more of their energy, determination, and resilience in the face of undeniable indifference by decision-makers to the global crisis these constituents know experientially to be true. They see it, feel it, and are committed to the creation of a new reality beyond.

Theirs is the most powerful denial of all, a counter-denial. They deserve our celebration and participation. They have moved past the politicians without conscience, the naysayers and saboteurs, the self-aggrandizers and politically compromised, by working, side by side, step by step, place by place, toward a future—in my view enabled and endowed by a vital ocean—where there will be clean water for all, food for all, energy for all, health for all, security for all, and community for all in a world sustainable for all yet to come. By their actions, they usurp the power, they deny denial, they govern.

Network Societies

W e often speak of "values," underlying concepts or premises on which we define, justify, and implement attitudes, behaviors, and actions. We speak of religious values, ethical values, economic values, community values—again, principles that guide us in our social, political, financial, and communal engagements and interests as individuals, groups, and nation states.

Today, when we speak of "consumption" for example, we acknowledge our right to exploit Nature to human advantage regardless of limits or consequence. Such a value statement then informs personal, corporate, and national choices and policies, sets priorities, and becomes a context for accepted behavior. At a time when fish abound, for instance, we harvest without limit. When fish become scarce, however, we react either by individualized indifference or by modified methods to include voluntary limits or cooperative agreements—changed behaviors that are based on modified values. Sustainability has emerged in the global lexicon as a new value proposition—that is, a new principle that provides a new response to the changing conditions, themselves a consequence of the previous application of the old value of consumption without restriction. At the local, regional, national, and even international level, such a value shift becomes an area of conflict between present interest and future interest, between individuals and collectives, between geographical areas dependent on the same resource, between nations protective of their proprietary demand on an ever-diminishing supply. To ameliorate and adjudicate such conflict, we look to communication and compromise agreement, to regulations and treaties, to a consensus built on reason and community interest.

But what if we can't agree? What if short-term profit for some overcomes the longer-term need of many? What if corporate interests contradict societal interests? What if governments cannot agree or even enforce the things on which they do agree? What if one nation state declares an economic, or political, or cultural justification for a specific harvest when inevitably it will deprive all the rest of us of sustainable access? What power can be brought to bear in such a case? How can the imposition of one value system over another be ameliorated or broken?

In 2014, some 30 Greenpeace activists were imprisoned in Russia for their attempt to protest drilling for oil that the Russians believe to be in their national interest. This is just one instance of such a clash of values. In the United States, 350.org and other organizations are protesting hydro-fracking and the Keystone XL pipeline from Canada across the country that they claim will have serious, unacceptable environmental consequences with no concurrent or offsetting public benefit. In his 2015 decision not to allow the pipeline, President Barack Obama agreed. The tactics here are confrontational and political, based on the perception that there is no middle ground, no reasonable resolution to the specific conflict, no willingness to explore or examine the possibility of a value resolution.

If this is the case, and change is held captive by un-compromise and denial, how can we move forward? How can we transcend the colliding interests and build a new forum for discussion and resolution? How do we build a volume of interest that expresses the argument for a new value proposition? How can we catch the attention of those willing to consider change and to work toward new policies and behaviors as an expression of progress? How do we change the prevalent mind-set?

We have seen the impact of social media in a new and revolutionary context: the Arab Spring for example, or other global initiatives that are issue-based and in search of a new constituency as political force. These represent a very different dynamic unification of interested parties outside the conventional parameters of an existing restrictive community or even a nation-state. These virtual assemblies are called *network societies,* a common space and communications system for like-minded people galvanized by an issue, a protest, and yes an alternative in contradiction or contravention to an accepted behavior.

This may be the way for those committed to the transcendence of entropic behavior and political paralysis to unite behind a change or a new value proposition to find commonality of interest, strategic efficiency, and specific acts and inventions for change. We are all *Citizens of the Ocean,* a group of individuals informed and motivated by ocean information, educational outreach, and global connection, as a means to defend and sustain the ocean. Indeed, the nascent W2O *Citizens of the Ocean* initiative can be one such powerful network society, linked as if arm in arm, allied against the bankrupt values of the past, and united as a force for the future.

From Natural System to Social System

In 1998, Mario Soares, the former President of Portugal, organized an Independent World Commission on the Future of the Oceans, that met, considered, and produced a report— *The Ocean, Our Future*[134]—that remains, in my view, the most prescient and clarifying analysis and set of recommendations for the sustainable ocean, bar none. Soares is an ardent advocate for human rights. His election to the presidency was a victory in the battle against the oppression of an ultra-conservative, colonialist dictatorship, which controlled the people of Portugal and Portuguese-speaking countries for almost 50 years. He is an equally passionate advocate for the ocean, and his leadership of the World Commission and its contribution to a strategy for the future must be acknowledged and never forgotten.

In his introduction to the report, Soares writes, "I have always seen the ocean as a realm of freedom, a prime medium of human contact—and therefore of dialogue, solidarity and coexistence between different cultures and civilizations... I have always seen the ocean as a school for democracy..."

That is a powerful estimate of the influence of a natural system on fundamental social behavior. It moves our thoughts forward to a place where we can understand that all our efforts on behalf of challenged marine species and habitat have a much higher purpose. The Independent World Commission was unique in its promulgation of that view. It conditioned its recommendations on public acceptance of that perspective, including its suggestion for the creation of a Web-based World Ocean Observatory to aggregate information and educational services about the ocean, to build increased public awareness and political will. In 2005, responding to this opportunity, I founded the World Ocean Observatory as a direct expression of that effort and point of view.

What disturbs me, however, is that much of the energy invested in ocean advocacy today does not support that approach; indeed, it remains focused on research and protection of species in the form of global observation systems, the census of marine life, and the growing world inventory of marine protected areas designated to preserve natural areas, the habitats, in which these species can continue and flourish. This is all to the good, but only recently has the policy discussion begun to move beyond this conventional thinking to incorporate social considerations through awareness and understanding of the predictable human impacts of such things as sea level rise, extreme weather, food and national security, acidification, public health implications, and ecosystem services that number among the most prevalent emerging concerns. This shift is also to the good, but must accelerate if it is not to be too little too late.

Soares goes on to state, "We need therefore to forge a new ethico-political relationship between humanity and the oceans, a relationship with a political and juridical basis which creates an atmosphere of sharing and solidarity and which provides for a new universalism centered on the knowledge of the oceans; a relationship capable of unifying the citizens of the world under one banner, a common, unique and irreplaceable asset: the sea which all the continents share, and which to a certain extent equalizes them."[135]

It has become clear that reliance on a narrow perception of the ocean as a natural system has not motivated such a relationship. The public has not responded to this strategy as an ethico-political call to arms. While our knowledge of the ocean has grown exponentially since 1998, universal unification of citizens under a one-ocean banner has certainly not occurred. Indeed, as I have cited before, a 2012 Ocean Project survey indicates that public awareness of ocean issues in the United States over the last decade has not increased at all.

I submit that the hoped-for increase will not come at all until we make a single, serious, simple shift in our thinking. We must change the premise for our ocean concern: that it is our culture and civilization at risk, not just the dying fish and poisoned places. Those phenomena are the symptoms of our failure to protect what can be better defined as threats to our freedom and democracy, by our indifference to the multiple social implications of ocean exploitation and decline, and by our lack of response to the ocean challenges we face and will accrue tragically to us all if we fail to act.

From Micro to Macro and Return

When confronting the challenges to today's ocean, we must inevitably make a passage from micro to macro and return. We first become aware of the problem nearby, typically a local manifestation in the form of a use conflict such as aquaculture versus inshore fishing or a natural phenomenon such as a red tide closing a beach to recreational access. There may or may not be a local solution. Yes, the conflict may seem to be resolved, just as the algae bloom may disappear, but the larger questions remain looming beyond the micro-perspective.

Research is typically the next waypoint, the investigation of a condition or problem identified by the gathering of data or observation over time and place that provides insight into what actually is happening and suggests additional questions and, sometimes, possible solutions. This research may seem somewhat distant, deep and detailed, ironically more general, less local in the scape of the problem and the scope of the inquiry.

Last summer, while waiting for a nearby island ferry, I noticed a large official poster announcing the closing of vast areas along this coast to shell-fishing due to the presence of intense algae and toxins most probably the result of the remarkably, unnaturally, high air and water temperatures measured since 2005. The red graphics were a dramatic expression of a serious local problem, a condition nonetheless most probably extended in both directions alongshore and surely the locus of an intense research and data collection effort in search of scientific under-standing and solution. This instance stands for many—an evident phenomenon detrimental to our relationship to the ocean that demands inquiry beyond the limit of its immediate impact and toward a universal explanation—it is happening everywhere. The situation has moved from micro to macro.

There is no question that our knowledge of the ocean is increasing exponentially through global scientific inquiry over the past decade. Through satellite surveillance, survey vessels, underwater vehicles, and fixed observation systems, enormous amounts of data have been, and will continue to be, collected exponentially about light, temperature, salinity, acidity, up- and downwelling, currents, earthquakes, hydraulic dynamics, marine species, known and new, volcanic activity, hydro-thermal vents, the mineral composition of the ocean floor, and much, much more. The data enters a parallel ocean of information into which will dive researchers who will extract value in the form of papers and reports, conclusions, speculations, and demands for more data. But take care; one can also drown in this sea.

I do not mean to belittle this macro-summation. It is powerful, implicative, and necessary work. The best use of data is its informing of policy, that is, its application and transformation into best practice in many different forms: new recommendations, voluntary modifications of behavior, regulations, laws, treaties, and other such agreements. At this point, the tide turns and the derived knowledge begins a cycle of return, from macro cause to micro effect, from the coastal site or deep ocean through the laboratory and back again. What is learned becomes guidance for the future and catalyst for change.

It offends me when I hear science derided by those who find the results inconvenient and contradictory to their interests. To me it is comparable to burning books, censoring art, or demeaning another's spiritual beliefs. The egoism and hypocrisy are all too evident. The irony is, of course, that in so many cases the advantages held by those who have these ideas are the result of previous science and comparable inquiry. I invite them to look at that chart of the closed coast as a red line signal of danger that begins there and, as the data reveals, extends its perimeter invisibly outward into the world ocean dissolved as acid, chemicals, and man-made poisons, yes, too the product of science, mis-used or excessively deposited in amounts, however microscopic, now globally measurable and proven detrimental to our survival.

As we think about the future, the passage from micro to macro and return corresponds to our critical thinking—our perception of a problem locally, collectivized and used as the stimulus for worldwide investigation and creative thinking, codified in response into responsible policy and reforms of behavior, as a new awareness applied through political will into direct action and change where we live, here by the nurturing ocean.

From Research to Responsibility

If we accept the notion that we must understand the ocean better before we can truly address its critical problems, then research and scientific inquiry must increase with urgency commensurate with the crisis. And, indeed, research has done just that, as best it can within a political and financial context sadly antithetical to this progress.

Funding for pure science has been diminished, both by the national and global financial circumstances we face, but also by the calculated efforts of those who ideologically oppose or fear the knowledge acquired. We have all heard of the North Carolina legislature in the United States attempting to outlaw climate change by statute. As absurd is a totality by definition, there may be no additional language that can characterize the magnitude of this collective, empty expression of denial. As the North Carolina economy depends in great part on new research being developed at its universities and science parks, this action excludes all reason.

Nonetheless, even in this atmosphere, ocean research is being advanced significantly by public and private entities in laboratories and aboard vessels worldwide. If you start to listen for it, you will hear ocean exploration and innovation announced constantly in the scientific journals and media accounts of experiments, projects, and breakthroughs. Oceanography, marine biology, and ocean engineering are fast-growing specialties in colleges and graduate programs; students in America's several maritime academies are now immediately employed upon graduation by companies involved in ocean-related enterprise. It is a coming thing.

But here is where research must lead to responsibility. In the many gatherings of ocean research and policy organizations I have attended, the concluding recommendations invariably focus on education and outreach as the pre-eminent need. In response, when I ask about specific institutional commitment to external communications as a measure of responsibility to the public outside of the institution's immediate, predictable, and limited audience, I discover that no resources are allocated, outreach staff are first to be laid off, and actual efforts are typically driven by near-term public relations and fund-raising, little more. In such cases, the individuals inside find little organizational support and therefore can make little or no contribution to the strategy outside deemed essential by the collective wisdom.

Once, interviewing the new president of a well-known ocean science institution, I asked what he thought it might take to transform the results of their research into policy. "Civil disobedience," he replied. I stopped the camera. Was he joking? Did he really want to say such a thing publicly? Would he be reprimanded by trustees or colleagues for what might seem beyond the traditional purview of his distinguished organization? He stood by his response, no question, it was that important to him, and I thought, "Now, there's a scientist unafraid of taking full responsibility for his discipline and endeavor."

In this regard, we are all in the same boat. We have concerns and informed opinions about things, be they social issues or environmental matters. But we are frustrated by the scale of issues, the forces larger than ourselves, the paralysis of institutions around us that seem no longer capable of action. We question what we can possibly do in the face of such opposition and lethargy. The crisis is so large; we are so small. How can we take responsibility for our concerns and opinions in any way that matters?

I believe scientists should advocate through responsible research and discovery in the public forum. Climate scientists have done just that, aggregated hundreds of project outcomes and reports into a collective call for action, justified by information. Yes, they could be wrong, but isn't the question more what happens if they are right? The evidence of sea level rise, changing water temperature, resultant shifts in feeding and migration patterns of marine species, increased severity and frequency of extreme weather, wind, and wave, resultant cost of response and reconstruction—all these have been documented and modeled for years now. How long can we reject responsibility for our indifference to this damage to human life and community? Isn't this what the research is for: to provide us the knowledge by which to prevent disaster and invent new ways forward to better our lives?

Don't we know what we must do?

From Consumption to Utility

"The pursuit of wealth for its own sake is folly." I read this declaration recently in *The Economist*, a publication that generally sets store by capitalism and markets.[136] It was spoken as editorial voice in a review of two new books on the limits of capitalism, a subject heretical in a world that thrives and declines by the measure of gross domestic product based on what appears to be insatiable consumption.

The argument over the real and moral manifestations of the dominant economic system of this time will not be settled here. But it can be addressed in the context of the ocean as a place where the pursuit of wealth, primarily natural resources, plays out in known and less known ways. The consumption of marine species as food, oil and gas as energy, coastal wetlands and estuaries as sites for tourism-related pollution, and soon enough minerals as the base parts of much making and processing are combined at the core of the supply system upon which we all rely. We consume these things without limit, or at least until we have used them all up. The system appears not to have failed us, those of us who have been the beneficiaries, not the victims, of its working. GDP grows as a result of our desires to live better, eat more, play harder, live longer, and otherwise continue an easy ascent up the scale of wealth and well-being.

Occasionally, the system fails us—a pestilence, a catastrophic natural event, a depression, a war, or an act of God, that is, things we may think are not of our own making. Science often undercuts such reasoning when it reveals that, indeed, such things may well be our responsibility for which we, not Nature or the Divine, must be held accountable.

I can argue that in fact it is we who have failed the system, not the other way around. Surely, war, for example, is ours to provoke and wage, no matter how we might justify our actions as religiously correct and exceptional. Such circumstance underlies climate denial, the unwillingness to accept that our pursuit of wealth, unrestrained and mismanaged, accounts for what is now polluted air, poisoned earth, acidic and hypoxic seas.

What measure might we take to make this different? What if we measured well-being by the meeting of our basic need for water, food, work, health, and community, supplemented and paid for by those interested and able to consume more without depriving others or exhausting supply? Not a new question, of course. But one that must be addressed again as we face the reality and increasing certainty that some, perhaps much, of this wealth may soon be denied us all?

What if we valued things first by their utility? A well, a bit of land and garden, a hoe and bucket, a hook and net, a roof, and stove, a book or brush, a place to help us when we're sick—what if everyone could have that first, and calculate our well-being from that utilitarian baseline from which to build our lives, every one of us safe and equal at the start? Those who have these things, and more, are far too often indifferent to this equitable foundation; those who do not have these things, and less, are far too often excluded from the discussion. What are we saying when we deride the safety net or government programs that apply such values to our basic human needs? What are we doing when we take resources without care or concern for their integrity or longevity simply to benefit ourselves? What does it mean when we consume things into extinction leaving nothing for anyone including our own children? Where is the logic in any of this? Why are we so fearful when basic human needs are promoted as basic human rights?

Capitalism may continue to serve us as a viable system, but

not in its present unrestrained, corrupted form where one can glut voraciously, break the law, defy regulation and treaty, deny the truth, and walk on free, irresponsible and indifferent to the consequences.

You do not have to look too far to find evidence of this decline. The media shouts the dire news; the land burns and floods; the weather extends into extremes; the jobs are lost, the investments fail, the opportunists hedge the markets, the politics become a paralyzed confrontation of pointing fingers, and the illusions become delusions evident to all, even to those who live only by the gross domestic product.

The ocean is a different place. It dynamism and life might provide an antidote to this polluted behavior. But not if we continue to treat it with the same ignorance as we have done the land. We can use the ocean to meet our needs, and it will nurture us. Or we can consume the ocean, and it will destroy us with power that we have already seen as comparable to the wrath of God.

From Mitigation to Management

To mitigate is to lessen the force or severity of a phenomenon— anger for example, or grief, pain, or physical attack. It is to make less severe, to become milder, softened, more gentle, appeased. Mitigation is a key word today for how we respond to natural challenges, frequently an engineered response—a dike or a drainage system that may defend or redirect floodwater away from an agricultural or settled area, or a much larger project like the major tidal control gates and barriers that protect London from storm surge up the Thames or the Netherlands from similar threat alongshore to a nation mostly at sea level or below.

Disasters occur when these mitigating factors are overwhelmed, be they collapsed levees in New Orleans during hurricanes or our disappointment and dismay when we have not been able to protect ourselves against an emotional challenge. What then do we do? In too many cases, we revert to our prior behavior—repair the damage, perhaps build the defenses more strongly, a response that does not truly address the cause of the traumatizing effect. Why did this happen? Will it happen again? Why did the system in place fail? How do we reconcile answers to these questions with actions that will do more than lessen the pain or severity of the circumstance the next time?

In the context of the ocean, climate change, sea level rise, extreme weather, acidification, mitigation seems a naïve, if not useless choice for the future. Have we seen any significant effort by the public to reduce their carbon footprint, to support any regulatory program to reduce emissions, mandate new standards for automobiles and trucks, or to accept any tax increase that might use market forces to reduce fossil fuel consumption? What we have seen is a political agenda, dominated by lobbyists and corporate contributions to political campaigns that have negated such legislative initiatives not only in the future but also in the past by the evisceration of previously enacted laws such as the Clean Water Act, Clean Air Act, and more. The environmental achievements of the past 20 years are under attack, the laws, and indeed the very agencies that have been responsible for whatever successes there have been. This is a perverse parody of mitigation, a backward-focused, mirror-image strategy that will inevitably make things more severe, more painful, more destructive, and more threatening and problematic for our children.

We are failing to manage successful response to these challenges, be they on land, coastwise, or in the deep ocean. We are failing to manage even within the structures that already exist that might enable solutions. We legislate, but do not enforce the legal requirements of the legislation. We set standards, but choose not live up to those aspirations. This must change, even if it requires individual sacrifice. This must change, and we must find the leadership to make it so.

We have schools for organization and management. We have institutes and universities researching and designing new administrative structures, applying new technologies, and inventing new procedures and policies. But I am amazed by how wary and closed we are today to innovation, how paranoid and protective we are when faced with change. When any one of us looks back over our lifetime we must admit that we have witnessed astonishing advancement in almost every aspect of our society. It is far from perfect, and certainly not everyone has shared in the benefits of this change, but progress it has been and we are the better for it. Why then would we suddenly resist this process now?

Coastal management is exemplary. Faced with ever-increasing migration to our shores, overbuilding, pollution, erosion, and growing inundation, we must apply the best management practices to overcome the reality of bad practice with new. We must use new management tools, such as integrated ocean and land planning, water recycling and watershed conservation, better sanitation, sewage treatment, industrial drainage systems, and storm protection engineering, revised building codes, improved air pollution controls, less impactful construction methods, new targets for tax incentives and public subsidies, use of alternative energy sources—all tools available to us now if only we can muster the will to insist they be applied.

Externalities

Externality refers to what lies outside a given perimeter; in modern parlance, it often refers to a disconnected or unconsidered consequence, sometimes positive, sometimes not, of a particular action. For example, a factory is built in a municipality, enthusiastically welcomed by the residents, justified as stimulus for jobs, taxes, and a healthy community, which then, as a by-product of its manufacturing process, releases high quantities of mercury as waste into the nearby swamp or river which then descends through the towns below into the watershed and into the ocean. That waste is toxic, and so it generates serious impacts along its downstream course, on the health of the citizens below, on the continuum of terrestrial and riverine life, and ultimately on the marine food chain where it is ingested by fish, thereafter harvested and supplied to our table. All of that consequence, none of it monetized or factored into the cost of the factory or the price of its product, is called "externality." A warning in my doctor's office recommends that pregnant women do not eat swordfish because of the toxic effect of excess mercury—the final externality to come should a child be born with a resultant birth defect.

Mountaintop removal, hydraulic fracturing, open pit mining, dams and highways, filled wetlands—these are just some of the many other examples of human-engineered intrusion into natural systems that are not typically planned or valued within the full context and cost of their use.

I watched a remarkable short film recently wherein a passenger tossed a plastic water bottle out the window of a moving car; the bottle bounced and rolled across the pavement, into the ditch that drained into a river, into a city, into a culvert,

drain, and canal, into the ocean. And there it descended, to the
ocean floor where it disintegrated into millions of tiny beads
of plastic, dissolved its chemicals into the water where it joined
the consequence of the disposal of millions of such bottles and
contributed to the mass externality that is today's ocean.

We are saturating the ocean with our unthinking consequence, be it plastic, or chemicals, or micro-particles—and
succumbing to the greatest externality of them all: accelerating
climate change that is already magnifying and amplifying the
threat to every nurturing part of our ocean world.

I recently attended a conference sponsored by the Climate
Change Institute at the University of Maine, a program that has
collected and interpreted climate data, extrapolated from ice
cores taken in the Artic, Antarctic, and Himalayas, and that has
developed several tools for visualizing the demonstrable change
in our natural environment over a 10,000-year period, and more.
The data, along with so much other climate science, document
the changing temperatures over time and the incidence of
man-made chemicals and deposits that have accelerated over the
past century at a critically increasing rate that is irrefutable and
deeply disturbing.

The conference was attended by state agency managers,
municipal officials, city planners, and interested individuals; its
purpose was to give us the opportunity to play "what if "—what
if we accept what the data tells us, what if we stipulate a certain
degree of increasing temperature, what if we accept so many feet
of sea level rise, what if we accede to the inevitability of extreme
weather events—what would be the specific consequences on
the life of our coast, inland, and further into the wild, unsettled
northern portion of Maine?

In that workshop, we accepted the actuality of climate

change, and then examined what would be the impact on our specific communities—alongshore, inland, and in the far north of our state, each with very distinct conditions to be affected differently by such risks. It was revealing and disturbing for certain, but it was also uplifting as we worked as groups of managers and residents from these areas to see what we might do, might do first, might do differently, and might invent to sustain our livelihood and place for the future.

We were not overwhelmed or discouraged, as much as we began to understand the comprehensive impact of what we might face, to analyze its complexity, and to agree on what steps might be taken locally, perhaps with resources already available to us, to meet the challenge. Indeed, there was a palpable communal realization in the room that a group of strangers, with varied qualifications and interests, could come together to solve the problem—once we agreed among ourselves that it exists.

In those few hours, we transformed plausible scenarios into possible plans of action. In many cases, we understood that certain circumstances already existed, that the risks were already evident, and that the need for response, regardless of the climate change debate, was a necessary step no matter what.

What would happen to fishing? To tourism? To jobs and taxes? To community health? And if we could identify those outcomes, what could we do about them—near-term, mid-term, and long-term—to mitigate the most immediate real consequence and to define the necessary change required to protect our livelihoods, our families, and these places where we live?

What did we do? We accepted the challenge, and we worked together to envision a way forward—indeed, we began an exercise to plan for the future. We rated the threat of certain outcomes; we defined a range of responses; we set priorities for investment of time and resources; and we began to understand that, beyond denial, within the contest of climate reality, there were things to be done, that could be done to visualize, design, price, and implement the community actions required to meet the challenge. We could see how something just might happen, just might work, and how that might accrue to hopeful community benefit.

It is simplistic and defeatist to deny the threat of climate change. Yes, it is complicated both to understand and to accept, and the easiest answer is to avoid the problem by denying its existence, or postpone its consideration, or leave it for the next generation. Excuses abound: too hard to do, too expensive, too disruptive to the status quo, too politically uncomfortable.

The externalities of climate change are real and dangerous. The hard question is: are we too cowardly and too irresponsible to confront them?

Pascal and Climate Risk Management

Considering the great climate change debate—whether it exists or does not exist as a major threat to our future—I am reminded of philosopher and inventor, Blaise Pascal's famous "wager" over the existence of God. If you believe in God, you can find solace in peace and salvation. If you do not believe in God, why not hedge your bet?

Climate change suggests a similar dilemma. If you don't believe it is real and dire, and it proves to be nothing, then doing nothing leaves you home free. But what if you are wrong? What if you do nothing, and thereafter succumb, unprepared, to the devastating consequences that might follow? Why would you not here too hedge your bet and at least consider, maybe even define and prepare for the possibility of the predictable risks?

Here is a list of climate change risks: increased average surface temperatures, altered air and ocean currents, extreme weather events, increased precipitation, heat waves and cold snaps, melting sea ice, rising sea level, positive feedbacks such as reduced albedo (reflection of solar heat from white frozen surfaces) or melting permafrost, methane release, abrupt changes in earth systems, ocean acidification, shifting growing seasons and ranges, species movement (extirpation, extinction), shifting disease vectors, algal blooms, heat-related waterborne pathogens, invasive species, and more.

Here is a list of climate change impacts: flooding, drought, fires, agricultural failure, food shortages, water shortages, infrastructural damage, water and well pollution, species loss, economic loss, and more.

Here is a list of vulnerabilities: environmental degradation, critical pollution, lack of inclusion in adaptation and planning, lack of technical and scientific expertise, lack of awareness, concern, and education, alienation from political power, regional geographical decline in island, coastal, and inland communities, poor governance structures, lack of leadership, lack of resources to meet the high cost of assessment, planning, mitigation, or adaptation, community disruption, social and psychological decline.

So what about that bet? None of this will matter to you if you do not accept the possibility of any of these risks. But, again, what if you are wrong? Are you willing to ignore even the possibility of these circumstances and trends, and leave us all to fend for ourselves and defer the consequence of neglect to our children?

I have always argued that beyond mitigation and adaptation the real solution to climate change is invention, the cooperative application of knowledge and experience not just to maintain or defend the status quo, but rather to imagine and create new solutions to the problems to be faced. I felt that power of invention in that place and took home renewed optimism that, as always, smart and well-intentioned people can come together to build a sustainable future. I wonder what Pascal would say?

Mottainai

The Japanese have long engaged me in various concepts that somehow resonate and shape my thoughts about how to live in this world. For example, *In Praise of Shadows*, a telling essay on Japanese aesthetics by Junichiro Tanizaki,[137] awarded the 1958 Nobel Prize for Literature, describes the appreciation of that ephemeral space where light meets dark, where bright contradictions give way to an inarticulate aura that is both complicated and simple, a dusky reconciliation of forces or ideas, a place where illusive harmony may be found if you are open to looking for it. This is the essence of the observation that a Japanese, looking into a bowl of rice, can see the shadow of each individual grain.

Wabi-sabi is another such concept: the value of a patina of use found in Nature, in abandoned places, and in artistic traditions, raised to an aesthetic transcendence that resonates and inspires appreciation for the elegance of utility and its meaning. These insights have purpose for defense against the raucous, unrelenting chaos of modern life. The antidote is found where? In Zen meditation, in adherence to tradition in the face of accelerating change, or the search for an alternative set of values to inform and found a different future.

The ocean represents such a healing space. It is of course a constant presentation of motion and light, a theater of sight and sound and feeling that draws us to and into it for recreation in every sense of that word and activity. Why do we continue to migrate to the coast the world over, which somehow soothes and lifts our spirits even if we don't know why?

There is another Japanese term that pertains: *Mottainai*, derived from a Buddhist term that refers to the essence of things. In a catalogue essay, *The Fabric of Life*,[138] for an exhibition of traditional Japanese textiles at the Portland Japanese Garden in Oregon, USA, Curator Diane Durston writes:

> *Applied to everything in the physical universe, the word suggests that objects do not exist in isolation but are intrinsically linked to one another. "Nai" 無い is a negation, so 'mottainai' is an expression of sadness for the disrespect that is shown when any living or non-living entity is wasted. "Mottainai!" parents say, admonishing their children not to waste a grain of rice or a scrap of paper. In a land where natural resources have always been scarce, people have long understood the importance of respecting the value of all things and of wasting nothing. It was the only way to survive in less affluent times.*

Wangari Maathai, the founder of the Greenbelt Movement in Africa, democracy advocate and political activist, and winner of the 2004 Nobel Peace Prize, responded to the "mottainai" concept during a visit to Japan and used it as focus for her call for an international campaign to reduce waste and recycle what we can that has continued after her death in 2011. To learn more about and to support this effort, visit www.greenbeltmovement.org.

There is yet another Japanese phrase: *Sato-umi*, defined on GreenBeltMovement.org as follows:

> *In Japanese, "s" means the area where people live, and "umi" means the sea. Sato-umi is an important sea-area that has been*

supporting culture and cultural exchanges through such things as fisheries and the distribution of products. It is an area that includes both Nature and human beings, as well as an area in which both high biological productivity and biodiversity are expected. Healthy Sato-umi provides numerous blessings: when the natural circulation function is appropriately maintained, when integrated and comprehensive management of the land and coastal area is performed, and when the rich and diversified ecosystem and natural environment are conserved. This "preferable coastal area environment" must be maintained with the cooperation of more people in order to accede this precious environment to future generations.

So all this conceptual language may translate to describe a new strategy for our relationship with the ocean: a place that reflects the outcome of our use, that respects and sustains the value of Nature, and that integrates and reconciles human needs and natural resources for the future of all mankind.

Mottainai!

AN OCEAN ETHOS

Another First Day on the Water

I am writing this in my home, in Maine, in the northeastern corner of the United States, on the shore of Penobscot Bay. It is a vast inward curve of the Atlantic with many wonderful, mostly unsettled islands that provide a nurturing scape for lobster and scallops, for incubating ground and shell fish, for coastal settlements and marine trades, and for voyagers in small boats who find shelter in the lee of these very beautiful granite, forested remnants of glacial movement and maritime weather.

Yesterday my wife and I had another first day on the water, this year's first glorious afternoon of sunshine, perfect wind, modest wave, and the sense of prospect and anticipation that character-izes the outset of many things. A first sip of beer. A first taste of a favorite dish. A first glimpse across a crowded room of someone to be loved. Call me romantic, but aren't those firsts always worth remembering in that they set the standard for our experience, as a set of beliefs and consequential behaviors that defines the things we value, determines what we want to conserve and sustain, and inspires what we revere as part of our life's core and meaning?

An ethos.

We are privileged to have this opportunity. Many do not. Many, however, do find another way to derive these same rewards from the ocean: the crowded beaches of the world's coastal cities, children playing in the waves of impoverished waterside villages, pilgrims submersing themselves in the healing religious waters of sacred rivers. It always amazes me how ingenious and pervasive are the ways that individuals find their access to ponds and lakes, streams and rivers, coastal wetlands and barrier islands, and the open ocean as a source for recreation and renewal, for the simple, quiet rewards of the best of human encounter with and community of Nature.

Water heals us in so many ways. It offers us a music of calm, movement, continuity, and connection, the sound of a system that works as natural solace and support against the challenges of modern life—the discontinuity and discord of life without water. We have spoken often here of water as a commodity that each of us, rich or poor, north or south, east or west, of whatever origin, needs in the same amount every day to survive. Water is so much more valuable than gold, oil, and financial instruments, and yet we ignore this essential value, pollute it, waste it, and otherwise throw it away in an exercise that is so profoundly ignorant of its contribution to our health, our true wealth, and our posterity.

That said, I return to what I believe is the essential premise for the design of our future. If we can envision the ocean as beginning at the mountaintop and ending on the abyssal plain, if we can relate to water as an organizing principle for how we live in and on the land, then we can understand that the protection of its integrity, free flowing and pure, relates directly to the most important requirements for successful living. We can understand the ocean as a system of literal and social unification. If we apply that premise, then we affirm the efficiency of the natural system to determine different patterns of settlement, preserve clean water for human consumption and agriculture, generate alternative energy, protect us from extreme weather and sea level rise, provide spawning and nursery ground for marine species, and offer the solace and peace that being by water seems universally to inspire.

Technology can advance this new perspective. We have the ability to invent new food, transportation, and energy systems, new planning principles, new cities and settlements, new financial valuations, new social relationships, and new individual behaviors that conform to, assert, and demonstrate the value of a new water-directed way of living. I call this idea: the new hydraulic society.

Where Does Water Come From?

Where does water come from? It seems such a simple question, and the answer is known from our earliest science lessons when we are introduced to the water cycle and the global circulation system that is so essential to our well-being now and forevermore. Water evaporates from the ocean reservoir, captured in clouds and fog and rain, from which it descends to become groundwater, seeping into the underground aquifer, or surface water distributed by lakes and streams. Some of the water is captured in ice as glaciers and high mountain peaks; some is retained deep in the earth, some perhaps prehistoric in its deposit, but there for now beyond our eager, sometimes desperate, digging and drilling.

All of it is finite in volume.

We know this cycle, and if we think about it at all, it becomes easy to understand the idea that the ocean where 97 percent of that volume is contained is the alpha and omega, the mouth and tail from this circle of sustenance. It becomes easy to see the "edge" of the ocean not at the boardwalk and beach, but rather at the distant snow-capped range where begins the long, convoluted flow of water down and across the land until it reaches its ocean origin...and the cycle begins again.

Essential to the sustainable ocean, then, is the protection and conservation of this fluid passage, the global hydraulics that can be compared to the circulation of blood through our bodies, themselves made substantially of water. Each of us is an ocean, with a comparable circulation, and a reliance on a healthy environment to sustain it. Extend the metaphor: if we treat those bodies with indifference, pollute them with excess and poisons, then we can expect them to succumb to obesity, disease, and collapse. If you think of yourself as the ocean, your family as the ocean, your community as the ocean, your nation as an ocean, then perhaps you will take the necessary steps to sustain the health of each of these many seas.

So, too, with the earth, and we return again to the geography of our living; the ocean, as I choose to define it, as a vast global system of interacting, infused water that extends from mountaintop to abyssal plain and connects us all—physically, financially, politically, socially, and spiritually.

This point lies at the core of any strategy for change. It establishes the context for every decision that follows—the choice to conserve hillsides and watersheds, lakes, ponds, and rivers; the planning for different settlement and systems, for new construction and reconstruction; the promulgation of new standards for economic development; the recognition of natural capital and new economic models as significant elements in the pricing of goods and services and the calculation of our gross national product; the re-engineering of the coastal zone; and the definition of new policies to maintain the quality of our air and water, to manage responsibly our ocean resources, and to govern the open ocean under an egalitarian and equitable set of international treaties and agreements that benefit us all.

Without our understanding of this absolute, this measurable, undeniable fact of life, all our efforts may be for naught, all our strategies may be half-baked, all of our results inadequate. We cannot build a new society, hydraulic or otherwise, if we build it on a weak and corrupted foundation. We cannot change behaviors if we do not accept and assert new core values. This clear and present understanding of the wisdom of Nature and the knowledge revealed can guide and protect us in our first steps toward sustainable practice and global renewal.

Where does water come from? That's one question, and we know the answer, but here's another, more difficult one: what will we do, who will we be, when that water has come...and gone?

Aqua

"I want to change the way you see the world." So writes Lincoln Paine in the opening line of his recently published *Sea and Civilization*.[139] To begin such a history with such a phrase suggests that the author's imagined readership looks at the world in a substantively different way, one diametrically opposed to a maritime perspective on the history of man on Earth. And therein lies a problem.

In truth, we have long seen the ocean as "a place apart," a dynamic scape of Nature beyond the edge, a distant horizon away and dislocated from the challenge of human survival on land. And yet, from the first day that the first intrepid explorer left shore in a dugout canoe or skin boat, reed or bamboo raft, the sea became a powerful part of world history, as source of food, avenue of trade, place of exchange, field of war, and locus of knowledge. East or west, this history matters, indeed amplifies its meaning, through the realization that the sea is equal to land as a primary stage for the drama of human enterprise, sustenance, and self-realization.

Today, our historical endeavors have exhausted the land. As we begin the 21st century, we discover that Terra has been polluted almost beyond redemption by burgeoning population and a consequent excess of consumption-driven exploitation of natural resources—coasts drained and filled; rivers dammed; lakes drained, ores, metals, and fossil fuels extracted; forests cut; and fields poisoned by fertilizers and pesticides in the name of maximized agricultural production. To put a blunt point to it, in the name of civilization, we have consciously and collectively destroyed the unique nurturing system on which that civilization depends.

But as we can now observe from space, *Terra* is more accurately *Aqua*, a planet more than 70 percent water, the penultimate source of our health and well-being then, now, and in the future. Indeed, if the land can no longer adequately provide, then we have no choice but to look beyond the edge, beyond the near horizon, to a vast ocean and natural system that is simultaneously now an integrated financial, political, social, and cultural system that is at once comprehensive, complicated, connected, and communal. If we understand that our future is based incontrovertibly on adequate and sustainable availability of fresh water, food, energy, health, security, and cultural resources, then we must also recognize that there is no place else to go for help but the ocean.

Tragically, as I have argued, we are showing dangerous signs of a continuing indifference to, even ignorance of this premise in our behaviors toward the sea. We live in megacities concentrated along our waterways and shores; we dump our waste and toxic by-products there; we harvest marine species indiscriminately and without limit to the point of their extinction; we corrupt the air to deposit acid in the sea to an extent that the pH of the water column is subtly modified, reproductive cycles are interrupted, and the seemingly infinite biodiversity of the ocean is pushed to the verge of systemic collapse. Ocean advocates sound the alarm, focusing primarily on threatened species and habitat, using the language of hope, but these best efforts are not working to urgently, easily engender a growing hopelessness and despair, and overwhelm our capacity to stop, protect, and sustain. We must move beyond hope toward real and lasting change, to transform these senseless, short-term behaviors, and to invent and create a newly imagined future.

We must build that future on a new and revolutionary system of values.

In *A Sand County Almanac*, Aldo Leopold, scientist, conservationist, and natural philosopher, wrote of the "land ethic," an ethical sequence defined as "a limit on freedom of action in the struggle for existence."[140] The first ethics were derived to deal with the complexity of population density, new tools, resultant anti-social uses, and the underlying conflict between the individual and society. "There is yet no ethic dealing with man's relation to land and the animals and plants that grow on it. Land...is still property. The land-relation is still strictly economic, entailing privileges, but not obligations."[141]

"All ethics so far evolved rest upon a single premise," Leopold writes, "that the individual is a member of a community of interdependent parts... The land ethic simply enlarges the boundaries of the community to include soils, waters, plants, and animals, or collectively, the land..."[142]

And, indeed, the ocean.

By placing us *within nature*, as opposed to our being its conqueror, Leopold changed both our social and moral relationship with the world around us and posited for us an ecological conscience, "a conviction of individual responsibility for the health of the land. Health is the capacity...for self-renewal. Conservation is our effort to understand and preserve this capacity."

When environmental advocates and policy-makers speak today of "sustainability," they are basically arguing for systems and behaviors that maintain and extend the value of the natural world for all parties who live within—plants, animals, and people—for all time. Our contemporary consumption-driven systems and behaviors are antithetical, and as the resources are finitely consumed, they limit our capacity for self-renewal, force decline, and deny a viable future. It seems illogical and suicidal, but that's what we are doing to ourselves.

The ocean can be no longer a place apart. It is essential as the last place where we can turn to survive. It is that dramatic, that critical, that urgent. What is most disturbing is the conscious indifference that characterizes our global leadership. No one seems capable of standing up for the future, willing to exercise conscience and lead us way from incapacity to viability.

Value changes are the most ephemeral, most important aspects of this opportunity. We live in a society that has been defined by historical events and cultural traditions that are hard to shift, an evolution of behaviors based on religious assumptions, economic theories, and sometimes tumultuous governance. Historically, the world has wanted to be organized around a collective global desire for political order, growth as a path to well-being, and capital defined first by the exploitation of natural resources and their transformation through manufacture; and second, more recently, by scientific innovation and technology. We debate the dichotomies—guns versus butter, free market versus managed economy, consumption versus conservation—and we conduct the arguments to a point now when we suffer from ideological adamancy, class differentiation, and political paralysis. It seems a critical moment. We can continue to suffer failed consensus and social stasis; we can experience continuing decline to collapse, chaos, even revolution; or we can regain our capacity for civilization by facing our problems, accepting the alternatives, and moving forward and away from default and defeat.

Sustainability is a new strategic and moral value that is advanced to this end. It accepts the finite capacity of Nature to support a burgeoning world population. It proposes new behaviors predicated on this knowledge, that we will only exploit resources to an extent that allows for their renewal and sustainability over time. We will incentivize and promote this new value system through financial tools, price structures, legislative action, regulatory enforcement, and cooperative action. We will stop taking it all, acting unilaterally and independently for unlimited profit, and will reorganize ourselves to maintain and nurture the natural systems that have sustained us, and can continue to sustain us, even as we grow in number, over time, if we will make it so.

But what more can we do to convince us at every level that sustainability is an essential core value for our future? Clearly the struggle is necessary to counter those who will not consider or accept even the idea, much less the concomitant action, required to make sustainability succeed. What else is required to convince the body politic that such destructive indifference, by individuals, corporations, and governments, is no longer acceptable?

Reciprocity

As a fresh context, then, consider the concept of *reciprocity*. Reciprocity is a state of mutual exchange, the categorization of an action by its motivation and consequence in relationship to another. Indigenous peoples have practiced reciprocity as cultural behavior through direct barter and giving of gifts. The cultural anthropologist, Claude Lévi-Strauss,[143] identified levels of such exchange, through language, kinship, and economics, a process that created bonds of social obligation present and future, an idea familiar through the popular notion of the "favor bank," a value on deposit that must be paid back in kind as a societal norm.

What if we accept the power of reciprocity as an additional standard of behavior at all levels, in all areas of exchange, with Nature? What if we acknowledge that the land and the sea provide us value, not for the taking and exhausting as an entitlement, but as the giving of a gift, the making of a loan, with a consequent obligation that we pay back that value through complementary behavior, equitable patterns of consumption, and forms of exchange that sustain the capacity of Nature through accepted future obligation? What if we accept such a reciprocal relationship and system of connection with Nature as our active contribution— *our obligation*—to ourselves, our children, and the public good?

Let me offer three illustrative statements, with examples of what I mean.

First: *By not taking, we are giving back.* If we choose to forgo or reduce our consumption of fossil fuels or plastic bags or tuna, we are leaving that value for others, a collective choice that taken to scale will extend or conserve that resource at a sustainable level.

Second: *By paying a fair price for what we need and use, we are giving back.* If we pay for our consumption at a level of true cost, we establish a new valuation system commensurate with changing realities. Some examples: withdrawal of subsidies for fossil fuels, reinvestment of such underwriting in clean technology; pricing water as the most valuable commodity on Earth; inclusion of insurance payment for disaster response and reparation from environmental destruction as part of regulatory requirement and permit fees; approval of government investment projects based on a neutral or positive comparison of public benefit versus private profit; increase in taxes and royalties to establish financial disincentives for polluting industries; allocation of penalties to support of non-polluting alternatives; and the definition of many other financial calculations and market applications based on the value added by environmental protection and sustainability outcomes.

Third: *By acting and applying these values, we are giving back.* We can also contribute by modifying personal, family, and community behaviors in every way possible to affirm these values through action. We can become a "sustainability" citizen.

We can set our own example. Sign petitions. Vote. Demonstrate when necessary. Communicate our commitment at every level, and hold others accountable in our daily purchases, our employment, our investments, civic organizations of which we are members, schools that we attend or have attended, churches that we belong to, recreational activities that we enjoy, and politicians that we support. We can communicate, advocate by example, and amplify our voices by joining other exemplars into a movement of giving back. By so doing, we counter the simplistic political recalcitrance that sustains the status quo, the impracticality of sustaining our way of life at present levels of consumption, the radical inflexibility and fearfulness that have brought governance to a standstill. What I am describing here is an affirmation of the democratic process and expression of popular will based not on narrow ideology but on our mutual understanding of the consequences for us all if we fail to act.

Reciprocity makes everyone a winner, everyone a builder, everyone a giver. It is a simple framework that allows us to understand another way of being, how to support, individually and collectively, a shift from our present way that is making us all losers, all destroyers, and all takers until we have nothing left. Is that really what we want for the land, for the ocean, for our children and their future?

Reciprocity. It seems so clear. Think what the land gives us. Think what the ocean gives us. Are we not obligated to respond? Let's start giving back. Let's adopt an ocean ethos as the transformative stimulus for changing the way we see the world.

HYDRAULIC SOCIETY

Cycles and Circles

One of the first concepts we learn in natural science is the water cycle: Earth's respiration and exchange of water evaporating from the ocean, massing into weather patterns that move around the globe, deluging the land to run down from the mountaintop across the foothills into the streams and rivers and watersheds until it returns to the sea again. That cycle of water—its continuity, clarity, and utility—is essential to our health, as water to drink, cleanse, irrigate, and sustain us as the only thing we all need in equal amounts to survive. We return to water again and again because of the ocean as penultimate source of supply, engine for global distribution, guarantor of purity, and sustainer of its nurturing parts, the plants and animals, including ourselves, who cannot live without it.

Indeed, there are cycles and circles in the ocean that occur and recur as currents and conveyors of heat and nutrients. Within this constant turning are consequent migrations that scientists continue to discover and measure that have implication for associated human interactions—fish populations, habitat, and localized meteorological conditions that correspond to food supply, patterns of work, location of communities, and the social requirements of living.

The water column itself can be visualized as a comparable circular exchange: the fall and rise of food, temperature, pH, and the presence of light that determines micro and macro conditions along the way in which some life forms flourish, others do not, until we reach the ocean floor through which passes the generating power of the Earth's volcanic core.

And then there are the winds, the circles of air, determined by temperature or, more recently, the sudden increase in emissions resulting from the energy of modern life, realized through undisciplined extraction, burning, and consumption of irreplaceable fuel stored in the earth but now released into the atmosphere in critical amounts, particles of pollution and poison that not only affect the weather, but also the life cycle of species downwind around the world.

Indeed, the Earth is parsed by circles of longitude and latitude that determine the measure of where we are in space, that guided the first sailors into unknown waters, explorers to unknown places and cultures, and merchants to unknown resources and riches. The seaman's log noted the position of the ship relative to the stars, the silhouette of the land, and the consistency of winds and currents, observations at the beginning of a system of trade, migration, finance, and societal integration that today we call globalization.

History documents such cycles in periods of awakening and discovery, competition, war, and the rise and fall of nation states, the exchange of philosophies and religions, and the intermingling of ideas and bloodlines that document the twists and turns of acculturation and civilization. Meaning is hidden in all of this, and wisdom, it would seem, might be still derived from such knowledge and experience.

Myths often turn around circular metaphors and cyclical behaviors of gods and mortals. They tell us of things past as an instructional manual for things to come. Change can evolve, slowly over time, or it can happen suddenly, without warning, at some moment when all the gravity of circumstance forces history to turn unexpectedly, sometimes explosively.

If we are so smart, why is it that we seem incapable of planning such a turn? We can engineer things, build instruments, scaled large and small, that extend the limits of our imagination, but we cannot seem to will our way out of our comfort zone, our complacency, when faced with ever-increasing, irrefutable evidence that the wheel is turning down and away from us before our very eyes.

The consumption-based society that we have built over the last centuries is at risk of collapse, the fall of its architecture and institutions into the sea. Recently, archaeologists found submerged buildings and statuary that spoke of a once great place and time. The underwater vestiges were mysterious—cold, devoid of light, and imprecise—as if flooded by regret and remorse and guilt for failing to meet the one great choice required to sustain itself in time. Continuity ended. There was no ensuing generation. The ocean took it all, and one wonders if that cycle had to be and why that circle was broken.

Security

At a recent academic meeting in Boston, Steve Murawski, an ocean scientist from the University of South Florida, quoted an interesting definition of security as "the protection of the flow of benefit."[144] The word is pervasive in our current usage: food security, property security, personal security, financial security, and national security. How often do we hear these phrases used to justify some ideological opinion, legislative option, social or legal right, financial regulation, or geopolitical act? Security has become a catchall word imbued with an implication of danger or threat to our benefit that must be prevented at all costs. It is used frequently by government to convince us that a certain behavior is best for the common good, even if it disrupts individual benefits, freedoms, and ways of life. Indeed, now one even hears the phrase "climate security," implying the need for protection against the ravages of Nature, typically extreme weather, but now also the consequences of changed air quality, acidification, loss of future food and health resources, even the economic, political, and social chaos that might occur following the physical onslaught of such weather. How do we protect what is near and dear, what is of the highest benefit to us—individual and community alike?

Environmentalists these days are focused on trying to understand and communicate the value of what they call "ecosystem services," natural processes that are essential to the success of many aspects of our lives and historically dismissed or undervalued in our engineered, manufactured, consumption-based world. The phrase is accurate—the global system of natural phenomena does serve us in myriad ways. Murawski described ecosystem services as acts: of provisioning (food, energy, employment, poverty), regulating (weather, sequestration, the water cycle), supporting (the global economy, environmental justice, governance), and acculturating (the adaptations and outcomes for civil society).[145] If you look at these human involvements, you will see that Nature is central and invaluable to them all. And if you look even more closely, you will see that the ocean is an inclusive and essential system that combines and connects us all through ties that bind.

Thus, it can be argued that the ocean as a pre-eminent ecosystem serves the world to such an important degree that it cuts across and includes all securities, that it represents an incalculable, multi-dimensional value not to be squandered or lost, and that the continuity of its benefit is an essential national geopolitical imperative.

But we don't think about things this way. We don't stand back to consider what serves us best beyond an immediate outcome. We don't think to preserve irreplaceable or non-renewable things if we can use them right now. We don't see the ocean, or all of Nature, as a phenomenon that sustains us and therefore must be sustained. We prefer to cut and mine, slash and burn, consume and discard, pollute and poison. Today, almost any suggestion counter to these behaviors is shouted down, almost any regulation or policy intended to protect or sustain is subverted, as an intrusion on what? Our rights, our well-being, our survival? It seems illogical not to see that our security is totally, irrefutably linked to natural security and that all this other stuff does not protect the flow of benefits. Ironically, our actions suggest we prefer to be insecure.

Let me ask you to think about two facts. One: the entire world population, today, 7 billion strong, now exists on 1.2 percent of the total finite amount of water on the globe.[146] In 2050, when the world population is predicted to grow to 9 billion, we will have not one drop more to meet that inevitable, insatiable, increased demand. Two: today we determine national policy, indeed fight wars wherein thousands are killed, for the acquisition and protection of the supply of fossil fuels that drives our cars, factories, and economies, fuels that will also inevitably be exhausted at some near term point in time. Add to this the critical impact of climate—drought, flood, deforestation, and erosion—and the situation will continue to worsen and destabilize politics and communities worldwide.

Where will we turn to solve these enormous problems? We will build a new hydraulic society. We will inevitably rely on the ocean for desalinated water, for a supply of continuous, dynamic energy through multiple renewable technologies, for protein beyond that generated by land, for the pharmacopoeia of medicines that will heal our diseases, and for the forms of governance that will allow us to exist successfully in a world where the needs of the global community must overcome the narrow and destructive causes of conflict. The ocean will provide us true security—provisioning, regulating, supporting, acculturating, protecting and sustaining us in its beneficial flow.

The 21st Century Working Waterfront

Civilization was built by the sea. An examination of world history argues that the globe was parsed by ocean exploration and exchange. Ships were the tools of discovery, settlement, conflict, and acculturation, and every nation or city-state in every period of time had its opening to the sea as its opening to the world.

The 20th-century version of the seaport reveals an accumulation of such functions that at the time were best placed on the waterfront, then available without limit or easily expanded by filled wetlands and new hard edges that created viable, valuable land for necessary purposes. The most obvious demand was for the workings of the port, space for landing and storing cargoes for intermediary time and place for further distribution as import or export value. Trade was the prime mover of nation building, and the ports of New York, London, Hamburg, and Hong Kong were among the most active in the 19th century. Those forces drove the locus of banks and exchanges, corporate headquarters and manufacturing centers, insurance companies, and all the associated vocations and endeavors required to sustain commercial enterprise at great scale.

As these cities grew, however, new demands emerged with equally impactful consequences for waterfronts. There were established the new functions of urbanism—water and sewage

treatment plants, power generators, oil tanks and grain storage
silos, and thereafter the necessary transportation infrastructure—
trains and highways, tunnels and bridges, and other built things
that condemned more marsh to fill, more edge to expand into
rivers and harbors, to feed an exploding appetite for enterprise
and its rewards. The 20th-century rise of the World Trade Center
in New York, indeed the historical making of most of lower
Manhattan, is a function of this process. Streams and ponds
disappeared, farms gave way to tenements, then towers, built and
rebuilt on land that once was water as both symbol and reality of
unimagined economic expanse.

The consequences of this cultural and physical record is
known, glorified or regretted, depending on your perspective.
But it is fair to say that this industrial function has left its mark on
waterfronts and that urban planners and city-dwellers have been
grappling ever since with the consequences and their alternatives.

What might the 21st-century waterfront look like? It will,
of course, reveal the requirements of changed values and new
technologies. Some waterfronts will still require vast areas for
the import/export of vehicles and large objects, containers, fuels,
and chemicals to and from the world. Some will retain that
function at a lesser scale, serving more coastwise delivery than
international trade. The functions requiring access to significant
volumes of water for treatment or cooling—desalinization plants
or nuclear generators for example—will stay, albeit in different,
well-fortified structures, presumably safer, more productive,
efficient, and economical. Some functions like waste disposal
or sewage treatment might be differently enabled though
improved technology, located elsewhere, inland and accessed
better by train or pipeline. Many things and the residue of many
processes previously disposed of in the ocean might find a

different place for processing and recycling. Warehouses may be converted to housing, manufacturing plants may be reclaimed or reprogrammed to different needs and systems. Edges may be reclaimed for recreational uses. In fact, much of this is already evident in many cities, New York among them, where Manhattan is soon to be ringed entirely by open space, walking and cycling trails, and Brooklyn has a new waterfront park that replaces dilapidated piers and warehouses with wonderful new public access to the harbor, and that, presciently designed, escaped serious inundation and destruction by Superstorm Sandy.

But what else should we be thinking for the waterfront? What will benefit the future welfare and health of urban populations? Desalination and geothermal energy options will certainly figure in our emerging need for fresh water and power. They demand enormous water access from somewhere, either outside the immediate city and linked to the distribution systems or inside the city in scale heretofore impossible by the limits of the technology in hand.

Will we grow our food using urban aquaculture? Will we expand our housing through floating structures accessible to the cultural amenities already extant in the city? Will we augment our underground transportation system, already taxed and vulnerable to sea level rise, with waterborne local transit, commuter lines, and delivery routes? Will we make a concerted effort to remove all waterfront functions not requiring water access to inland places serving regional requirements? Will we design our cities around this premise made real and practical? Will we make the waterfront work for us anew as a necessary and fulfilling reality in the future?

Hydraulic New York

I have used the phrase hydraulic society as a proposed new organizing concept and strategy for ocean conservation and related social behavior, particularly in the population centers, where the growing world population is now concentrated with enormous impact on climate, watersheds, coastal areas, and the deep ocean.

The concept of water harvesting and management is certainly not new to history. In Fatehpur Sikri, for example, a 16th-century city in Uttar Pradesh, India, home then to a population of 200,000, the design for collection, distribution, multiple use, and recycling of water collected from the adjacent landscape and aquifer was built directly into the architecture to supply water for storage, irrigation, cooking, hygiene, gardens, fountains, and simple cooling systems.[147] Today, this technology long abandoned, the town population is just 33,000 and water supply is crude and inadequate to the present frequently drought-stricken needs.[148]

How then can we envision such a system for a city of 10 million or more? We need only to look to New York City, in the United States, for a real and compelling example. The city utilizes 4 million cubic meters, or 1 billion gallons, of fresh water per day, collected and supplied from millions of surrounding acres in protected watershed areas conserved as a natural filtration system. The land was acquired at a cost of $1.5 billion, thereby relieving the city from the obligation to construct filtration plants at a cost of $10 billion or more—a savings of $8.5 billion. Along with this was the added value of the highest water quality *and* the protection of substantial forestland to promote air quality, sustain plant and animal habitat, provide recreational opportunities, and prohibit additional development and sprawl in the intense urban agglomeration that is New York.[149]

The approach has been in place for almost two decades, but requires constant maintenance, improvement, expansion, and new technologies to deal with other associated problems such as leaking infrastructure, combined sewage and storm-water runoff beyond the capacity of treatment plants, escalating energy costs for pumping and operations, and pollutants, generated by manufacturing processes, automobile exhaust and residues, even high concentration of chemical and salt used to melt the winter snows. Thus, New York has continued to invest in additional filtration facilities (one underground with a golf driving range to be built on top), repairs to regional aqueducts, a third major supply tunnel, new and expanded sewage treatment plants, a new ultra-violet disinfectant system for micro-biological contaminants, and major new combined sewer overflow containment basins to hold almost 100 million gallons of untreated water until it can be run through the system after the peak subsides.[150]

But the New York plan has other serious elements:

- To reduce consumption through conservation;

- To assess and improve the hydraulic capacity of tide gates, obstructed pipes, clogged collection sewers, and storage areas;

- To capture the first inch of rainfall from 10 percent of the city's impervious surfaces through street trees, swales, and sidewalks rebuilt and retrofitted, porous pavement for roadways and parking lots, constructed wetlands in parks, captured runoff from schools, multifamily residential housing, new and retrofitted factories, vacant lots, and rooftop collectors—even rain barrels to be provided to low-density single-family houses.

All of this is to be coordinated through a multi-agency task force to coordinate planning, mitigate bureaucratic overlap and contradiction, reduce costs of duplication, competitive management, and purchasing, and otherwise integrate government agencies with environmental advocates, civic and community organizations.[151]

This approach, entitled *The Green Infrastructure Plan* and proposed as official policy, does represent a huge public investment—over $1.5 billion over the next 20 years—but it has been developed in cost-benefit comparison with other, more conventional graywater approaches and is predicted to maximize treatment per dollar invested, reduce operating cost of treatment per gallon, increase capacity through conservation and new forms of collections, extend treatment to volume heretofore untreated, and integrate conservation values, economic efficiency, and public/private collaboration into a new, vastly improved system of water treatment and example of a *new hydraulic society*.

How does this affect you and me? Remember, every drop of this water, before, after, and forevermore, ends up in New York Harbor, the Atlantic, and the world ocean where it, and water quality improved by other megacities following New York's lead, will benefit us all directly and by example.

Circling the World

In 2009 I visited India to work with the Indian Maritime Foundation toward the development of a multidisciplinary ocean curriculum for introduction into India public schools. The physical journey was exhausting; 14 hours by plane through myriad time zones, into an otherworldly physical, temporal, and cultural place. The outcome of that visit, however, requires frequent communications, email messages, exchange of large data bundles, tele-meetings, and eventually a distance learning connection that will link W2O resources and lecturers to Indian classrooms and teacher training programs in ocean and environmental science.

The communication seems so simple, until I think about it again and question exactly how does that connection work so efficiently, mostly problem free, at little cost to me and my colleagues thousands of miles away. While I am not certain how my message travels, it is likely that it moves at astonishing speed along the global network owned wholly or in consortium partnership by Tata Communications, one of the world's largest telecommunications companies, headquartered in Mumbai, which has recently completed the first global cable system between North and South America, Europe, India, Africa, the Gulf, China, and Asia, in effect, has *circled the world*.[152]

Tata Communications' Global Network comprises major ownership in 125,000 miles of terrestrial network fiber and over 300,000 miles of subsea cable, with a Trans-Atlantic and Trans-Pacific data transfer capacity of one terabit per second, all underwater, invisible, on the ocean floor. The complete system provides service to the 195 independent nations recognized by the United Nations, and indeed to other territories and disputed regions, a truly worldwide connection.

The Tata Group is not well known in the United States where we take great nationalistic pride in corporate conglomerates and successes. This is not meant to be an advertisement for Tata, but in this time of anti-corporate fervor, it might be good to know something about its structure, reach, profits, and values—its measures of worth that are impressive, dynamic, and very unusual.

The Tata Group strives to be the poster company for globalization. It comprises over 100 operating companies in seven business sectors: communications and information technology, engineering, materials, services, energy, consumer products, and chemicals. The group has operations in more than 80 countries across six continents. The total revenue of Tata companies, taken together, was $83.3 billion in 2010–11, with 58 percent of this coming from business outside India. Tata companies employ over 425,000 people worldwide. The major Tata companies are Tata Steel, Tata Motors, Tata Consultancy Services, Tata Power, Tata Chemicals, Tata Global Beverages, Tata Teleservices, Tata Indian Hotels, and Tata Communications. Products include steel, cars, software, tea, commodities, consulting and financial services, tourism, and communications. There are altogether 31 independent, publicly listed Tata enterprises with a combined market capitalization of about $79.36 billion. Tata is big, diverse, and profitable.[153]

But here's an innovative and compelling difference. Two-thirds of the equity of Tata Sons, the Tata holding company, is held by philanthropic trusts that have created national institutions for science and technology, medical research, social studies, and the performing arts in India. The trusts also provide aid and assistance to non-government organizations working worldwide in the areas of education, healthcare, and social development. The combined expenditure of the trusts and the companies amounts to around 3 percent of the group's net profits in 2011, a considerable sum, beyond taxes, of wealth returned through philanthropic donations. In the United States, while some corporations have foundations, the percentage of profit to charitable distribution does not come close. The donation of the personal fortunes of Bill Gates and Warren Buffett are admirable, but they are individual contributions, not ongoing corporate engagement.

Much of the Tata profit is derived from endeavor that involves the ocean, as a site for cable communications, transport of goods, tourism, and related financial return. As the ocean is a global public space, Tata has chosen "to pay a fee" for this use through partial ownership by the trusts and subsequent contributions to research, health, education, culture, and the eradication of poverty around the world. It is probably not perfect, but it is unique, hopeful, and worthy of emulation by all corporations that exploit Nature, land and sea, mostly indifferent to the physical or social consequences of their enterprise.

A Pledge for Change

The reports from the COP-21 Climate Summit in Paris in December 2015 are in. Many experts and activists from around the globe worked hard to formulate serious policy recommendations and priorities, and went to Paris to advocate for inclusion of ocean sustainability in the final report. The details of that recommendation included seven focus areas, from integrated governance, to climate change mitigation, to biodiversity protection, to the prevention of unregulated fishing, to the needs of small island nations, to the control of marine pollution, to the building of a "Blue Economy" that advances alternative policies and behaviors. The final outcome did not include any of these areas. In fact it omitted specific ocean recommendations altogether.

Those good people are right to be disappointed, terribly disappointed. We need now to be honest in our assessment of future strategies and tactics. We need evermore to persevere. But how? It is surely time to reassess the process of political engagement and action for the ocean, not so much the policies themselves, but how we work to implement them. Government has revealed its inability, indifference, or subservience to those interests that will continue to corrupt our land, our water, and our seas with no regard for the earth or for our children who will inherit a wounded world. To counter this paralysis, we need to mobilize ourselves into a vast army of *Citizens of the Ocean* to demonstrate our commitment through individual responsibility and collective action. As one small step forward in this direction, I invite you to visit WorldOceanObservatory.org/content/citizens-ocean and take the Citizens of the Ocean Pledge as follows:

I pledge:

1.   To consume at home or in restaurants seafood that has been clearly labeled as sustainably harvested or raised and to advocate to suppliers, markets, and chefs that only such product be distributed or served.

2.   To refuse plastic containers and to only choose those that can be reused or recycled.

3.   To avoid all products using non-biodegradable packaging, Styrofoam, and plastic wrap.

4.   To conserve, harvest, and recycle fresh water whenever possible at home, at work, and at organizations with which I am associated.

5.   To do my best to reduce dependence on fossil fuels and production of CO_2 emissions. I will endeavor to reduce my personal annual consumption by 25% using alternative transportation and conserving energy at home.

6.   To adopt alternative technology—more fuel-efficient, hybrid or electric vehicles, solar and wind energy production, and other options—whenever possible.

7.   To advocate against the use, runoff, and disposal of agricultural and lawn fertilizers, pesticides, chemicals, paints, oils, industrial waste, debris, detergents, sewage treatment, and storm drain outflow into streams, rivers, ponds, lakes, and watersheds that all lead to the ocean.

8.   To leave all upland natural areas, waterways, coastal areas and beaches cleaner and better than when I found them.

9.   To oppose development within the coastal zone that compromises the environmental health of the shoreline, pollutes associated maritime resources, and restricts access and support of marine trades and working waterfronts.

10.   To encourage local schools and civic organizations to support environmental studies, programs, and values.

11.   To support local conservation and advocacy organizations involved in community-based conservation activities upstream and down in support of a sustainable ocean.

12.   To require my choice of candidate for local, regional, statewide, and national office to commit to these outcomes as part of their political agenda before they are elected, and to hold the activities of government to these same standards.

13.   To build the "Citizens of the Ocean" network by sharing this pledge and link actively with my family, neighbors, and friends worldwide.

These are all things we can do as individuals when government is too slow or fails. At first, they may seem distant from the ocean, but they are not. Every such activity has direct and immediate impact on the ocean in known and measurable ways. Inherent in this pledge are individual choices that penalize those who don't care or subtract from the effect of the indifference of others. Each choice adds up to a collective choice, a different pattern of consumption, a market consequence, a financial condition, and a natural outcome that contributes to the sustainable outcome that was not realized at Paris. It's a beginning.

The Architecture That Comes Next

B ill McKibben, Founder of 350.org, the global communications campaign for building public awareness of the impact of global warming, concludes his 2010 book, *Eaarth: Making a Life on a Tough New Planet*, as follows: "We'll help build the architecture for the world that comes next, the dispersed and localized societies that can survive the damage we can no longer prevent. *Eaarth* represents the deepest of human failures. But we must live on the world we've created—lightly, carefully, gracefully."[154] McKibben is a truth-teller; he analyzes the damage we have done to our terrestrial and marine environment, the crises we face, and then outlines ways we can carry on, and thrive, through decentralized regional self-sufficiencies, community-based systems for energy, water, food production, health, and political discourse. His is a determined, quiet voice, albeit speaking with a global megaphone, advocating responsible ideas and reasonable solutions for survival that are resilient, practical, and hopeful. We should listen.

Bill McKibben advocates a new way of living on the land, but, at some point, I submit that we will come to understand that the ocean is the ultimate answer to our plight. When we have finally exhausted the fossil fuels, diminished the fields, and altered the climate to the point where even Bill's world may not be feasible, we will turn to the ocean for everything the world population will need to survive.

Let me give you one example of this new thinking: "an integrated biotectural system,"[155] a process of multidisciplinary engineering on a highly cross-professional level, that will enable the integration of conventional architectural design with natural elements toward the conceptualization and implementation of new structures and institutions that will address these future needs. Basically, this works through the layering of synergistic technologies, overlapping functions that support and amplify outcomes, with minimal contradictory effects, combined in a facility unlike any we have known before.

Recently, in a fascinating Rice University thesis by Matthew Genaze on hydrology and architecture, I discovered a project that combined known technological functions heretofore built separately—water collection, waste-water treatment, hydroponic farming, residential living, a public bath, and a forested park—into the design of a single urban tower, thereby integrating fresh water supply with food production with home living with personal health with community recreation, in one structure in a new city.[156] A provocative, perhaps very practical idea.

Another example, beyond theory, is the "seawater green-house" that uses the sun, the ocean, and the atmosphere to produce fresh water and cool air, re-creating the natural hydro-logical cycle within a controlled environment. This idea has been developed by a British designer, Charles Paton, whose company, Seawater Greenhouse Ltd, assembled in 1992 a prototype on a site in Tenerife, the Canary Islands.[157] A second seawater greenhouse was constructed on Al-Aryam Island, Abu Dhabi, United Arab Emirates, in 2000, and a third system and joint research facility was completed in 2004 on the Batinah coast near Muscat, Oman, in collaboration with Sultan Qaboos University. In 2010, Seawater Greenhouse built a new commercial installation on the Spencer Gulf, near Port Augusta, South Australia, now independently operating as Sundrop Farms Pty Ltd, that harnesses the sun's energy to desalinate seawater to produce fresh water for irrigation, produce electricity to power the greenhouse, provide the energy to heat and cool the facility, and generate biological residues, biomass that can be used to help create and enrich the surrounding soil, or alternatively digested to make bio-methane as fuel.

Another similar initiative, larger in scale, is the Sahara Forest Project that has won $3.5 million in funding to construct a 10,000-square-meter site in Qatar that will combine the seawater greenhouse concept with concentrated solar power to produce electricity from sunlight to generate thermal energy to drive conventional steam turbines. In this case, in addition to the outcomes already described, the project designers, as quoted in *Wired* magazine indicate, "the saltwater will also be used to cultivate halophytes or sea-loving plant species as well as algae, which can be used for large-scale bio-energy production." This project was developed by collaboration between Seawater Greenhouse, Exploration Architecture, and Max Fordham Consulting Engineers in London, and the Bellona Foundation in Norway.[158]

As we plan for the day-to-day needs of this changing world, we must not abandon the inventiveness and imagination that have characterized the history of world civilization. We speak now of mitigation of climate effect, adaptation to rapidly changing environmental conditions that are upheaving our lives. But, I believe, beyond that, we must free our imaginations to invent our way into the future, and it will serve us, and our children, well.

Reuse

I have spent a lifetime with words. As a writer, teacher, and endless talker, I have spent my years arranging words to devious ends: to create a fictional world, to expose ideas, to persuade to a cause, to exhort friends and strangers to a purpose I believe in. Words are like stepping stones; they are rock solid by definition, set in sequence, sometimes straight, sometimes curvilinear; words take you from one place to another over time;

words are an extraordinary tool by which to lie and by which to tell the truth; words are something we all hold on to.

In the language of conservation, we are familiar with the words "reduce" and "recycle." By "reduce" we mean "conserve," take less, consume less, a means by which we can extend limited supply or, in some cases, manage a resource in a renewable, sustainable fashion. Conservationists live by this principle; whether they protect land or marine areas, their motivation is to prolong, indeed secure, the vitality of a place or species in an antagonistic economic and cultural world. By "recycle," we mean the return of consumables to their component parts: plastic bottles to plastic toys, aluminum cans to aluminum foil, glass jars to glass windows, rubber tires to rubber gaskets, steel ships to steel girders and rebar, wood debris to wood pulp and paper. Recyclists transform our manufactured things into base materials that can be used again in the making of new products to accumulate. These two words frame a process, from the beginning of things to their rebirth as something else—all good, albeit not good enough.

But there are words in between. Talking with a friend the other day, we discussed "reuse" as such a word, different from the others, that describes the making of existing things available for exchange with others. Examples? Well, those always surprising T-shirts worn by African children, discarded in the United States and Europe and shipped in bulk to Africa to serve as new clothing for people who need it. We read accounts of cell phones reused in similar manner, distributed to women in India who use them to network, bank, and create small businesses. When you think about it, there many examples closer to home. Antique and thrift shops. Garage sales. Vintage clothing stores. Video and auto rentals. Bicycle networks for urban transportation. Architectural salvage. In every case, existing things are reused by others for what they were made for, an efficient, monetized system that both conserves the inherent value of the item and redirects its utility from someone who doesn't need it to someone who does. Creative people have taken this idea to scale: citywide tag sales, for example, a massive urban redistribution of goods that empties attics and storage units, not into the dumpster, but to neighbors and strangers in a local exchange.

Failure to reduce, reuse, or recycle equals waste. And in a world of burgeoning population and limited resources, waste is anathema. In the context of water and ocean, examples of waste abound. Oil companies, once resource value is extracted, leave behind all sorts of things: obsolete rigs and derricks, rusting barrels, slurry and sludge, polluted land and water. Today's latest energy trick—hydraulic fracturing—leaves behind land bereft of agricultural capacity, polluted aquifer and surface streams, and reservoirs of poisoned water that must be contained and isolated from the already limited freshwater capacity of the locality, the region, the world. There are myriad other examples: watersheds mined and quarried releasing toxic chemicals to become "brown-fields" costing millions in public funds to attempt some pitiful cleanup of waste left behind by companies and investors long gone. Consider the location of many of our nuclear plants, not just in Fukushima, Japan, but in North America and Europe, located on rivers and coasts for access to free cooling water but vulnerable to leaks or meltdowns and the almost insurmountable problem of how and where to store their waste.

Take the most pressing ocean example: the decline, and many argue, collapse of global fish stocks and resultant catastrophic loss of protein for global sustenance. Will we reduce our harvest; voluntarily limit catch to conserve species for the future? Will we use 100 percent of every fish caught? Will we recycle by-catch as fertilizer, animal food, or fish products for human consumption? Will we reuse our coral reefs, coastal wetlands, mangrove swamps, and other marine habitats for their essential, undisrupted incubation of fish species, their vast potential for medicinal development, or their massive contribution to water filtration and storm protection?

Our forebears reused things all the time. Why can't we? Walk the beaches and see what you find: so many things we do not need, do not recycle, do not think someone else might want. We just threw it all away.

Bad Trash to Good Cash

Let's talk about recycling. For millennia humans have maintained and reused tools and resources as part of an essential economy based on what is available, what is the need, and what is the best way to meet that need without waste. The behavior was reality; there was no choice. But as we multiplied and responded with innovation and technology, we discovered that we could make more than ever before, into goods and necessary services; we could build and earn our way beyond scarcity to a new standard of making, consuming, and living that today is both system and expectation of surplus, even excess.

Waste and its management are the new challenges of this day. How do we dispose of toxic tailings and spoils, plastic containers and packaging, discarded automobiles, old refrigerators, outmoded televisions, superseded computers, or out-of-fashion smartphones? Where does it all go? Into dumps where we attempt to cover and contain its seepage and deterioration; into the groundwater and watershed and ocean where it does invisible damage to the land and sea and all that lives in it or depends upon it.

Take that to scale, and you have poisoned aquifers with water unfit to drink, lakes and streams hostile to native species, an ocean surface pocked with vast clusters of floating debris, and a water column corrupted by a solution of poisons we cannot see, taste, or feel—until they are made evident through algal blooms, dead fish, and sick people.

We recycle what, and how much of this waste? We collect aluminum cans, some glass, paper, and cardboard and a small percentage of the plastic discard, and turn them into similar products for similar uses. We feel good about this. Not everyone does it.

We also have some bright new ideas. For example, we recycle discarded ocean plastic into clothing and soap bottles and surfaces for parking lots; we recycle fishnet and line into carpet tiles, skateboards, and doormats; but when you really consider what percentage of everything we produce and then recycle to be produced again, it must add up to a pittance. How do we turn bad trash into good cash?

Here are some thoughts:

- First, what if we refrain from creating the trash at all by conserving or using less of the things that enable its making? Use less plastic by not using plastic bags, rejecting plastic packaging, substituting reusable containers, glass for just one example. These small individual protests, and many more such similar actions, are easily done now by many of us and our families at home.

- Second, what if we recycle more, by insisting that all plastics be recycled? If every piece of plastic detritus was collected for reuse, would we need to produce any more? What if all engine oil and fast-food frying fat were recycled? What if all manufactured items were made of recyclable products or, if not, carried a penalty deposit for the true cost of their safe disposal? What if we held corporations responsible for their industrial waste; enforced, not diluted or contradicted, regulations put in place to protect human health? Such regulations are justified by the right of the public to be protected from such premeditated impacts health impacts. Some of these have been tried and successful; some have been subverted by the narrowest interest that asserts mean shareholder return over basic human rights. These, too, are achievable through political will.

- Finally, what if we built a new economy on a recycling ethic, a price or tax structure built on the inherent value of reuse, the concept that an item is more valuable if it can be used longer or can be reused in a way that exploits and affirms its economic basis again and again in a cycle of maximum utility and return? What if it costs more, not less, to purchase a non-recyclable item built from a waste-based process? This would not be a new principle on Earth; it too is achievable as the revival of a principled behavior that attacks waste at its irresponsible, anti-social core.

Without substantive recycling, in these ways or others, we perpetuate waste. Waste is excess. Excess is pollution. Pollution dirties our air, corrupts our land, fouls our water, poisons our ocean, and diminishes our future.

Urban Mining

One does not often consider the concept of deep-ocean mining, especially when there are so many environmental issues related to mining on land, but there does exist today a project off the coast of Papua New Guinea where a multinational corporation was engaged in scouring the ocean floor to recover gold, silver, copper, and other rare and precious metals, deposited there because of geological conditions resulting from intense historical underwater volcanic events. The project, only financially viable because of increasing prices in global markets for such resources, was also destroying the local concentration of hydro-thermal vents, the biologically unique so-called Black Smokers, home to myriad heretofore unknown marine species and extraordinary biodiversity with enormous implication for the future of human health. That local subsistence fishing was also significantly disrupted and royalty payments for such activity within national territorial waters were minimal, paid mostly to the central government, with almost nothing for the impacted coastal communities, is yet another negative consequence of this new form of unsustainable natural resource extraction, a distant phenomenon of which the public is hardly aware.

The situation is the result of the enormous amounts of gold, silver, and precious metals that are being consumed by the exponential demand for electrical products such as cell phones, hybrid cars, satellites, medical devices, and new tablet computers, some 100 million of which were sold in 2013, a number expected to double in the coming year. According to the Deep Sea Mining Campaign, more than $21 billion was invested in such production in 2013—just in gold alone, 320 tons, more than 7.7 percent of the world's supply and roughly 2.5 percent of the total US reserve at Fort Knox.[159] This situation became critical in 2010 when China, a major supplier and processor, especially of rare earths, announced it would limit exports, thus threatening supply for Europe and Japan and causing Lockheed Martin, the American military contractor, to seek an alternative source as a key investor in the Papua New Guinea ocean mining project.

But, as the Deep Sea Mining Campaign points out, there is an extraordinary alternative to this endeavor, yielding a recovdinary supply sufficient to meet this expanding demand without disrupting the ocean floor at all—the mining of so-called e-waste. Rather than being lost as the various devices become obsolete, replaced, or discarded—these rare metals already dedicated to this production are recovered and recycled. In the case of gold, up to 85 percent of that extant metal can be recovered and recycled efficiently and effectively—thus, some significant amount, especially as the price of gold has increased from the $300 to $1,500 an ounce in recent years, a market reflection of the new demand.

Would it not be better to mine that abandoned supply already in hand than destroy a pristine environment, devastate communities, and otherwise add unnecessarily to what has already been extracted and is available? Ironically, what is required here is a profit motive—the realization that mining this urban waste is more practical and advantageous than the more dangerous and politically volatile ocean mining approach. Cannot crude processing technology be replaced, in both the developed and developing countries, with new systems already proven 95 percent efficient, not just to sustain this cycle of supply and the production energy already invested, but also to create many new jobs, new national revenue streams, and solve what is a serious local and international waste management problem with critical environmental impacts that otherwise remain unaddressed? Is this not a powerful enterprise, justified by multiple justifications for investment in this recycling approach by national governments, donor nations, the Global Environment Facility, or the World Bank? Isn't this exactly the kind of catalytic stimulus that these institutions are meant to facilitate?

In the 1960s, Jane Jacobs, the prescient American analyst and critic of modern urban development, proclaimed "cities as the mines of the future."[160] The conditions that drive the need for these rare metals are essentially land-based and urban—as a function of ever-concentrating global centers of burgeoning population, ever-expanding consumption of technological devices, and ever-amplifying consequence of deleterious waste. Just as we have learned to recycle paper, glass, iron, steel, even water, we must now also learn to recover these new elements as well, mine their density and availability, and invent a new conduct toward sustaining the value of these most precious metals already in hand. If we do so, we will simultaneously solve three important problems through a single dramatic action: first, we can remediate profitably an existing toxic situation; second, we can reuse and restore the value of what we have already taken; and third, we can do no further harm by destroying pristine ocean environments and existing coastal communities in the name of unnecessary requirement.

The Arctic Council

How then to resolve this conflict between natural resource exploitation and biodiversity protection, at one point an easy relationship until the world economy grew to a level of demand that shifted the balance from infinite to finite supply, from moderate to excessive demand. The ebb and flow is visible on land, for example, in the history of the American "rust belt," the middle states that flourished as the primary producer of iron and steel, then collapsed in the face of offshore competition and labor costs, now to feel the hope again of revival in the face of the fracking boom producing new supplies of natural gas, indifferent to the negative environmental consequence, that will eventually be exhausted and return these communities to even greater destitution.

This conflict underlies the growing controversy and opposition by many to comparable energy-driven development in China, Africa, and other developing states with growing financial and social aspirations already enjoyed by the developed world. It seems to be an unstoppable, repeating pattern that will endure regardless of lessons already learned.

How do we move beyond this deleterious cycle? If you look to the ocean, specifically to the northern Arctic regions, above latitude 40 degrees north encircling the North Pole, you see an area rich in resources of every kind, home to indigenous peoples, unspoiled by its isolation, but now ever more accessible due to the actuality of global warming that has raised temperatures, melted glaciers and sea ice, opened passages and areas heretofore impenetrable except by a hardy few, and otherwise become available to meet the critical global need for energy and water. It is seen by some as a last great wilderness that must be kept forever wild, and by others as a vast new opportunity for exploitation and consumption.

We have discussed earlier the so-called "new north." But we have not explored its potential as a laboratory for policy and management in which we can experiment with new structures of governance, new cooperative limits on resource extraction, new protections for extraordinary biodiversity, and new relationships with the communities and peoples who live and work therein.

In 1996, through an international declaration formulated in Ottawa, Canada, The Arctic Council was formally established as a high-level intergovernmental forum "to provide a means for promoting cooperation, coordination and interaction among the Arctic States, with the involvement of the Arctic Indigenous communities and other Arctic inhabitants on common Arctic issues, in particular issues of sustainable development and environmental protection in the Arctic." The participating

Arctic Council Member States are Canada, Denmark (including Greenland and the Faroe Islands), Finland, Iceland, Norway, the Russian Federation, Sweden, and the United States of America, each of which contributes US$58,000 per year toward a Secretariat budget. As the Council evolved, two new related non-voting categories emerged: *Permanent Members*, United Nations organizations and programs and other governmental agencies with Arctic interests; and *Observers*, various non-governmental organizations with comparable concerns.[161]

The Council has five areas of designated interest: Environment and Climate, including climate change and environmental protection; Biodiversity, including an Arctic Biodiversity Assessment and a Circumpolar Biodiversity Monitoring Program; Oceans, including search and rescue, Arctic Ocean review, emergency preparedness, marine environment, shipping, oil and gas; and Arctic People, including health and well-being, indigenous people needs today, and languages and culture. What is interesting about this, of course, is the integrated activities that balance needs and demands, plan for outcomes and consequences, and address the sustainability requirements of the ecosystem and the people that live there. The activities are structured so that no single demand of any single interest can be imposed at the expense or deterioration of another. The Secretariat for the Council is based in Tromsø, Norway, and is charged with managing the activities, organizing the various meetings, producing reports, and executing an annual work-plan that is determined by the council members.[162]

One can look at this as a structure designed to protect vested national interests, not unite them; to defend resources, not exploit them responsibly; to control the local citizens, rather than assimilate their needs and values. One can also look upon this as a model structure of governance, based on common interest, sustainability, and community integration. Time will tell if this will create a new mode of international government, corporate, and social behavior, more cooperative than competitive, more planned than unregulated, more progressive and protective than regressive and destructive. Such a demonstration of new conduct might well demonstrate how even on land where old conduct has done its worst, we might change our ways for the better.

Operation Surf

I attended Blue Mind 3, a conference organized by peripatetic ocean advocate Dr. Wallace J. Nichols, where neuroscientists, artists, and ocean managers were invited to investigate our emotional response to the ocean.[163] Through poetry, art, sound-scape, photographs, film, and research presentations on brain function, the intent was to explore the cognitive benefits of the ocean on human health and well-being.

It may be that we intuit this connection, through a kind of cumulative cultural agreement that being by the ocean, river, lake or pond instills a kind of peacefulness and calm, an alternative to the noisy, frenetic disorder of our lives from external circum-stance, constant motion, accelerated expectation, the exigencies of time and occupation, and the resultant internal stress. Obviously, the increasing demographic of migration from inland to the coasts, as well as the desire to recreate or vacation by the ocean, are strong indicators of this phenomenon. While the classic liter-ature of the sea documents such elements as fear, exhaustion, depravation, and intense interpersonal relations aboard ship, the anthologies nonetheless often express a composite portrait of romance, revelation, solace, and strength derived from constant, insistent experience with Nature.

One of the neuroscientists at the meeting displayed a slide of an early sea chart—much of the space unmarked as unknown, with artistic depictions of violent weather and terrifying monsters in the margins. His next illustration was a map of the brain, showing various places where emotions have been measured by experiments and studies, indicative of relative change in laboratory animals when tested with different or intensified stimuli. We take our proof where we can, be it through an enthusiastic postcard from abroad or a graph of electrical response in a lab on a campus just over town.

The conference discussion focused on empathy—the understanding of one's feelings and the attribution of such emotion to a thing or another. Empathy allows for a compelling link between a perception and a reality, between me and the ocean, between me and you as we experience the ocean together. If we can create empathy, the discussion went, we can extend understanding and awareness of the ocean's value beyond economic calculation, policy, and governance—even beyond science— touching and reaching people in ways that will deepen their knowledge and commitment to the natural world around them. To do so, we must use every strategy available.

No matter what you think about this idea, let me give you an example of how it works. One presenter, Van Curaza, described the work of Operation Surf, a non-profit organization in San Luis Obispo, California, with a program to expose wounded military to the healing power of the ocean through adaptive surfing taught by world- class instructors. According to Curaza, the participants "are being treated for various kinds of trauma including multiple amputations, spinal cord injuries, traumatic brain injury, burns, and Post Traumatic Stress Disorder."[164] Curaza, the founder and director of the organization, understood the value and contribution of the surfing experience to his own recovery from alcohol and drug addiction. He realized the rehabilitative effect and increased confidence, and resolved to extend those benefits to men and women whose bodies and lives have been dramatically and painfully altered by war. The ocean becomes for them more than a place for exuberance, rather a place to advance physical recovery, to demonstrate prowess, to build relationships and bonds with others, and to regain the psychological strength with which to transcend trauma, to return to their families, to reengage in positive and remunerative work, in the military and elsewhere, and to regain the wholeness of mind and spirit that will enable their survival and success. The video showed astonishing examples, not just of individual joy and dramatic accomplishment, but also of attitudinal transformation—if I can do this, then I can do anything. It was poetry, art, sound, and personal achievement all as one, an expanded presence of mind and mindfulness that transcended a wounded body to become a viable foundation for a life for individuals who at that point of violent accident, and thereafter, must have thought they did not have a future.

What a gift. This is empathy for real—a physical and emotional connection between victim and therapeutic environment, between wound and cure, between despair and possibility—all in the redemptive context of the sea. The literature and the science are affirmed: the ocean provides both tangible and intangible qualities for our lives—indeed, it is an immersion that we cannot live without.

Law of Mother Earth

Just when you think the world is impossible, the world surprises. Looking forward into the future one can easily despair over the scale of change required, the intractability of vested interests and governments, and the human energy and imagination required to make any change for the better. We talk of hope, but when specific actions are considered and expressed, all the reasons against often overwhelm the possibility.

Enter Bolivia, where in December 2010, in response to an understanding of the impacts of climate change on the nation's economic and community health, the National Congress voted to support an act to protect the well-being of its citizens by protecting the natural world—its resources, sustainability, and value—as essential to the common good.[165] The act was supported by Bolivian President Evo Morales; revisions of the national legal code were explored; over 2,900 specific conservation programs and anti-pollution projects, conceived as expressions of the practical application of the law, were implemented in all 327 municipalities; $118 million was invested; and full legislation enabling this new social and economic model is expected to be ratified soon.

The language is astonishing. Here are the binding principles that govern:

1) *Harmony*: Human activities, within the framework of plurality and diversity, should achieve a dynamic balance with the cycles and processes inherent in Mother Earth;

2) *Collective Good*: The interests of society, within the framework of the rights of Mother Earth, prevail in all human activities and any acquired right;

3) *Guarantee of Regeneration*: The state, at its various levels, and society, in harmony with the common interest, must ensure the necessary conditions in order that the diverse living systems of Mother Earth may absorb damage, adapt to shocks, and regenerate without significantly altering their

structural and functional characteristics, recognizing that living systems are limited in their ability to regenerate, and that humans are limited in their ability to undo their actions;

4) *Respect and defend the rights of Mother Earth*: The state and any individual or collective person must respect, protect and guarantee the rights of Mother Earth for the well-being of current and future generations;

5) *No Commercialism*: Neither living systems nor processes that sustain them may be commercialized, nor serve anyone's private property:

6) *Multiculturalism*: The exercise of the rights of Mother Earth require the recognition, recovery, respect, protection, and dialogue of the diversity of feelings, values, knowledge, skills, practices, transcendence, science, technology and standards of all the culture of the world who seek to live in harmony with Nature.[166]

The Legislation continues:

Mother Earth has the following rights: To life, to the diversity of life, to water, to clean air, to equilibrium, to restoration, and to pollution-free living. And it further outlines the obligations of the State and the people to these principles and rights as a binding societal duty.

The Bolivian economy relies heavily on natural resource export activity, earning a significant part of its foreign exchange thereby. But this moves forward nonetheless, as an endeavor initiated and supported by Bolivian political groups representing some 3 million voters. Bolivia attempts to move forward, to show us another way, and nearby Ecuador, with similar intent, is right alongside.

The Law of Mother Earth—not just an idea, more than a vision. Something new. Something real. Change must begin somewhere, sometime; perhaps Bolivia is inventing the social model and role of governance that will demonstrate how globally we can transcend the divisions and conflicts, beyond the destruction and despair that we feel, toward an harmonious, effective, efficient, and equitable society connected by the true value of nature as sustainer. If so, should we not pay attention?

SOME OF US ARE DREAMERS

Waves' Collision

As my frustration builds over the continuing degradation of the world ocean, and the outrageous indifference and unwillingness of many governments and other vested interests to do anything about it, I search for ways to reach into peoples' minds and consequent actions to make a difference.

Harsh statistical description is one strategy. The repetition of facts concerning climate, acidification, persistent ocean pollutants, the poisoning of marine species and their habitats, overfishing, all forms of waste from manufacturing, accident, and deliberate disposal, and so many other factors, would seem to be a powerful motivator for engagement. And for some it is. But dire description can intimidate and dissuade as much as it can motivate, and in so many conversations about the ocean I hear so often a resultant despair and helplessness expressed by those who see no individual way to make a difference. What can I possibly do about it?

Political and community action is another strategy. There are numerous organizations fully engaged in ocean conservation and the promotion of regulatory structures to define and contain the abusive practice, financial subsidy, and lack of enforcement of existing laws and treaties that enable degrading conditions to continue. By joining these organizations and collectivizing concern and financial capacity, some steps can be effectively taken, but when the effect is calculated today through connection to and awareness of specific ocean issues, the outcome is wanting, almost negligible.

A third strategy is an attempt to motivate action through an emotional, rather than only logical, connection. I have described above the idea of reciprocity as such a concept, the notion that as a recipient of the ocean's bounty of water, food, energy, health, and spiritual sustenance, you are obligated to give back, to return the favor, to accept the gift of responsibility for the ability of the gift to keep on giving.

Finally, there is the concept of empathy, an emotional sympathy and understanding heretofore considered ephemeral but now subject of study by neuroscientists that can locate and measure chemical reactions in the brain coincident with feelings of sympathetic identification with someone, something, or some idea expressed by both mental and physical response. If one can empathize with the ocean and its creatures, one can define and exploit new and different motivational strength to catalyze behavioral change.

Whatever works! Whichever strategy advances the engagement, so be it. But why not all four? Why not an overlapping consensus of empathetic response, leading to reciprocal obligation, leading to individual, political, and community action, leading to a new measurements of the reversal of outlawed practice, invigorated enforcement rule of law, newly sustained species and revivified habitat, conserved resources, and alternative perspectives and technologies that will save the ocean from ourselves. How to make this so?

Before the Deluge

How do we get beyond the complicated circumstances of our world? How do we deal with the individual and community consequences of actions that consume our terrestrial and marine resources, incite conflict and confrontation, and force us to decisions that make no sense and prolong the worst practices and behaviors that slowly consume our world, our values, and our lives? Dour thoughts, I suppose, and as I think about this condition these verses from an old Jackson Browne song, "Before the Deluge," sound and resound in my head today.[167]

Some of them were dreamers
And some of them were fools
Who were making plans and thinking of the future
With the energy of the innocent
They were gathering the tools
They would need to make their journey back to nature
While the sand slipped through the opening
And their hands reached for the golden ring
With their hearts they turned to each other's heart for refuge
In the troubled years that came before the deluge
Some of them knew pleasure
And some of them knew pain
And for some of them it was only the moment that mattered
And on the brave and crazy wings of youth

They went flying around in the rain
And their feathers, once so fine, grew torn and tattered
And in the end they traded their tired wings
For the resignation that living brings
And exchanged love's bright and fragile glow
For the glitter and the rouge
And in the moment they were swept before the deluge

Some of them were angry
At the way the earth was abused
By the men who learned how to forge her beauty into power
And they struggled to protect her from them
Only to be confused
By the magnitude of her fury in the final hour
And when the sand was gone and the time arrived
In the naked dawn only a few survived
And in attempts to understand a thing so simple and so huge
Believed that they were meant to live after the deluge

These words speak to me emotionally as I consider the challenge that we face in response to the evidence of wholesale abuse of land, air, and sea. The implication is enormous. Dreamers and fools, we've stood before the deluge, and are now faced with the consequence of making plans for a future built on the fecundity of nature, not knowing, perhaps not even caring, if that wealth is squandered, never to be available again. This is not a naïve sentiment; the evidence is overwhelming in example after example where we have insulted and exhausted the land, poisoned the air, and polluted the water to the point where there is no oxygen even for marine animals to survive. Is it not a reasonable conjecture, then, that if we continue in this way we too will be swept before the deluge, indeed the fury of a final hour? It is a dire and depressing thought to be sure; that said, should we not do something about it?

And so Browne's concluding chorus:

Now let the music keep our spirits high
And let the buildings keep our children dry
Let creation reveal its secrets by and by
By and by...
When the light that's lost within us reaches the sky

We have the light within us; actually, it is no secret, we know what to do to sustain life beyond the deluge. We have the knowledge, but do we have the will?

Therein lies the challenge, the hard part by which we give up something known and familiar to create something new, to abandon one set of premises and values to invent and apply another that will guide us and our successors back to the water planet that will sustain us. Now, let the music keep our spirits high...and express our dream as to how we might build a new just, equitable, and sustainable society around the ocean, water, and their eternal and nurturing cycles.

VI. A NEW HYDRAULIC SOCIETY

GETTING THERE

Planning with Water

The World Economic Forum met in 2015 at its usual "watering hole" in Davos, Switzerland—an annual gathering of national leaders, economists and corporatists, the occasional celebrity, and many others who, like moths to flame, use the event to circulate with the self-declared best and brightest, promote their ideas, and otherwise network with movers and shakers who are, or want to be, among those who are shaping the world agenda.

In advance of the meeting, a survey was conducted by WEF among some 900 leaders in business, politics, and civic life that concluded that the most important global risk faced today is the world water crisis. "The world is not doing enough," the report asserts. According to Circle of Blue, a program of the Pacific Institute and one of the best Web-based sources for water information, this is a major shift in world attention, explained in part by climate and weather phenomena, drought, pollution, and other limits on water that dramatically affect vulnerable populations, be they in California or the American southwest, China, India, southern Europe, or Australia.[168] "Though the problems of floods, drought, and inadequate water supply that were projected more than two decades ago have come true, little is being done to address them effectively. Leaders are especially ill-prepared for widespread social instability..." Circle of Blue quotes Bob Sandford, chair of the Canadian Partnership Initiative, as follows: "We didn't realize until recently how much our economy and society relied on hydrologic stability."[169]

Well, that is not entirely true. China, for example, has been building massive water transfer systems to move water from areas in the south to the more arid north where drought, industrial irrigation, and flagrant pollution have brought scarcity as well as economic and political crises. A recent analysis by researchers at the Leeds Water Research Center at the University of East Anglia in the UK, published in the *Proceedings of the National Academy of Sciences*, suggests that this extraordinary expenditure of public funds and labor may not be sufficient to meet increased economic and population growth.[170] Dabo Guan, Professor of Climate Change Economics at the University's School of International Development, is quoted by *Bloomberg News* describing the system as "pouring good water after bad."[171]

China, India, Australia, the US—all are grappling with these conditions, certainly not theoretical anymore, but immediate, devastating, and disruptive. The rising price for grain and rice resulting from severe drought has been suggested as being among the major contributors to social unrest, perhaps toppling a government in Egypt and crippling a regional economy in Australia and escalating prices in food-dependent markets throughout the southern hemisphere. These are not problems easily dismissed or ignored. Indeed, we already fight wars for water, in the Middle East for example, as much as for oil or religion.

The old solutions do not serve these extreme events. It may be that the old engineering ideas and designs like the Tennessee Valley Authority in the US or the diversion of northern rivers in

India cannot meet the challenge of exponential demand, degraded supply, and global warming. That proof may be now visible to us all, even those leaders gathered in the Swiss mountains to contemplate the world condition and its most critical needs.

There is a direct link between water abundance and human well-being, between adequate supply and the sustainability of any community, rich or poor. Northern California is a region of great fecundity and wealth in the US, entirely dependent on water from the Rocky Mountains distributed by engineered solutions. Water rationing, inadequate supply at key points in growth of fruit and crops, and weak and declining harvests can bring even such a community to its knees. The response cannot be conventional, more of the same; the time for that has passed.

There is of course no alternative plan. Or is there?

Suddenly the commodity around which the world has organized its economics and geopolitics is no longer oil. All the calculations are rapidly changing, even as the energy companies and their investors double down on what surely they hope will be a return to the good old days. Suddenly the communities suffering from the consequences of fracking or exploding pipelines find leverage to fight back against what has been so cleverly packaged as beyond them and essential to the national interest. Ironically, nations like Denmark and Germany where quality of life surely compares favorably with the United States, suddenly find their support of alternative wind and solar energy systems a demonstration of progressive prescience that now provides a stable mix of technologies to hedge against reliance on a single source now brought down in a world of volatile supply, sanctions, and political unrest.

What then is the most valuable commodity on Earth around which a new, more viable, more realistic system of value can be built? It is water, the one natural product that every person, rich or poor, from anywhere around the globe, must rely on for life—to drink, to irrigate, to sanitize, and to otherwise support the basic elements of living. The collapse of oil, then, could be seen as a unique opportunity to shift our value system to an alternative based on water, priced by its utilitarian necessities, distributed equitably as if it is worth more than black gold or bullion or whatever arbitrary standard we have based our economic calculations in the past.

Of course we need energy to grow, not just for growth's sake but to meet the known requirements of a world population that is increasing dramatically by the millions from year to year. If we cannot provide basic living for these, in the form of health, shelter, food, and employment, not to mention the continuity of the quality of life that we enjoy, then we should prepare to accept our responsibility for the unfortunate consequences. It does not take much imagination to envision the outcomes; we see them in the disrupted conditions of poverty, political volatility, and social injustice in those places and among those peoples already deprived of what we take for granted.

If those global leaders at Davos have come to an understanding of hydrologic stability as an evident, valid requirement for the future, then indeed the time is now for the alternative plan that addresses the what and how such a system can be built from the ashes of coal and dirty oil and their lingering consequences that have proven so antagonistic and detrimental to communities worldwide.

Is it possible to construct a new system on the true value of water? What decisions must be made? Do we need new technologies and more money, or can we actually change by using the technologies already in hand and re-allocating existing assets?

Can we finance such a change with funds divested from the extraction industry and reinvested in alternatives? Can we move

the oil subsidies away from a dying industry to bring the new
alternatives to scale? Can we take back the definition of our future
from those who see it only as a replication of our past? Can we
make—and execute—a new plan?

Of course we can. It is, in fact, already in progress, perhaps not
so publicly known, perhaps not so clearly understood, but there
are amazing examples of a kind of progress based not on resiliency
to post-traumatic duress but on a sharpening vision of the future
that will leave the reactionaries in the detritus of their petro-dollars
and polluted dreams. What can it be? It is a world built around the
movements and cycles of water, and the ocean sits at its center.

This may seem a drastic idea, but I think not. I submit that
there is compelling logic here, a recalculation of value, a strategy
for action, indeed even a plan that might enable necessary change
away from a destructive status quo toward a realizable future
using existing technology and re-allocated financial assets.

How would it work? Let me give you an example of a
planning initiative that speaks to the why and how. The Nile
River Basin comprises 3 million square kilometers along a
6,695-kilometer course starting at headwaters in Rwanda and
Burundi, supporting millions in 10 riparian nations along the
watershed, and descending to Egypt and the Mediterranean
Sea. The basin accounts for 10 percent of Africa's land-mass, but
includes 25 percent of its burgeoning population. The river's
erratic flow, and the associated activities supported by that
flow, have been severely impacted by climate change factors—
temperature rise, persistent droughts, extreme weather, flooding,
expanding areas affected, and the inevitable socioeconomic
consequence in terms of energy and food production, health and
sanitation, employment, poverty, and regional security.

To understand the gravity of the problem and to begin

defining its solution, the UN Environment Program (UNEP), in cooperation with the Nile Basin Initiative with support by the Swedish International Development Agency, retained the Danish Hydraulic Institute, one of the world's largest and most accomplished hydraulic engineering and design organizations, to gather all available data regarding all activities and needs throughout the watershed, and to generate from that data a complex hydraulic model through which to project climate change effects, growing demand, and multiple requirements for water resources throughout the entire basin over time.[172]

The DHI, a nonprofit consulting firm chartered by the Danish Government, has developed proprietary software capacity that can assimilate massive amounts of data, process and visualize it, and make it adaptable for testing impacts of projected future conditions and scenarios.[173] It is an astonishing planning tool. The Nile model includes rainfall-runoff, lakes, reservoirs, dams, wetlands, and irrigation water demands.[174] The projections applied cover two 30-year periods—from 2020 to 2049 and from 2079 to 2099. Comparing the changing capacity with population growth, rural and urban shifts, agricultural and manufacturing needs revealed not just what amount of water might be available, but also how that water can be efficiently and effectively managed. From this information, very specifically located in a place, a region, a settlement, or a nation, decision-makers were provided with informed conditions on which they could evaluate and place water-dependent uses, target limited financial resources, and understand the management practices and professions for which to train personnel to operate the system in the future.

Take a moment to think about the implications of this, not only for the Nile River, but also for all the other multi-state and transnational watersheds around the world that could benefit from a similar understanding of the hydraulic reality on which their future viability will depend. For such a system to work, local knowledge, communication, cooperation, consensus agreement, implementation, evaluation, and further planning and action are required—all bringing together managers from nations sometimes antagonistic over other issues, but understanding that without such agreement and collaborative action, the absence of adequate water supply at any point along the line will lead to deprivation, dissatisfaction, and unrest.

Apply this methodology to any waterway you know—in the United States, to the Mississippi River, the Colorado River, the Columbia River, the Connecticut River; or to any number of the rivers in Europe, the Middle East, the Asian continent, and South America—and you immediately see how decisions made upstream or down, indifferent to conditions downstream or up, are the instigators of competition and conflict that most often does not serve anyone well.

The Nile Initiative is just one amazing example of planning with water. Take your thinking one step further: if nations can find consensus and compromise around water as an egalitarian human right, what else might they find possible through this first success? What other agreement might be found through the understanding and experience derived from one system that unites us all?

Water as an Asset Class

I expect to see in the near future a massive expansion of investment in the water sector, including the production of fresh, clean water from other sources (desalination, purification), storage, shipping and transportation of water. I expect to see pipeline networks that will exceed the capacity of those for oil and gas today.

I see fleets of water tankers (single-hulled!) and storage facilities that will dwarf those we currently have for oil, natural gas and LNG. I see new canal systems dug for water transportation, similar in ambition and scale to those currently in progress in China, linking the Yangtze River in the South to the Yellow River in the arid north.

I also hope and expect that these new canal ventures will be designed and implemented with a greater awareness of the environmental and social impact of such mega-projects. India will have to engage in investment on a scale comparable to that seen today in China to produce clean water in the best locations and transport it to where the household, industrial and agricultural users are.

I expect to see a globally integrated market for fresh water within 25 to 30 years.

Once the spot markets for water are integrated, futures markets and other derivative water-based financial instruments—puts, calls, swaps—both exchange-traded and OTC will follow. There will be different grades and types of fresh water, just the way we have light sweet and heavy sour crude oil today. Water as an asset class will, in my view, become eventually the single most important physical-commodity-based asset class, dwarfing oil, copper, agricultural commodities and precious metals.[175]

So writes Willem Buiter, an economist at the Global Markets division of the international bank, Citigroup, in an essay entitled, *Thirsty Cities—Urbanization to Drive Water Demand*, for the July 2011 Citi investor analysis and strategy newsletter, about the future of water as an investment and trading commodity. The paper surveys the growth of world population and its concentration in urban areas, consequent rising demands, resulting pressure on existing supplies, and investment implications. The report lists 12 companies with "material exposure to water" deriving significant percentages of their total revenue from water testing, individual and industrial treatment, pumps, chlorinators, and filters, disinfection systems, chemicals and softeners, automatic sampling devices, meters, plant engineering and construction, management and operations for large corporate and municipal users, and the design and implementation of desalination plants.[176]

Economists do see the world differently from you and me. Here are some quotations from that essay that are instructive:

"From an economic perspective there is nothing terribly special about water. It is an ordinary, regular commodity, a private good...(that) can be allocated effectively and efficiently by markets, and provided by private profit-motivated producers."[177]

"Many production and consumption activities whose primary purpose is not the production or consumption of water, have water pollution as a by-product/joint product or externality. Internalizing and/or pricing and charging for these externalities is clearly a hugely important political and social enterprise for the future."[178]

Buiter asks,

Is water a merit good?

A merit good is a commodity of which a particular society believes that it should be provided to individuals or households on the basis of need, rather than ability and willingness to pay. Provision should therefore not be based on consumer choice (alone)." 199 "Merit goods...have about them a whiff of paternalism and of the philosopher-king technocratic right to nudge the indigent and/or ignorant into directions and towards actions deemed to be in their best interest, if only they knew or were able to commit appropriately.[179]

Buiter continues,

Before getting to the nitty-gritty of how to allocate, distribute, ration or price water, I will dispose of a couple of pervasive fallacies and non-sequiturs: Fallacy 1: Water is essential for life: therefore it should come free. We disagree. Water is indeed essential for life. That is why it should be priced or physically rationed to reflect its scarcity value. After all, food is essential for life—should food be free? Opportunity cost—the value of the last pint of water you use for purpose A in its best alternative use—should guide the allocation and distribution of water... (and) Fallacy 2: Water comes free from God: therefore it should come free. We disagree. And the rebuttal is independent of whether one believes in any kind of Deity. After all, diamonds come free from God. Should diamonds therefore come free to everyone who wants them? Scarcity and opportunity cost are the drivers of fair and efficient allocation and distribution.[180]

This is one economist's analysis, in one investment publication—but it is a representative argument, and very much in opposition to those who see present-day disputes over water as a major cause of instability and war, fear the financialization of water as a dangerous force against individual and community health, define water as a public trust, and argue that a basic allocation of water is an essential human right. We must understand that the commoditization of water is well advanced. Investors are already attempting to control water as an asset class through ownership of all aspects of management and distribution. This is a dangerous and one that must be protected against lest this most essential public resource be captured and diverted to exclusive, private gain.

This may be the single most important debate of our time.

Freshwater Trade

A key function of the ocean is as a conduit for international trade in commodities and goods. We are all aware of the transformation of forest products into paper and packaging, minerals into automobiles, oil into plastic and all the products derived therefrom. We are all aware of the bulk freighters, container ships, car carriers, and oil tankers that ply our oceans in every direction in the complicated network of worldwide exchange that is the essence of the global economy. Now that function is being applied to the most valuable commodity of all: fresh water.

According to company press releases, S2C Global Systems (now the VIPR Corp.) has acquired a 50 percent interest in a license to export up 3 billion gallons of fresh water per year from Blue Lake in Sitka, Alaska, to buyers in Asia, the Middle East, and India. The potential value of these sales is estimated at $90 million per annum. A pipeline from the lake and a deep-water loading facility are already in place.[181]

Recently, S2C Global Systems/VIPR Corp. announced the expectation of distribution of this bulk water in India through a "world water hub" that will include a berth for a Suezmax vessel capable of holding 41 million US gallons, a dedicated tank farm, and a distribution complex for packaged water. The company predicted additional sales and distribution through trans-shipment in smaller vessels to such out-ports as Umm Qasr in Iraq. While the company did not announce the hub location "for security reasons," it is rumored to be near Mumbai on India's west coast.[182]

The Sitka Economic Development Corporation has also indicated additional interest in bulk water sales in queries by the American Water Company and Aqueous International, a subsidiary of holding company based in Luxembourg.[183] Elsewhere in

Alaska, on Adak Island in the Aleutian chain, applications have been filed for 1.5 million gallons per day to be sold from three reservoirs with substantial excess capacity.[184]

There are multiple ironies and contradictions in all this, of course. The physical transfer of Alaska's surplus to India's growing need is an expensive proposition, especially if new ships and onshore facilities need to be constructed to expand the transaction to profitable scale. Water demand in the lower 48 states is at an all-time high, exacerbated by drought, profligate use, and exhausted local supplies. California is a significant example, with many municipalities imposing water rationing and over half a million acres of agricultural lands lying fallow due to inadequate irrigation. The Governor has indicated a need of a 20 percent reduction in consumption to meet statewide needs for the future without substantial increase in supply from some other source. The distance from Sitka to mid-California is about one-sixth the distance to Mumbai.

These are just a few new examples of the growing monetization of fresh water as the most valuable commodity on Earth. Comparable circumstances in Australia, the Middle East, and elsewhere have brought the freshwater crisis to the fore worldwide and we will certainly see more such entrepreneurial endeavors as demand grows and conservation efforts do not keep pace. What to do? Turn off your faucets, collect rainwater for your lawns and gardens, and consider every drop of fresh water you consume as if it is liquid gold.

Virtual Water

As we continue to work toward a fuller understanding of the presence of water in all aspects of our lives, we begin to look deeper into the hydraulic systems beyond the obvious—the ocean, the glaciers, the mountain ranges, streams, lakes, rivers, and wetlands—to the place where water lies hidden, unrecognized for its significance to our health, our diet, and our way of life. Of course, we know that we need—or at least the UN has established that we need—a minimum of 40 liters of fresh water per day to sustain our bodies, ingested by drinking to support physiological systems, hygiene, and the other mechanics of living successfully. We know our bodies are approximately 65 percent composed of water, evident in our blood, our organs, our muscles, our respiration, our digestion, and even our tears. We know these things, but we don't always know their true value, until we become dehydrated, deprived of sustaining water, and these systems begin to slow down and fail.

What we may not know so well is what is called "virtual water," the water that lies "behind" things, that is used to produce almost everything we incorporate into our daily routines but is not listed on the label or calculated into the price.

The most obvious example is foodstuffs we consume, the amount of water that is used in production cycles to irrigate, wash, clean, and process the products on the supermarket shelves. UNESCO estimates that it takes, for example, 2,500 liters of fresh water to produce a hamburger, 1,000 liters for a liter of milk, 75 liters for a glass of beer, and 70 liters for that apple a day. A kilogram of beef requires some 15,000 liters, "considering an animal of 3 years, for 200 kilogram of resultant meat, 1,300 kilograms for the grain and 7,200 kilograms required for feed, as well as some 24,000 liters for drink."[185] A kilo of pork takes 4,800 liters, of chicken 3,700 liters, of citrus fruits 2,000 liters, of bread 1,500 liters. A kilo of coffee requires 21,000 liters, a single cup of black coffee, 150 liters.

Virtual water calculation can be applied to so many other things we use. For example, a kilo of cotton requires 19,000 liters of water to produce, a fact that translates into 8,200 liters for a pair of jeans. Multiply that by all the cotton in all the clothes we wear, and you have a virtual cascade. And then there's energy required for the processing of foodstuffs and clothes and all the rest. According to The Energy Collective, all the increase in US energy production in 2010–11 can be allocated to the 27,000 shale gas wells drilled and hydraulically fracked, each requiring some 5 million gallons of water, amounting to some 135 billion gallons of water consumed and removed as result of contamination from the aquifer, the water-shed, and availability for additional use.[186] The number is astronom-ical, and that's for just one year, in one nation, for one product in the energy mix. Then add the water required for plastic, packaging, chemical production, fertilizer, irrigation, manufacturing, and all the other processes in our consumption-driven economy and life-style, and the number grows beyond comprehension.

There are so many examples and statistics you can drown in them. Here is one last: Think of all the water lost when food is left on the plate, wasted, or processed foods extend beyond the use date and are discarded. We lose not just the water, but also the associated nutrition, the energy consumed to produce, the trans-portation cost of shipping from here to there, the uncompensated labor, and the deficit subtracted from the global economy forever.

We are a planet crying out for water, and we don't seem to hear the call. That's not virtual; that's real. We are what we drink, and without water, we are nothing.

Non-Revenue Water

To move forward, however, we need to understand and incorporate water in *all* its value forms. There is, for example, what is referred to by hydraulic engineers as "non-revenue water," that is what has been produced by collection but cannot be valued because of the utility lost to leakage and other forms of waste.

If you think about your own water usage, you can begin to understand what I mean. Whether or not you draw your water from a well or a municipal systems, picture in your mind how that water flows through your home, what it provides, and where might be the places or behaviors where the value of that water is lost. Showers, toilet flushes, food preparation, car washes, lawn and garden irrigation—these represent the major functions of water in the home. For how long do you or your children shower? How many times a day do you flush the toilets? Do you leave the water on when you brush your teeth or wash your dishes? These are all typical points where each of us loses the value of water down the drain, rarely recycled, mostly wasted.

If you take this one phenomenon, and add to it the theft of water or inaccurate metering, or free use for fire-fighting and other such unpaid-for civic necessities, it totals (as estimated by the Danish Hydraulic Institute) more than US$14 billion lost by water users, managers, and utilities each year due to non-revenue water.[187]

To understand this water loss, the Hydraulic Institute conducts comprehensive water audits, identifying and analyzing the various stages along the distribution chain. The process examines water supplies, owned and imported, to calculate total system input. Against this is measured water supplied and exported, consumption authorized and unauthorized, billed and unbilled consumption, apparent and real losses to construct a balance sheet that reveals revenue water minus non-revenue water showing either surplus or deficit derived from the existing system.

These analyses can reveal weaknesses and inefficiencies along the way, and can reveal strategies for repair, modification, and increased economies to make the system better. Localized pressure tests and flow meters can point to very specific, reparable problems, reduce leaks and blow-outs, and reduce maintenance costs and failure rates, diverting funds to upgrades and replacements. Similar tests can discover areas of deteriorated pipe, broken connections, mal-functioning valves and pumps, and failed or tampered meters. In its entirety, the water audit gives a real-time picture of a system that may have been constructed decades previous, sporadically maintained or improved, and in need of a major overhaul or modernization. Finally, this information can provide the data required to make management and financial decisions, accurately predict and allocate budgets over time, and provide a schematic for capital improvement, investment in new technologies, a model for a better systems with far greater efficiency and return, and dramatically reduced waste of the most valuable commodity on Earth—all this, from a reasonable evaluation of usage in the home or along the path of distribution.

Beyond scale, what, then, is the difference between water consumption patterns in the Nile Basin and what we might do at home? Indeed, what we do domestically is a key locus where a change in behavior results in shift in the data set, representing both baseline information but also measure of resultant improvements. If you take the larger view then, what you do each day with your water is part of an enormous hydraulic reality by which precious water moves through a global natural, financial, and political system of distribution and redistribution, through cycles and conveyors and upwellings and anthropogenic interventions that too often corrupt or poison the water consumed. Removing any water from that system, even a single drop, denigrates it and denies it for the future.

If we can understand the peculiarities of our plumbing and habits at home, then we can fix them. The same holds true for a municipal water system. And the same holds true for a watershed.

And the same holds true for the ocean, the greatest water system on Earth. Understanding the problem allows us to invent its solution. If we can understand how our patterns of water use and profligate waste are connected, perhaps now we can look to solutions evident and possible through planning with water.

But What If We Don't?

The truth is that unlimited consumption, pollution, outdated treatment and distribution systems, and diversion from direct human need to the exponential demands of industrial agriculture are evident in most cities and nations where population growth has created an ever-increasing demand. When you examine these specifics, you find that *water management* has been ever problematic, taken for granted, an essential resource otherwise left unconserved and unprotected against any change in use, demand, or circumstance.

Let's take a look at the city of São Paulo, the largest and richest metropolis in Brazil, some 20 million inhabitants located in a country of glaciers, mountains, the Amazon River watershed, other river systems, and a collection of large dams designed to exploit to the maximum what seemed to be inexhaustible water— Brazil, "the Saudi Arabia of water," as repeatedly described in press and financial reports.[188]

But, in a February 2015 article in the *New York Times*, São Paulo is described as "a dystopian situation" where the city water pressure is critically diminished, taps are beginning to run dry, rationing is predicted, basic sanitation and hygiene are threatened, and water anarchy may be the outcome when the available supply is finally exhausted.[189]

How can this have come to pass? First, the vast amount of

water available has grown a pre-emptive culture of unlimited consumption and expectation. So much water has nurtured a pattern of indiscriminate use and social and political indifference. The economy of the city, indeed the nation, is based on an assumption of unlimited supply. The waste of "non-revenue" water, leaked, stolen, wasted, or otherwise not used or paid for as a result of rusted pipes, pumps, and valves, and long-deferred system maintenance or equipment replacement over time, became catastrophic—some *30 percent* of the São Paulo water supply was estimated to be lost to such mismanagement—one-third discarded, useless and without compensating return![190]

As city grew to megacity, from slums to industrial areas to commercial towers to suburban homes, the luxury of water was a given. But that same expansion and growth has had its concomitant, contradictory side effects in the form of vast volumes of water required for manufacturing, polluted, deposited in the local rivers, and removed from the water cycle, thereafter unavailable for human use. To meet the demand of growing population and need for urban space, wetlands were filled, surrounding areas were cleared and constructed, and reservoirs were left inadequate to store the increase volume required. Deforestation of the rain forest changed the local microclimate of the region, increasing runoff, erosion, and rainfall patterns. More importantly, the more extreme changes in global warming and weather patterns, rising temperatures, and storms resulted in the larger effect of reduced mountain melt, induced drought, increased the demand for irrigation, and otherwise rapidly constricted the water capacity of the nation and undermined the economy on which the nation depends.

The city of São Paulo is now faced with drastic water-rationing, perhaps supplied just two days per week, the need to truck water from sources away, the threat of a resultant black market for water, compromised sanitation and possible resultant spread of disease, regional competition between water haves and water have-nots, financial decline, increased unemployment, and even the cancellation of Carnival celebrations and related tourism. Add to this slow but steady degradation the sudden impact of extreme drought, and a city, and a nation, long thought to have inexhaustible water, finds itself faced with water rationing, expensive transfer by tanker or truck to meet the emergency need, inevitable social unrest, even anarchy, and a demand for accountability for the failure of an essential system to meet an essential need. The disruption of the predictable supply of water on the basis of daily need is a certain prelude to social and political unrest.

The politicians and managers, for whatever reason, postponed or ignored the problem, and one assumes will be held somehow accountable. But that is not good enough. This crisis, long in the making, will also be long in its solution. It will require time, immediate action, leadership, community engagement, and major investment of public funds. And São Paulo is not the only city in Brazil, in South America, North America, Europe, or Asia where similar conditions exist, an incipient crisis evident as a predictable result of climate change, lack of foresight, indifferent management, irresponsible policy, failed investment in alternative systems and behaviors, and political cowardice. San Francisco, California, and Bangkok, Thailand, have announced comparable crises resulting from many of the same circumstances. And there will be many more still to come.

To remedy the situation, every element of its cause and effect must be re-examined. Let me give you another illustrative, more positive example—the city Olomouc, on the Morava River, capital of Moravia in the east of the Czech Republic. While dramatically smaller than São Paulo, with a regional population of some

500,000, the city nonetheless evinces a comparable catalogue of critical symptoms: an old and outmoded water network, growing population, area expansion, urban renewal and reconstruction, public demand and expectation of service, and impact of the consequence of climate change, in localized but inevitable effect, on past weather patterns, industry and agriculture, and social behavior. What to do?

To its credit, the municipal government commissioned the Danish Hydraulic Institute to do a complete analysis of the city's overall water system and management plan including its current demand and future needs. The new plan would integrate and redevelop regional collection and distribution, connect elements such as the sewer network, storm water drainage, and watershed culverts and creeks, and provide a process for design and cost estimation of recommendations derived.[191]

Commissioned in 2012, the consultants produced a plan through the year 2030 by first mapping the regional drainage area (some 63 km of streams and channels), the 310 km drainage system, and 328 km water supply network; second, creating computer analyses and models to evaluate and simulate present and future conditions; and third, making recommendations for a reconstruction plan that prioritized the necessity of repairs and assessing the technical and financial aspects of future developments.

DHI describes the scope of work as follows: evaluation of network conditions; solving existing variations in water supply pressure; examining combined sewer overflows and interrelation with flow protection measures; identification of flood risk zones; integration of infrastructure improvements in city investment plan; calibration of sewer and water supply models; analyzing and updating existing sewer and water supply systems; and setting guidelines and conditions for new municipal construction. In effect, using the most sophisticated mapping, data management, and modeling software, the consultants could provide a single comprehensive visualization of integrated existing conditions, indicate weakness and priority for repair and maintenance, model impact of changing future conditions, suggest resultant infrastructure improvements, and estimate costs for municipal investment over a 20-year period. Suddenly, unlike São Paulo, Olomouc had a plan. The challenge, of course, will be to apply it, finance it, and adapt it to the inevitable changing conditions the future will bring. The politics and the costs will be real and difficult, no doubt, but the plan at least provides a structure for a significant governmental response to the need of the community to manage its most important socioeconomic resource.

Olomouc sits as a small inland city on a river somewhere in between the mountains and the sea. These habitations are both reality and symbol of the water connections and cycles on which we have and must depend. This water sustains the agriculture, industry, health, and myriad other social benefits of each place along the way, from upstream to downstream to the ocean and back again. The water provides, the watershed distributes, the ocean collects and circulates, and the cycle turns like history, like fate, like the circle of civilization.

So let's give a cheer to the good fathers of Olomouc! And let's send our prayers to the good people of São Paulo who have not been so well served by their good fathers. And let's understand the difference between complacency and foresight, between indifference and engagement, between denial and acceptance, between avoidance and active participation in the building of our future around water.

California Dreamed

California dreamin'. Many of us have grown up with the promise of California, that place out West where the other coast meets up against the rest of the world, that has grown from a frontier opportunity and golden dream to a magical place that feeds our bodies with fruits and vegetables in fulsome variety and amount, and supplies our minds with new ideas from conservative to progressive, new laws that slowly find their way east, and new ideals for what is ideal, healthy, and good.

But today California, like many other places on this Earth, faces a fundamental challenge to its existence, its economy, its lifestyle, and its sense of place and self. What is different? It's the water.

Or the absence thereof. Here are five *New York Times* headlines from the past few weeks: "California Drought Is Worsened by Global Warming, Scientists say."[192] "California Imposes First Mandatory Water Restrictions to Deal with Drought."[193] "In California, Spigots Start Draining Pockets."[194] "Mighty Rio Grande Now a Trickle Under Siege."[195] "For Drinking Water in Drought, California Looks Warily to Sea."[196] The articles describe a sudden, painfully evident phenomenon that strikes at the heart of the financial, political, and social well-being of the state, a sociogeographic unit that exceeds the area and economies of many nations and makes an enormous contribution in production, taxes, and innovation to the rest of the United States and the world. California, truly, is too big to fail. And fail it might if it cannot come to terms with the demand for and supply of most nurturing water.

It was that water, of course, that built California and opened the West. Yes, there was western expansion, the lure of found gold, free land, benign weather, and infinite opportunity. The California dream, once begun, has never really ceased its powerful attraction, to the first settlers, to Chinese laborers, to Dust Bowl refugees, to agricultural innovators, to migrant workers, to manufacturing giants, to dot.com and Silicon Valley innovators. The psyche extends from Baja to Puget Sound, as Portland and Seattle expand on the concept even as they object to those California license plates they see now headed north. Where do our children look for a future? Again and again, I hear of the best and the brightest abandoning the declining urban infrastructure of the Atlantic cities for the lure of a future out West that still appears golden.

That success was built on water—on the diversion of the great western rivers, large engineering projects, the dams and canals that brought water from the mountain ranges to turn the desert green, nurture the trees and plants and vines, and send that resultant bounty worldwide. California politics revolved around water rights and management. California markets epitomized the possibility that the increasing population and food demands of the US could be met, and then some through export of output and experience. As long as the water, like the center, was able to hold.

California is looking now to conservation, restriction, rationing, pricing, and sourcing a new, heretofore unnecessary, too expensive supply from desalination of the ocean. No water now will be exempt from a true value calculation and real cost, and the resultant distress will be palpable in California and other western states in the US, just as it has been in South America, the Middle East, and in Africa where water has been at the center of civilization for all time.

This cannot and will not be a quiet, evolutionary fix. As we continue to argue here, the solution lies in an entirely new value proposition, built around the rightful use and distribution of water, that will change our behavior, realign our strategic investment, re-allocate our assets, and change how we govern ourselves worldwide. There is promise here—perhaps a new California dream—but only if we listen, accept responsibility for the future, and talk action.

Resource Planning

I sit on the Planning Commission of my small town in Maine where we have no ordinances or zoning, and we do not plan. It is an ideologically driven mind-set that argues that government has no role to play in governance. What we do primarily is to get ourselves in trouble, by applying situational, ineffective solutions to the complaints of neighbor against neighbor that would in any other community be covered by some community-accepted master plan and reasonable regulation and enforcement.

This behavior is analogous to many situations we find along watersheds and river systems, the coastal zone, and the ocean beyond national jurisdiction. In a stunning investigative series entitled "The Outlaw Ocean" by Ian Urbina in the *New York Times*, the dark side of activities in the deep sea were described in four stories of indifference to any international restrictions on irresponsible commercial fishing, of piracy, slavery, and murder. Urbina and the *New York Times* are to be congratulated for the courage to pursue these harsh, very real abuses and to give ample space for their publication and distribution. Those of us who live and work ashore may suspect these things, but to see them revealed in their stark reality wherein responsibility and respect for human life are without any import or regard is an awakening to an immediate need for some kind of useful and humane order.[197]

Management of marine resources remains our primary tool to counter the myriad challenges presented by the ocean today: the depletion of fisheries, pollution of coastal zones, conflicting uses within the coastal zones, demands for exploitation of deep-sea resources for energy, mining, and pharmacological purposes. Add to that the impact of climate change—sea level rise, extreme weather, acidification, and much more—and the ocean environment demands a critical management response to mitigate, adapt, and invent revolutionary strategies to sustain its resources in space and in time.

Management strategies have been primarily local and hard earned. Coastal conservation efforts, marine protected areas, networks of marine protected areas, regional management schemes, and, most recently, experiments in "marine spatial planning" have served as a an evolutionary, opportunistic response. But, clearly, these have not been enough.

In her 2010 publication, *Ocean Zoning – Making Marine Management More Effective*, Dr. Tundi Agardy, Executive Director of Sound Seas, Director of the MARES Program at Forest Trends, and Science and Policy Director of the World Ocean Observatory, argues clearly and cogently for a radical management shift: ocean zoning as an up-scaled, enhanced, and integrated system that "overcomes the shortcomings of small-scale protected areas; recognizes the relative ecological importance and environmental vulnerability of differing areas; allows harmonization of with terrestrial land-use and coastal planning; better articulates private sector roles, responsibilities, and market opportunities; minimizes conflict between incompatible uses; and moves us away from fragmented sectorial efforts towards integrated and effective ecosystem-based management that fully includes all uses of, and impacts on, the oceans."[198]

Dr. Agardy goes on to assert that zoning is simple, straightforward, systematic, and strategic and that it clarifies rights and creates shared management responsibilities. The parceling

of the ocean into areas according to their human-use values
is radical and certainly difficult in the face of vested interests,
conventional thinking, and local, regional, national, and international politics, but it provides "a framework that can evolve
out of existing use patterns and cooperative agreements toward
meeting the larger goals of biodiversity conservation, conservation of rare and threatened species, maintenance of natural
ecosystem functioning at a regional scale, and management of
fisheries, recreation, education, and research in a more coordinated and complimentary fashion. The integrated approach
inherent in zoning is a natural response to a complex set of
ecological processes and environmental problems and is an efficient way to allocate scarce time and resources to combating the
issues that parties deem to be most critical."

Ocean zoning is, no doubt, as controversial as frequently
as it has been on land, but there are serious benefits to be
earned through economies of scale, pro-rated costs, reconcili-
ation of competing interests, and more effective conservation.
Many encouraging experiments are already underway: at the
Great Barrier Reef Marine Park in Australia, in Barbuda in the
Caribbean, in New Zealand, the United Kingdom, Italy and the
Mediterranean Sea, along the coasts of Europe, the northeast
Atlantic, and Africa, and in the small island nations of the Pacific.
The need is there, and there are indeed encouraging signs. But we
must adopt such radical tools if we are to truly meet the insistent
freshwater and ocean management challenges, to reverse degradation, and to improve full ecosystem health. We must put all such
tools to use, realizing of course that they are only as good as those
who wield them.

NATURE'S TRUST

On Law We Build

We are overwhelmed by the daily litany of environmental disaster. We see the pictures and hear the voices of places and people whose lives have been tragically affected by the global compulsion to grow, not just to meet the needs of ever-increasing population but also to feed a system driven by unrestrained consumption of goods and services derived from the excessive and unsustainable extraction of natural resources. Knowing full well the inevitable collapse of such a society, we nevertheless carry on, indifferent to the destruction around us, the alternative possibilities, and the exponential risk to the lives of our children. We face a global despondency that finds form in a poisoned landscape, poverty, political disaffection, and social unrest. Some live well at the expense of many who live miserably; income disparity grows; vested interests corrupt the political process to near paralysis; the world, even from the most privileged perspective, looks nervous, angry, volatile, delimited, lost.

We ask ourselves, "What can we do?"—and we can do some things for ourselves, for others, for the local community, even for causes we believe can make some contribution toward far greater change and improvement. But these efforts often seem insubstantial, inefficient, disconnected from the larger need to manage our way from the evident failure of past systems and ideas to the very different, limited world of the future that cannot survive without a new paradigm around which to organize a successful, civilized response to the needs of a new age. As I have argued before, we need a plan and we need a principled strategy to base it on.

I have proposed the ocean and global water cycles as that paradigm—as a galvanizing strategy with a compelling logic and application that will release us from the addiction to fossil fuels and associated system of compromise and destruction, and connect us to new values and behaviors that will guide us as we enter the turbulent unknowns of the 21st century.

Pass over for now the objections, attacks, and clamoring justifications of those who will lose purchase and benefit in this new world. That part will be vociferous and dangerous; we know its defensiveness and aggression already. But think for this moment on just what it is we want in that stead, and how we can achieve it in a democratic society based on the rule of law. Is it a hydraulic society as proposed here? Or is it another idea, a better idea that meets the mandate for change and viability as a system beyond? Whichever, we need a new idea and system of law that will enable an alternative to collapse or chaos.

As an advocate for the ocean and the global water cycle as that idea, I have been unable to establish the principle and precedent on which such a system of law might be based—until now, with the discovery of a fresh and astonishing contribution to the discussion by Mary Christina Wood, Professor of Environmental Law at the University of Oregon, in her book, *Nature's Trust: Environmental Law for a New Ecological Age*, published in 2014 by Cambridge University Press.[199] Permit me this metaphor: In designing the gateway to this future, the components of an imagined arch may be in place as elements of content, standards of performance and behavior, the most useful technologies, the financial assets in place, and the workers straining to build an edifice like never before. But without the keystone, the architecture will fail. I see as all the blocks in place save one—the one that will provide the incontrovertible internal vector of support to enable the construction to stand and endure over the challenging circumstances of time.

Professor Wood asks two fundamental questions about environmental law: "First, does the field of law work to keep society in compliance with Nature's own laws? Second, can it be effective in confronting the ecologic challenges now coming at us at horrifying speed?"[200] Her answer to both is a resounding yes, based on—and here is where I found the breakthrough surprise—principles established as far back as Roman law, rooted again in English common law, incorporated in the US Constitution and the writings of its authors, manifest in the governing documents of other nations, upheld often in landmark decisions by the judiciary in those nations, and providing a system of principle and precedent on which environmental legislation and the mission of governmental environment agencies were predicated in the 1970s when the need for conservation and regulation became evident and the conservation ethic, its definition, practice, and implementation, evolved. The keystone principle is known as *the public trust doctrine*, a civic and judicial understanding that asserts that natural resources such as waters, wildlife, air remain common property belonging to the people as a whole. The doctrine "rests on a civic and judicial understanding that some natural resources remain so vital to the public welfare and human survival that they should not fall exclusively to private property ownership and control. Under the public trust doctrine, natural resources such as waters, wildlife, and presumably air, remain common property belonging to the people as a whole. Such assets take the form of a perpetual trust for future generations." Is not such a doctrine exactly the legal foundation we need? And there it lies, to hand.

For the Common Good

In fact, this public trust doctrine was the foundation for the many innovative legislative actions in the 1970s that, through the Clean Air and Clean Water Acts, the Endangered Species Act, and other such laws, led to the creation of the Environmental Protection Agency, other government agencies, and various regulatory programs and bureaucratic systems wherein conservation was central to the mandated mission and established as a progressive response to a need recognized from the emerging detrimental consequences of consumption-driven, unregulated industry and agricultural on which the postwar system of "growth" and "value" were based. We enjoyed the benefits of such enterprise for certain, but then realized that there were unforeseen, damaging results that needed the controlling hand of government.

What followed on the surface seemed generally a good thing, with certain changes and protections enacted that suggested that environmental protection was secure and appropriate to the challenge. But, as Professor Wood argues, there followed almost immediately a succession of compromises—small, incremental changes that allowed for the rules to be bent, standards diminished, certain activities disqualified from the most stringent oversight and enforcement. Lobbyists, campaign contributions, vested interest in short-term reward, and the cynical rotation of industry and governmental political appointees worked with insidious effect. Woods cites again and again myriad examples of innumerable licenses and permits that from the outset were exceptions to the law, not a right guaranteed by it, now evolved and aggregated into a seemingly impenetrable web of validated destructive bureaucratic compromise that *de facto* from the beginning diluted and eroded the principles and protections, and enabled the vested extractors and exploiters to consume and harvest, make and discard the natural elements of healthy land, air, and water, the sustainable resources that the original legislation was meant to protect. Given the state of nature we find ourselves in today—the condition of the air we breathe, the water we drink, and the exhausted land around us—one might argue that the entire regulatory effort of the past decades, despite the occasional management success and judicial affirmation to the contrary, has only delayed the inevitable, indeed has been a devastating failure. That is very hard to accept, but it may be cruelly true. What would the American landscape look like if we had no legislation at all? Would it be habitable today? And why would we not take every possible step to defend against it happening again? Is there law on which such defense may depend?

Professor Wood cites many legal decisions, precedents, and arguments. Three will serve us there. In the first, *Illinois Central Railroad v. Illinois*, a case involving a length of the Lake Michigan shoreline to a private railroad, the Supreme Court stated "the decisions are numerous which declare that such property is held by the state, by virtue of its sovereignty, in trust for the public. The ownership of the navigable waters of the harbor, and the lands under them, is subject of public concern of the people of the state."[201] Second, in *Geer v. Connecticut*, the Court stated "the trust is for the benefit of the people, and not…for the benefit of private individuals as distinguished from the public good."[202] And third, in *Alabama v. Texas*, Supreme Court Justice William O. Douglas wrote, "the marginal sea is not an oil well; it is more than a mass of water; it is a protective belt for the entire Nation over which the United States must exercise exclusive and paramount authority. The authority can no more be abdicated than any of the other great powers of the Federal Government. It is to be exercised for the benefit of the whole..."[203]

We are not lawyers here, but the point to be made is that there is an historic and durable foundation in law for the responsibility of government to assure the conservation and sustainability of submerged waters, rivers and watersheds, and the species nurtured within—in effect, the entire system of Nature—as a public trust protected against destruction and waste, private exploitation and gain, depletion, and the diminished health and livelihood of human communities from one generation to the next.

If this is so, cannot the law be used to restore, rebuild, and revalue Nature's enduring sustenance for our continuing, successful habitation of our planetary home?

As a Public Right

As we consider how we will be able to change our behavior and somehow recoup the loss to our environment on land and sea, we come down to a basic conflict over ownership and control of our natural resources. Do these elements and systems belong to the public or do they belong to the private interests that historically have been licensed and permitted to use them? Are they public property or private property? Do the corporate entities that have privatized access, extraction, processing, and distribution of those resources have an obligation to sustain them for the ongoing benefit of the public, or can they use them to exhaustion, keeping most of the profits for themselves and their limited shareholders? Does the public have the right to establish standards for utility, define sustainable methodology, demand accountability and compensation for indifference, irresponsibility, and accident? Can the pricing of such activity actually be democratic and inclusive of all costs in a highly competitive capitalist corporate society? If there must be change, if the consequences have become so dire, how do we confront the vested determination, the systematic entropy, the judicial compromise and political capture of the systems for change? How do we do this? And how do we do this in time?

Again and again, the argument comes down to ownership and control of natural resources as private property, to the role of government to uphold the fundamental principles, interests, and protections of the governed, to the paralysis resulting from such ideological conflict, determination, and inflexibility, and to the ability of the public to rectify a condition that has become manifestly evident, illogical, and detrimental to the collective interest, and even suicidal, given the critical exhaustion and inequality that we know ourselves and see around us.

It is as simple, and as dreadfully complicated, as that.

The evidence becomes clear in the rapidly growing disparity between rich and poor, north and south, developed and emerging nations. On the one hand, we see enormous wealth concentrated in closed control by totalitarian states, oligarchs, and corporations, individual fortunes capable of enormous political influence, corrupt financial schemes and practice, and the most luxurious quality of life for a few; while, on the other, we see increasing global poverty, declining health and education, economic disruption, physical dislocation, political disenfranchisement, and the most egregiously failed quality of life for so many.

What does it say about us as individuals, communities, and nations that we would allow such tyranny to stand? If water is both the symbol and reality of this predicament, does that mean that we will keep whatever remains for ourselves, fight over it even to the death, deprive others of it even if it means thousands more will die by its lack and our indifference? Is that how we want to live? And if or when the collapse of our water system affects us in such a way, is that how we want ourselves, or our children, or our communities to die?

This condition cannot, will not, must not stand. The public trust doctrine asserts that natural resources are ours to own and to control, and that we have therein the legal foundation by which to take them back and change how they are used for the benefit of all mankind.[204] We have argued that their value and distribution is a basic human right. We have thereby a strategy grounded in law, a fundamental principle and tool for natural resource sustainability that we have allowed to be eroded by multiple exceptions to the rule. The corporate permit holders and licensees, and the governmental agencies we created to regulate and control them, have failed us, and we have lost the knowledge of our rights, even as we have lost the value of those resources to unsustainable, irresponsible consumption.

In *Nature's Trust* and the public trust doctrine, Professor Wood provides us a strategy by which to take back those rights: "First, it provides tangible legal principles to guide local decision makers in environmental management and sustainable resource use. The fiduciary standards of protection, no waste, and maximization of societal value...can offer beacons of duty for recognized decision making. Second, trust principles provide legal levers by which local communities may assert ecological rights against federal and state environmental agencies... Finally, third, Nature's Trust provides a framework by which local trustees can assess and quantify their global obligations to planetary assets..."[205]

We have three courses from which to choose: (1) we can do nothing, and accept the consequences; (2) we can engage, as so many are today, in resistance to protect for ourselves what is left behind; or (3) we can resolve to use the legitimate tools of law, civil engagement and disobedience, and the force of invention to combat and to change what appears presently destined to destroy us.

We have turned to Nature for support and healing and improvement of our lot since the beginning of time. Why would we not trust Nature now?

Civic Action

When we find a failure of governance or the regulatory systems, we have always as recourse taking the issue to court to apply the legal tools of law. We know that judicial principle and precedent can be a basis for an argument intended to redress wrong and restore justice. If you accept that the principles on which American environmental law was based in the 1970s have been compromised and excepted subsequently to dilute protections, regulations, and enforcement to an unacceptable circumstance, then we have but one tactic to fall back on: lawsuits to force the issue, reassert the principles, and reverse the destructive trend. And that is exactly what citizens in Europe, the United States, and elsewhere have chosen to do.

In the Netherlands, some 990 Dutch citizens have filed suit against their government for "failing to effectively cut greenhouse gas emissions and curb climate change." According to the website Climate Progress, "The plaintiffs will ask the court to force the Dutch government to reduce its greenhouse gas emissions by between 25 and 40 percent relative to their 1990 levels by 2020—reductions that the Intergovernmental Panel on Climate Change (IPCC) has said developed nations must make if the world wants a 50 percent chance of avoiding a 2 degree Celsius increase in global temperature. Currently, the European Union has committed to reducing its emissions 40 percent by 2030, but the Netherlands has not made any specific commitments, saying instead that it intends to adopt any international agreement that comes from the Paris climate talks later this year."[206]

The class action was supported by the Urgenda Foundation, a Dutch organization devoted to sustainability and climate advocacy. The Netherlands is certainly vulnerable to extreme weather and sea level rise; indeed have been leaders for centuries in the design and construction of dikes and coastal barriers and other engineering systems to protect the 2 percent of the national land mass that is below or at sea level. The urgency of the changing circumstance has not been lost on the Dutch government, and various new schemes to innovate and protect against further inundation have been put forward. But the plaintiffs argue that that same government has been not aggressive enough in addressing the root problem, requiring much stricter emission controls and faster shift to alternative and renewable energy generation. The judicial proceedings will take place over the coming months, and Urgenda is mobilizing publicity and support from citizens in Holland and throughout the European Union.

A similar, extraordinary movement has been quietly underway in the United States led by the Oregon-based nonprofit Our Children's Trust (OCT) devoted to "a game-changing, youth-driven, global climate recovery campaign, securing the legal right to a healthy atmosphere and stable climate" through legal action, youth engagement, and public education and film.[207] The organization, along with five individual teenagers, and two other nonprofit organizations representing thousands more, partnered to bring a federal suit to the US Supreme Court designed "to require the federal government to immediately plan for national climate recovery according to the scientific prescription of Dr. James Hansen and other leading international climate scientists that will restore our atmosphere to 350 parts per million (ppm) of CO_2 by the end of the century and avoid the disastrous scenarios of 2°C of warming. This lawsuit relied upon the long-established legal principle of the public trust doctrine, which requires our government to protect and maintain survival resources for future generations."[208]

On December 8, 2014, the Court declined to hear the case, and Our Children's Trust responded as follows:

> *Our Children's Trust has been building new federal cases on behalf of youth to secure science-based climate recovery policy nationally, and will return to the Supreme Court if necessary. We will expand our efforts to enforce individual states' responsibilities to preserve the atmosphere for the benefit of future generations, and we will advance select global and local efforts to do the same. Piecemeal legislative and executive actions not based on nature's laws will simply never get us where we need to be. We need judicial declarations that government must act systemically to stabilize our climate.*[209]

OCT is pursuing legal remedies in state courts with some successes. Cases are pending in New Mexico, Oregon, Massachusetts, Colorado, Washington, and North Carolina, with courts in Alaska, Texas, Arizona, Kansas, Montana, and Pennsylvania issuing developmental decisions along the way on which the pending suits are based. In addition, Our Children's Trust has sought administrative rule-making decisions in various agencies in all 50 states as another means to make the argument and compel consideration of the legal principle.

OCT asserts: "Specifically, these court decisions have rejected many legal defenses raised by our opponents, including non-justiciability, standing, separation of powers and sovereign immunity. In support of our youths' positions, and in face of argument to

the contrary, the courts have validated critical climate science
and reserved for the courts the exclusive right to determine
whether a particular commons resource is protected by the Public
Trust Doctrine for benefit of present and future generations, and
whether there has been a breach of that trust."[210]

We need a children's crusade based on the public trust
doctrine to take back our future with Nature. With this work, in
the US and abroad, the crusade has already begun.

A Danger of Dams

What we may not need, however, is our traditional reliance
on massive engineering projects to solve all our problems.
One of the greatest expressions of such hubris has been the
construction of ever-larger dams to transform the energy of
free-flowing rivers into massive reservoirs of water for controlled
release and hydro-generated energy. In the United States, and
in Egypt, India and China, enormous dams in remote places
have become symbols of national pride and emerging economy
designed to bring energy to distant cities and growing urban
populations and industrial enterprise.

The construction of these dams required equally enormous
investment of capital and labor, financed, supervised, and
subsequently managed primarily by central governments or
their specially designated authorities. In 1957, the historian Karl
Wittvogel published *Oriental Despotism*,[211] a survey of the reliance
of ancient society on the control of water, examples again in the
Middle East, India, and China, of similar engineering projects
where dams, reservoirs, canals, and distribution systems facilitated
the growth and sustenance of a sustainable societies on a scale
far greater and more successful as a result of abundant water and

its provenance. Such projects could only be managed by a power great enough to command the financial resources and the slave labor required to build such cities, many of which, like Angkor Wat in Cambodia, collapsed to be subsequently consumed by the encroaching jungle leaving only archaeological remnants behind to remind of such historical feats, indeed perhaps to mask the lessons learned. To construct modern dams requires an equally authoritative regime—either by legislative decree or dictatorial fiat. The Aswan Dam in Egypt, the engineered river linkage projects in India, and the Three Gorges Dam and north–south canal water transport systems in China are all examples of a similar pattern—central government, unlimited finance, cheap labor, and no fear of opposition or consequence of the environmental damage, social dislocation, and cultural destruction that followed.

Nepal, the Himalayan nation and impoverished economy, was devastated by a major earthquake in April 2015 that left many thousands dead, many more thousands unrecovered, and the country bereft of resources to respond or to restore what was their simple modicum of life. The quake measured 7.9 magnitude, destroyed homes 100 miles away, caused avalanches, destroyed bridges, and blocked roads, bringing the country and humanitarian response to a standstill.

Isabel Hilton in an excellent report for *The New Yorker* magazine reveals a chilling sidebar to the larger earthquake story, the rescue by helicopter of 280 Chinese workers from the construction site of the Rasuwagadhi hydropower dam on the Tishuli River, some 86 miles from Kathmandu, the Nepalese capital that suffered major damage. The 350 Nepali workers were left to fend for themselves. According to the Three Gorges Corporation, the construction company owned by the Chinese government, the dam was "severely damaged."[212]

"The Rasuwaghadi dam," reports Ms. Hilton, "is one of

three contracts won in the area by the Three Gorges Corporation, and one of thirteen planned along this stretch of the river. The company, which has been repeatedly implicated in corruption in China, has also won the contract to build the controversial seven-hundred-and-fifty megawatt West Seti dam, which, at US$1.6 billion, will be Nepal's biggest-ever foreign investment."[213]

What does it mean that the Rasuwaghadi was "severely damaged"? What would be the catastrophic downstream destruction if an aftershock or larger quake caused the dam to collapse? Here is the most disturbing paragraph in Ms. Hilton's report:

"Geologists argue that the risks of building dams in earthquake zones go well beyond an earthquake-induced collapse... But the most fiercely debated risk, since the 7.9-magnitude Sichuan earthquake in 2008, which killed seventy thousand people and left nearly twenty thousand missing, is that of 'reservoir-induced seismicity'—the theory that the weight of water behind a dam, coupled with the seeping of water into the fissures in rocks below, can produce shearing stress strong enough to worsen, or trigger an earthquake."[214] What I think this suggests is that the first tremor can create further tremor within the water reserve and the underlying geology so as to amplify the quake into reverberation increasing the probability of collapse.

Yes, Nepal needs this energy for its own security, development, and financial stability. But what is being wrought here? These mega-projects—and there are many more of them—are fed mostly by glacial melt, a phenomenon put in question by the already evident effect of global warming on the glacier as source. Thus, these dams may be over-engineered for a future inadequate supply or under-engineered for the risk of an earthquake zone.

The danger here is the failure to understand that water is power, physical and political, with inherent force not always acquiescent to our ambitions and prideful dreams. We attempt to control it, to master it at our peril.

Can There Be a New Conversation?

World governments are conducting a new conversation regarding the inherent tension between the elimination of most trade constraints advocated by corporations, investors, and some economists, and environmental protections advocated by environmentalists and labor who point to the already adverse impact of such unregulated exchange as evinced by actions taken by the World Trade Organization and the North American Free Trade Agreement (NAFTA).

The conflict has risen again in the proposed Trans Pacific Partnership under negotiation and consideration by 12 countries from Asia and the Americas and pertaining to complex and complicated attempts to manage a global economy that now includes the growing, successful trade-based economies of Pacific nations. The debate is intense and further confused by the lack of information available to the public and even to many of the elected officials who must vote to accept conditions of which they are not fully aware. The deliberate secrecy may have its justifications, but not in a society that prides itself on transparency and open discussion of the issues. Deliberations have been going on for eight years, and still we know virtually nothing about the specific terms and possible impacts.

Enter Edward Snowden and Wikileaks that in 2014 published the draft chapter on environmental issues, many of which directly affect the ocean. In January 2015 an analysis of the draft chapter was published in *The New York Law Journal* by Stephen L. Kass of the New York firm Carter Ledyard & Milburn that provides interesting insights into the prospective terms of the proposed agreement.[215]

Past such agreements hardly referred to environmental issues at all, and the consequence is the basis for much of the current opposition. The TPP environmental chapter has subsections on fisheries protection, endangered species, climate change, corporate conduct, conflict resolution, and enforcement. It addresses compliance with prior multilateral environmental agreements such as the Convention on International Trade in Endangered Species, the Convention on Marine Pollution, the Ramsar Convention on Wetlands, the International Whaling Convention, the Convention of Antarctic Marine Living Resources, and several more.

Environmental groups' reaction to these terms is mixed. Many, including the Natural Resource Defense Council, the Sierra Club, and the World Wildlife Federations, have actively objected that the new agreement dilutes the required standards and enforcement obligations of these prior commitments by allowing individual nations options to dilute, ignore, or fail to enforce—in other words, to weaken environmental protections already established.

Further, according to Kass's analysis, "alleged violations of TPP environmental commitments are subject to a lengthy three-stage consultation process...virtually guaranteed to require several years of negotiations which, if successful, lead to arbitration before a specially constituted arbitral panel whose only power, at the end of that undoubtedly length additional proceeding, is to issue a report determining whether the alleged violation has occurred and, if so, to require the disputing parties to 'endeavor to agree'...on a mutually satisfactory action."[216]

If you follow that, you will have followed a long and inconclusive quasi-judicial process that takes you right back to where the disagreement started.

With regard to illegal, unreported, and unregulated fishing, Kass points out that while the language includes numerous and welcome commitments to protection of wild fish stocks, marine mammals, and ocean pollution, the document "suffers from the ineffective enforcement provisions," as well as weak language on certain practices—shark-finning, for example—trade in threatened and endangered species, and fishing subsidies that create known unfair practices that contribute to overfishing and declining stocks.

Regarding climate change, the language seems even weaker, allowing actions to "reflect domestic circumstances and capabilities," which Kass concludes in the US "means no foreseeable federal legislation." There is recognition of an option to reduce dependence on fossil fuel subsidies that encourage wasteful consumption, but that too is delimited by existing dependence and policies that fail to curtail consumption demand and correlative government policy and corporate profit. Given the exceptions, conventional behaviors, and voluntary commitment, it seems as if climate action comes down to "sharing information and experiences."[217]

Kass makes one key observation regarding US involvement and leadership leverage in this debate: our lack of political creditability and standing as a result of our failure to ratify other earlier relevant treaties, from the Kyoto Protocol on climate to the UN Convention on the Law of the Sea—failures that do not provide moral or actual leadership by which to hold others to account.

That water, ocean, and climate issues are included in this proposed international agreement is to be of course welcomed. But not as "blue wash," language that means nothing when it comes to international behaviors in the ocean left unchanged because we could not mean what we say, or say what we mean. We have had enough "double-speak" and hypocrisy, enough political collusion and failed governance. Meaningless agreements, unfulfilled

commitments, and unfunded pledges have characterized the
conversation for decades. We must now have innovation, fresh
perspective, and young voices in the mix if we are to have a new
conversation and a real path to change.

WHAT NEXT?

The Old Economics

We know the ocean as a natural system. We know too that
beneath that surface lies the challenge of governance; like
the land, the ocean too is a political system, equally complex
and vital. But, ultimately, is not the ocean an economic system as
well, a place of infinite value that can be parsed and understood
for its invaluable contribution in goods and services toward
global sustainability and survival? Let's assume here that the
superimposition of these three systems creates an even larger social
system that is the true scape of change and betterment for our
future. Let's postulate this equation: Nature + Politics + Economics
= Social Vitality and Viability in a growing, evolving world.

In her provocative new book, *This Changes Everything,* journalist Naomi Klein introduces her argument with the words of
science fiction author Kim Stanley Robinson with this quote:
"...I've imagined people salting the Gulf Stream, damming the
glaciers sliding off the Greenland Ice Cap, pumping ocean water
into the dry basins of the Sahara and Asia to create salt seas,
pumping melted ice from Antarctica north to provide fresh water,

genetically engineering bacteria to sequester more carbon in the roots of trees, raising Florida 30 feet to get it back above water, and (hardest of all) comprehensively changing capitalism."[218]

Klein's book is a well-researched, challenging, compelling analysis of the climate situation, the interests resistant to change, the extraction industry, and the fallout—physical, financial, and psychological—that has so paralyzed a coherent global response. Why? she asks. "I think the answer is far more simple than many have led us to believe: we have not done the things that are necessary to lower emissions because those things fundamentally conflict with deregulated capitalism, the reigning ideology for the entire period we have been struggling to find a way out of this crisis. We are stuck because the actions that would give us the best chance of averting catastrophe—and would benefit the vast majority—are extremely threatening to an elite minority that has a stranglehold over our economy, our political process, and most of our major media outlets."[219]

So, there it is, nasty old capitalism, resultant irresponsible behavior, the tyranny of short-term gain, profit now, and the indifference to the consequence in any place or generational time. Toward the end of her book, Klein points to "the moral imperative of economic alternatives." She lists any number of projects that suggest different values and approaches; she points to specific hopeful populist movements; she foresees a critical moment when "suddenly, everyone" will understand the need for revolutionary action. How will we react? She concludes: "Because these moments when the impossible seems suddenly possible are excruciatingly rare and precious... The next time one arises, it must be harnessed not only to denounce the world as it is, and build fleeting pockets of liberating space. It must be the catalyst to actually build the world that will keep us all safe. The stakes are simply too high, and the time too short, to settle for anything less."[220]

So, what is next? What is the possibility of a post-capitalism economic model that might evolve to support the new values and behaviors in a new era of alternative technology, political action, and finance? Enter The Next System Project, an initiative to explore "new political-economic possibilities for the 21st century," created by the Democracy Collaborative, an institute based at the University of Maryland, with the goal to change the prevailing paradigm of economic development—and of the economy as a whole—toward a new emphasis and system based on:

- Broadening ownership and stewardship over capital
- Democracy in the workplace
- Stabilizing community and emphasizing locality
- Equitable and inclusive growth
- Environmental, social, and institutional sustainability

The project is directed by Gar Alperovitz, James Gustav Speth, and Joe Guinan, who are recognized for their work in environmental history and economics and their engagement in addressing our future needs across the full systemic spectrum. "...we believe," they declare, "by defining issues systemically, we can begin to move the political conversation beyond the current limits with the aim of catalyzing a substantive debate about the need for a radically different system and how we might go about its construction... There are real alternatives. Arising from the unforgiving logic of dead ends, the steadily building array of promising new proposals and alternative institutions and experiments, together with an exploration of ideas and new activism, offer a powerful basis for hope."[221]

The ocean cries out for "the next system." We must move to

the new paradigm with urgency, in time to oppose and reverse the forces that are rapidly affecting the global water cycle in the so many ways we have discussed here before. What are the alternative economic approaches? How will they work?

The New Economics

If unregulated capitalism has failed us in the context of sustainability of natural resources and community health, are there other financial systems that might enable us to reformulate value and reward new behavior with more employment, responsible return, equity and justice? The Next System Project was initiated to answer that question by identifying alternatives, fostering conversation, evaluating fresh ideas, and proposing hybrid or new solutions. According to their first project report, "A political economy is a system, and today's system is NOT to meet basic needs but to prioritize the generation of corporate profits, the growth of Gross National Product, and the projection of national power."[222]

From my perspective here coastwise, we live with the benefits and the deleterious consequence of that fact every day. But what can we do about it? To use an ocean metaphor, we are each just one fish somewhere on the food chain, alone in a vast environment over which we have no control. Who are we to make a difference? How do our actions contradict corporate power where even shareholders cannot force management to divest, adopt sustainability practices, uphold environmental and safety standards, tell the truth. How can we influence something as formidable as Gross National Product? How can we counter military incursions and financial impositions on countries without our economic or military resources, but nonetheless vastly rich in the natural resources that we require to continue and expand our higher standard of living? How do we delimit such projections of power, the resultant social devastation and consequence, when we don't have the facts or a government representative of our collective will, or leaders who will stand for transparency and justice even when it threatens their re-election? "Our goal is not to answer all the questions," states the Next System Project report, "...we seek to define sufficiently clear options...so that we can radically expand the boundaries of political debate in the United States and help give greater clarity of long term direction to activists, researchers, practitioners—and to millions of others, young and old, who are increasingly angered by the immorality and insecurity of the existing system and want to somehow realize America's long unfulfilled promise of freedom and democracy."[223]

The number of alternative theories and structures is surprisingly large. Here is a partial list as enumerated by the report: Worker Ownership and Self-Management; Localism, a small-scale, decentralized, ecologically oriented sector of entrepreneurial individuals, small businesses, and households; Reinvigorated Social Democracy, a continuation of some capitalist endeavor tempered by strengthened regulation, industrial policy, full employment, and national economic planning; Beyond Growth Ecological Economies, a decoupling of well-being from natural resource consumption toward prioritization of resource efficiency, renewable energy, consumption taxes, and changed to the historical market economy; Socialism and Reclaimed Public Ownership; African American Cooperative and Related Strategies, an inclusion in systemic change in such issues of discrimination, policing, racial violence, and mass incarceration; Community-Based System-Changing Ownership Solutions, a pluralistic society focused on municipal enterprise and local community ownership and democratic governance; and more.

Clearly there is much theoretical work to be done. But what might be tangible outcomes? I was drawn to the embodiment of the Next System plan to be made manifest in fully articulated models of how one city, one state, one region, and one nation might be reorganized today on the basis of these new ideas, institutions, strategies, and principles. The national model is devoutly to be wished: a portrait of a nation reorganized "over time to achieve genuine democracy and economic equality, ecological sustainability, a peaceful global foreign policy, and a thorough-going culture of cooperative community based on non-violence and respect for differences of race, gender, and sexual preference."[224]

Now wouldn't that be a world for our children to live in? Is it so idealistic as to be impossible? I think not, in that this kind of creative thinking represents known and unknown strategies by which to invent our way out of a dilemma. And, as we have often discussed, there are many examples of individuals, groups, companies, communities, regions, and states that have found ways to apply these ideals in spite of the contradiction around them. Suddenly, you hear the phrase "bottom up" everywhere, a reflection of this growing populist reorganization of ideas and power that most relate to local well-being and success and defy the existing "top-down" paralysis.

But here's a problem: it can't all be just about systems. There needs to be substance, a real organizing principle around which all these systems in whole or in part can combine and recombine to make palpable, measurable, successful, sustainable change in government, institutional, community, and individual behavior.

What is that substance? Need you ask?

WATERMARKS

Inventory and Measurement

As we continue to consider the prospect for global water resources—indeed for the water cycle by which that water is distributed through the ocean, atmosphere, and watersheds—we need first to make a major adjustment to how we measure the water we use, how we value it, and how we allocate it and to whom for what purpose.

That is a huge undertaking given the fact that we have fundamentally taken water for granted and used it, while certainly knowing its essential need, with little restriction. Recently, I was visiting a friend at his new small farm in the high desert region of Oregon, purchased as a retreat from his urban center in a beautiful, distinctive microclimate both wet and dry and bordered by picturesque mountain views. There were flat fields with large watering systems everywhere. At one point, he turned on pumps and began to let water collected in a pond and drawn from wells on his 40 acres to flow without purpose into the adjacent river. As a member of a local Irrigation Association of other similar properties in the area, he was allocated a certain volume annually to use—or lose. This water was being deliberately wasted, not to irrigate crops or to be sold to others, in the midst of a drought that had brought California agriculture to the south to crisis and was moving north where rainfall and other water sources were beginning to show comparable declines with implication for similar results. All agreed this behavior was absurd, and all realized that the historical attitudes and structures for water management in this locale were obsolete and inadequate to the changing circumstance. This problem exists worldwide, suddenly now in places where water supply has seemed secure, but long extant in places distant and poor and dry where the inhabitants have been living on marginal water for centuries.

What is required is a complete overhaul of water inventory and use measurement in a new green economy. In 2012, the United Nations Environment Program (UNEP) issued an invaluable Report by a Sustainable Water Management Working Group that addressed the need and opportunities for change to water concepts and frameworks, data collection and access, and methodologies for quantifying water use and environmental impacts through such tools as water registers, accounting, scarcity indicators, use assessments, corporate monitoring, and stewardship techniques.[225]

The Report describes the present situation of a world economy based on a global ecosystem reliant on unrestricted natural capital to provide material inputs for production, then consumption, leaving the system to absorb the waste outputs and continue with no consideration of sustainable supply, growing demand, pollution, or enhanced efficiency or conservation as part of the process. The Report then envisions "a green economy" incorporating natural capital and ecosystem services, sustained and resilient, with a more efficient economy of manufactures and financial capital, and human well-being, social and human capital, with enhanced social equity and fair distribution of use and burden. What follows, despite the jargon of such reports, is a very new and very sensible way of understanding water as a "service"—water cycling as a supportive service, water flow control, purification, and waste treatment as a regulating service, and water for plants, fish, and organisms grown in or around the ecosystem as a provisioning service—all measured, monetized, and distributed within a very different set of social considerations and resultant actions.

The Report contains some existing, effective examples of

present-day best practice. For measuring water use, it cites the
Jordan Water Information System, a body of data that depicts
water use patterns, reveals physical water flows, provides analyses of indirect water consumption and collateral demand, and
suggests ways to integrate and economize on national supply
and future needs. A second example focuses on Singapore, a city
of 4.4 million, that despite ample rainfall and aquifers has been
challenged by the consumption requirements of both its growing
population and its emergence as a major global manufacturing
economy. The key to its success has been made possible by a Public
Utilities Board that currently manages the entire water cycle of
Singapore—to include sewerage, protection and expansion of
water sources, storm-water management, desalination, demand
management, pricing, community-driven programs, catchment
management, and public education and outreach, leading to
wastewater treatment and reuse on an unprecedented scale.
The board also administers electricity and gas, applying similar
systems and values.

This integrated holistic approach is devoutly to be wished,
not always necessarily as a mammoth centralized system, but
certainly as an attitude and approach that pervades water and
ocean management at every level of government planning,
management, and implementation. What is required is a willingness and commitment by individuals, institutions, corporations,
and administrative agencies to define a "watermark," a design
impressed into our very being that will guide us as citizens to
the balance of water use—how much, for what, at what cost, for
whom—that is essential for our future.

Water Accounting

The UNEP Report recommends ways forward that require new tools for measurement and management, such as *water registers* to document actual conditions within a place and understand how allocation can work fairly and adequately in a time of scarcity. *Water accounting* will be required by which managers can prioritize register information. Existing management structure, typically discontinuous and localized, may need integration and reorganization. *Scarcity indicators* will need to be established to forewarn managers for planning and future delivery. Demand must be analyzed by sectors and cycles, understanding who needs more water when, seasonally for example. Beyond agriculture, every industry from manufacturing to commerce to tourism will expect stable and consistent supply that in times of extreme and changing weather—storms, floods, and droughts—must be implemented by policy, planning, and engineering adequate to the condition. A system for regulation, conflict resolution, and pollution control must be defined, affirmed, and enforced. Environmental impacts of commercial water extraction and trade must be considered in the context of local requirement, appropriate compensation, and effective sustainability practice to protect the resource from unlimited demand and exhaustion.

Such management cannot be seen as a tyranny, but rather as a means to add value to every aspect of the water cycle. Homeowner conservation patterns; fair rates and new management efficiencies; corporate analysis of cost-effective change; value criteria that enhance investors' estimate of company value, translating physical economy into reputational value; and creating resultant water plans that pertain to product manufacture. All these requirements, according to the report, involve input from interests representing "environment, agriculture, industry/economic policy, energy, trade, foreign policy and development cooperation."

If this seems like an enormous change, well it is, and it isn't. In fact, many of these approaches and initiatives exist today in isolation and disconnection. Water management structures may exist in adjacent places, river basins, and neighboring states, sometimes in conflict, sometimes in cooperation. The over-arching reality of water scarcity may find a *de facto* consensus inevitable, and thus integration and continuity management may find its absolute inevitable rationale. In many places, watershed planning is already in place forcing retrofit and future development to conform to these new standards. Some areas, California in the US for example, have been forced to deal with the sudden undeniable condition of drought that has revealed their allocation systems to be completely unprepared. Some agricultural users have understood their dependence on water-intensive fertilizers and pesticides, fodder and feed, and the value of alternatives to reduce the inevitable cost implication of increased water pricing on the profit and loss of their business. Some nations have taken dramatic steps in system change—Australia, for example—where meters have been installed to monitor irrigation use, allocations have been modified to meet entitlement needs seasonally and annually in response to weather conditions, caps have been placed on individual or regional water use, and a system for water "trading" has been created to allow a user to consume more only if a matching user to consume an equal amount less is found. A viable water "market" has emerged, standardized contracts have been created, and trades executed driven by the age-old rule of supply and demand.

These signs indicate that change in water use, management, and value, voluntary or by necessity, may not be so impossible after all. This change is coming, like it or not.

Water Footprint

The new water paradigm should begin not at the top of the user pyramid, but at the bottom, with a better calculation of our own water footprint, a measure of the amount used to produce each of the goods and services we use, directly and indirectly, including "virtual" water and externalities. There is an excellent online tool to help us understand this process—the Water Footprint Network, founded in the Netherlands by Professor Arjen Hoekstra, and intended to assist individuals, companies, municipalities, and governments with water assessments, to design stewardship plans, and to offer training for new methodologies and project implementation under this new aqua-centric approach.[226]

The Network assesses three types of water as follows:

Green water footprint *is water from precipitation that is stored in the root zone of soil and evaporated, transpired or incorporated by plants. It is particularly relevant for agricultural, horticultural and forestry products.*

Blue water footprint *is water that has been sourced from surface or groundwater resources and is either evaporated, incorporated into a product or taken from one body of water and returned to another, or returned at a different time. Irrigated agriculture, industry and domestic water use can each have a blue water footprint.*

Grey water footprint *is the amount of fresh water required to assimilate pollutants to meet specific water quality standards. The grey water footprint considers point-source pollution discharged to a freshwater resource directly through a pipe or indirectly through runoff or leaching from the soil, impervious surfaces, or other diffuse source.*

Each of these requires an evaluation and strategy particular to use, place, and time, for an individual, a business, a product, or a nation using a standard that, according to the Network website, "has been applied and tested worldwide across many sectors and includes detailed instruction and guidance on the following:

- *How to calculate the green, blue and grey water footprint to understand the geographic and temporal allocation of water resources for industry, agriculture and domestic water supply*

- *How to conduct a water footprint sustainability assessment which includes criteria for understanding the environmental sustainability, resource efficiency and social equity of water use, for both consumption and pollution*

- *How to use the results of the water footprint accounting and sustainability assessment to identify and prioritize the most strategic actions to be taken in local, regional, national and global scales, individually and collectively.*

The Network provides an extensive data site, called *WaterStat*, a comprehensive collection of research and statistics about international, national, scarcity, pollution, and product water footprints against which to compare baselines and set objectives.[227] The website also makes available a free online assessment application that allows the user to complete both a *geographic assessment* to explore the water footprint of a river basin, its sustainability, and ways to reduce consumption; or a *production assessment* to quantify and map operational and supply-chain water footprints of a specific facility or product, to maintain sustainability, and to identify ways to reduce use going forward.[228]

I admit it is facile to suggest such a radical change to how

we interact with all elements of the water cycle without understanding the who, what, where, and how such actions are implemented down to the lowest level of use or production. But there
is a vast community of water scholars and hydraulic engineers
available for such research, planning, design, and organization,
that must be reprogrammed and reassigned to this new way of
measuring and assuring the value of water as an organizing principle of a new society.

Why not try it for yourself? Go to Waterfootprint.org and
use the personal water footprint calculator. I just did, and my
footprint was estimated at 772 cubic meters of water a year as
follows: Food 654 (57 cereal, 335 meat, 7 vegetables, 18 fruit, 108
dairy, and 130 others), Industry 16, and Domestic 102, a total of
772 cubic meters! Image the volume if you can. The terrifying
thing is that the global assessment using the same criteria is
1,243 cubic meters—471 more! I am a water-miser. What can I
do to lower my footprint further? Eat less meat and dairy, more
vegetables and fruit; make sure every member of my household
is equally water conscious; and spread the word about changing
our "watermark"—not just as a response to dry or drought, not
just for a healthy me or family, not just for the here and now, but
for everyone, everywhere, for a healthy planet.

So what is the real cost of all that water that is typically
under-valued by the under valuation of water in general and by
the resultant negligible price factored into the accounting of what
is purchased as raw material, transformed, and sold?

The Water Footprint Network has conducted studies of
specific manufacturing operations in an attempt by some corporations to understand the true environmental impact of production. Volkswagen provides an astonishing case study wherein it
began to analyze the freshwater consumption of three specific

car models—Polo, Golf, and Passat—along with their product life cycles on both inventory and impact assessment levels.

Here, quoted from the Water Footprint Network website, is a description of the scope of the inquiry, from a 2012 UNEP report entitled, *Measuring Water Use in a Green Economy*:

> *In order to obtain a regionalized water inventory, which is a prerequisite for a meaningful impact assessment, the total water consumption is allocated to different car material groups as a first step. The water consumption in these groups is then assigned top-down to the corresponding countries on the basis of import mixes, location of suppliers, production sites, etc. Based on this, country- and watershed-specific characterization factors are calculated and selected impact assessment methods for water consumption are applied to estimate the environmental consequences. In this water footprint study only freshwater consumption was considered. It is complemented by additional impact categories like eutrophication, acidification, human- and eco-toxicity.*

> *At the inventory level, the water consumption along the life cycles of the three cars was: for all three cars, more than 90 per cent of the water was consumed in the production phase. Water consumption takes place in 43 countries, with less than 10 per cent of the total consumed directly at the production site in Wolfsburg, Germany, mainly from painting and evaporation of cooling water. More than 70 per cent of the total relates to steel and iron materials and polymers and 20 per cent to special metals (gold, silver, and platinum group metals). The study shows that impact assessment results can lead to different conclusions from purely volumetric water footprints. However, water use and consumption figures are not complete*

in current databases and regionalization of inventory data,
which is a necessary and inevitable step... We therefore recom-
mend improving the quality of water data and establishing
spatially differentiated water flows...[229]

I could not find the actual number of gallons of fresh water required to produce the Passat you may drive, or the additional water that it takes to maintain your car with parts and service, to operate it over so many thousands of miles, or even to discard or recycle it at the end of a lifetime of use.

But let's think of it this way:

Every vehicle consumes 90 percent of its water use in its production. Parts manufacture and assembly takes place in over 40 countries, in each case dependent on the water supply available then and there and thereafter wasted or unavailable for alternative use such as hygiene or agriculture. In your mind, if you begin with the idea of a few gallons of water to support the production of one small part, and then incorporate that part, and that water, into the total flow of a single assembly, and then add that assembly to other assemblies similarly water-dependent, and then integrate all those pieces—transportation, chassis, engine, systems, tires, lubricants, and fuels—into a fully aggregated volume of water flow, what began as an insignificant amount has now grown into a tsunami of water required to put just one Passat on the road. Now multiply by models and years and brands and numbers of cars owned, and you might drown in the sea of water captured by just one aspect of our global system of manufacture and consumption.

Now consider this: if climate and irresponsible water use and management further delimit the amount available for all uses just in the critical climate and under-supply we know today, what will the inevitable change in water valuation and consequent increase in price mean for the cost of a Volkswagen or anything else on earth? It will be simply unaffordable. Just as for years we have been living the delusion of endless fossil fuel, we are now living in an even more devastating delusion of endless water. What has been seemingly a dream is becoming a nightmare, and we have no alternative but to wake up, face reality, and change assumptions and behavior along the full systemic extent of the water cycle.

To solve the freshwater problem that is now evident around the globe, we must first understand how much water is actually available, how much we use, to what purpose, using what system, in what condition, and with what realistic capacity given rapid climate change and its visible and continuing catastrophic effect.

The answer is complicated and can only be found in the understanding of "watermarks," measures of use at every level of supply and demand—for the individual, for separated uses or uses not heretofore integrated or included in the general calculation, for corporate manufacture and processing, and for the externalities of virtual water as hidden in almost every product that affects our lives.

Even if these disparate elements are recognized, measured, and integrated into a larger discussion, the problem still cannot be solved without addressing the larger national policy question and a revolutionary new governance approach that, taken together with complementary international policies, adds up to a global solution.

The Water Footprint Network describes the situation as follows:

> ...Traditionally, countries formulate national water plans by evaluating how best to satisfy water users. Although countries consider options both to reduce water demand and to increase supply, they generally do not include the global dimension of water management. They therefore seldom consider

explicitly options to save water by importing water-intensive products. In addition, by focusing on domestic water use, most governments are unaware of the sustainability of national consumption. Many countries have significantly externalized their water footprint without determining whether imported products are the cause of water depletion or pollution in the producing countries. Governments can and should engage with consumers and businesses to work towards sustainable consumer products. National water footprint accounting should be a standard component of national water statistics, supporting the formulation of national water and river basin plans that are coherent with national policies on, for example, the environment, agriculture, industry, energy, trade, foreign affairs and international cooperation. Water footprint and virtual water trade accounts are a relevant input into various governmental policy areas, such as national, state, river-basin or local water policy; environment; agriculture; industry/economic policy; energy; trade; foreign policy and development cooperation...[230]

To assist this effort, the Network suggests a new international classification system for water-related ecosystem services based on "provisioning, regulating, and maintaining," with subcategories to include *nutrition*: terrestrial and animal foodstuffs, freshwater plant and animal foodstuffs, marine plant and animal foodstuffs, potable water, biotic and abiotic materials and energy sources; *regulation of waste*: bioremediation, dilution and sequestration; *air, water and mass flow regulation*: atmospheric, physical environment, and water quality regulation, pedogenesis and soil quality regulation; *lifecycle maintenance and habitat protection*: pest and disease control, gene pool protection, cultural, aesthetic, heritage, and spiritual consideration, and recreational and community activities, information, and knowledge.

And these are just the elements to be analyzed on land! Each and every one of these requires a new assessment of the failed status quo, with consequent invention, engineering, and implementation, with myriad consequent decisions and actions, and each and every one of these constitutes a changed impact on the particular challenge, in the particular place, felt thereafter along entire regional water collections area and watershed, and ultimately reaching the ocean. This is not an easy process, without many difficult questions and no easy answers, but when, as today, cities like São Paulo, San Francisco, and Bangkok are exhausting their drinking water supply, when the reservoirs and rivers run shallow or dry, when the water-dependent crops cannot grow, when we can no longer stay clean or healthy, then this problem will find its urgent, irrefutable logic and we will change the "watermarks" we know today dramatically and forever.

VII. The Once and Future Ocean

THE NEW PARADIGM

Imagining a Way Past Dire, Dour, Despair, Done

"Water remains a chaos until a creative story interprets its seeming equivocation as being the quivering ambiguity of life."[231] This aphorism by Ivan Illich suggests the purpose of what I am proposing to do here: to provide "a creative story" to equate the once, an equivocal situation in the reality of the accelerating corruption and decline of the Earth's resources as a result of our intervention and disruption of the processes of Nature, with the *future*, our unambiguous survival through the change required to present a new system of value and behavior that will enable life to come.

The prognosis is dire and dour. So much more could be included to demonstrate the crisis we face. The research is demonstrable and compelling. The disasters are palpable and continuous. The damage is visible destruction of our physical world, our health, our livelihood, and our community. There is no dearth of well-intended studies, articles, and books that document the facts. There are efforts at every level of society to adapt or mitigate to these conditions; there are attempts at invention, small steps taken locally, regionally, nationally, and internationally, hopefully designed and advanced toward evolutionary policies and decisions. All of these progressive endeavors are good, but are they good enough? Does it not seem that for every advance there is a devolutionary decline? And are not many of our challenges, the acidification of the ocean as just one example, fixed in their enduring consequence even if we could reverse all negative input today?

We approach solutions the best way we know how. We engineer, we calculate, we demonstrate; we score small, certain, hopeful victories. We isolate each problem on the assumption that, once well understood, we can invent a set of isolated corrections, improvements, and solutions. Sometimes these work, and we are hopeful. Other times we realize the depressing extent of the problem and our helplessness in the face of faceless forces that seemingly mock our commitments and pitiful actions. We are paralyzed with despair. Are we done?

Some withdraw, and lead self-contained lives in denial. Some flee, in search of any life better than the one they have. As the human species cannot live successfully without the contributions of Nature, the destruction of the air, land, and sea leads demonstratively to decline, retreat, and social entropy. We begin to think more and more exclusively of ourselves; we care less and less about others; and we see the way forward as a dour inevitability. The disparities accelerate and we defend our perimeters, our conventions, and our contributions to what can be arguably portrayed as *collapse*—of individual determination, collective will, and social integration. The science fiction writers have explored the extrapolation of this physical and mental condition to dystopian limits, and the speculation is not pretty.

Perhaps we are just too aware—a function of the constant illustration of deteriorating systems by news feed and photo, by post and tweet, to a level of psycho-cacophony that overwhelms our senses and exhausts our mental function, a collective and corrosive pessimism generated by knowing too much about everything. Such a position is pointless and absurd. What is required, as a contradictory force, is an *idea*—a *new* idea.

I do not believe that we can act going forward based on past premises and behaviors. It seems clear that the most formative strategy of the late 20th century—the worldwide extraction and conversion of fossil fuels for energy to drive an unrestrained capitalist society—has proven now bankrupt and left a fundamental ecological deficit—a real debt to Nature—along with an inequitable social structure, and a psychological fear of change or challenge to the vested interests and status quo. The organizational principles and extreme realization of their consequence have left us socially isolated and intellectually bewildered. What seemed unlimited prosperity and growth has peaked, and without fundamental, even revolutionary change, we are without a place to turn, without a galvanizing force for the renaissance of civilization.

In a contrarian spirit of optimism and renewal, I submit that the place to turn is the ocean, as defined herein as an integrated global system of natural, economic, political, social, and spiritual manifestation that begins at the mountaintop and descends to the abyssal plain and circulates in dynamic cycles internally and externally across and around the world, connecting us all. The goal of that oceanic turning is what I call *the new hydraulic society*. To survive and thrive, then, we need a radical shift and transformation—earth renewed, energy sustained, air rendered clean and clear, and water in adequate amount, carefully stewarded, equitably distributed, and valued as the most necessary element for the sustenance of every aspect of human life. The ocean pertains directly to all this, and will make a primary, novel, regenerative contribution to each and every one, an aggregated process of change that will result in an entirely new context for successful, sustainable, and peaceful living. The ocean is the vast, focusing prism through which to envision the creative story of a passage from dark equivocation to the quivering ambiguity of life. It is the new paradigm.

Earth, Fire, Air, and Water

Like a medieval philosopher then, we begin with the four elements and examine each in a 21st-century context of modern science and technology, of policy and governance, of institutional management, community organization, and individual practice.

EARTH. The planet is challenged to a point where, while still fecund, it has become delimited by the demands of population growth, settlement, and the consequences of agricultural and manufacturing industrialization. The corporation, so paradoxically defined by the US Supreme Court as a "person" with all the accordant rights, has come to dominate in physical and financial scale, disenfranchising the rest, commandeering the economic distribution and return, and otherwise abandoning most responsibility for its detritus, its measurable waste and resultant human effect. The condition of the earth deteriorates before our very eyes in the reality today of dying fields, dying rivers, and dying cities. The deteriorating conditions, both rural and urban, become shocking to our satisfied selves, suddenly comparable to scenes from the third world societies that have never achieved our standards of living. Drought becomes more than an occasional threat. The dry forests burn spontaneously; the reservoirs decline; the crops wither; the associated businesses morph into empty storefronts and main streets. We see how quickly our traditional patterns of water use can generate such outcomes. We begin to see, feel, and understand the finality of land without water.

How does the ocean affect all this? Every child in school is taught the basic concept of the water cycle and the role of the ocean as the penultimate reservoir of 97 percent of the water on Earth. We are taught the circle of evaporation, atmospheric collection, distribution, and deposit on land as snow and rain that then spreads across the watershed to determine where to farm, fish, and live. If you follow the path of civilization over time, you will follow the water where ancient cities formed along the Tigris and Euphrates and along the rivers of Africa, South America, and Europe, water that transformed desert into fertile growth, now stifled by the cycle stressed and interrupted. There was a reserve discovered in the aquifers, but now too we are pumping them dry.

Nature in all its myriad forms, shapes, and sizes cannot exist without water. Earth as its habitat cannot endure without water to provide its basic life support. The ocean determines the governing factors of volume, temperature, and circulation that are the dynamic parts of a planetary biological system of fertilization and growth without which habitat is corrupted, modern cities too will certainly die, and we will pass with an ephemeral exhale of mist, just gone.

If we do to the ocean what we have done to the land, we are beyond hope. The evidence builds. Radiation from the Fukushima tsunami inundation of three Japanese coastal nuclear plants has spread in a morbid plume far into the Pacific. The toxins from manufacturing by-products can be found in the flesh of creatures in the Galàpagos Islands, brought there by the very same ocean currents that brought the exceptional concentration of nutrients that sustained the extraordinary animal life found there. The incalculable amounts of plastic discarded into the ocean, ground or dissolved into micro-particles, now finds its way into the marine food chain to work its way up to our dinner tables. The presence of oil spilled and leaked from the thousands of offshore wells remains in the water column, alongshore, and in the reproductive organs of marine species well after the so-called cleanup is over and the penalties are absorbed as rounding on the energy company balance sheets.

This cannot continue. Thus, the first steps to protect and possibly restore the land is to do no further damage to the ocean, to mitigate damage done, to regulate and terminate all license and activity that contains any such risk, and to assert the reality of the ocean as a global commons that must be sustained by every nation-state, every individual, without exception. The vapid, extenuated process of the global conversation must be accelerated at the United Nations and in the individual legislatures worldwide regardless of short-term impacts. The losses typically cited as inhibitions to such meaningful dialogue and actions are nothing compared to the losses, once thought to be long-term, suddenly prevalent now. The calculus is obvious. On our reaction, the earth depends.

FIRE. Literally, land in Australia and the United States burns, and those attempting to control the wildfires and protect property are faced with water shortages as a result of the drought-reduced reservoirs and streams. They search for supply far and wide, water to be diverted from other uses and users. They dance for rain. They are turning to the ocean to fill the tankers to bring that water to combat the flames.

But fire is also energy, energy that has been sourced primarily from land-based fossil fuels that may well have reached not the peak, but the bottom of supply provided by technology-induced processes to eke out the last barrel of oil or gas from fracking, a process fraught with now evident, serious, and unacceptable environmental consequence for the land.

We return to the ocean. Not by drilling in the Artic or in ever-more irrational places like Africa and Cuba. That desperate corporate behavior only exacerbates the dangers and extends the problem into areas that have not yet been affected by what the rest of the world has known. No, we return to the ocean as a massive energy machine that through wind, wave, and tide can provide alternative output that is less environmentally destructive and can supplement and eventually meet energy demands on land, redefined and repriced realistically, and subsidized at a level equal to the mostly invisible subsidies, loopholes, and exemptions that have characterized government support of the oil industry historically.

Wind has already proven its viability, in Denmark and Germany in particular. Other countries follow. In the US, a few prescient companies have attempted to initiate ocean wind to scale, but they have been met with tremendous opposition by legislators influenced by corporate lobbyists, political contributions, and by neighbors who fear their ocean views will be sullied. There are small-scale experiments with tidal energy, a long-lived small tidal project in Nova Scotia, Canada, and the testing of various tide-driven energy generators in the US and Europe. Wave energy has followed a comparable slow track, with various machines designed and tested but no project of real scale in place. Often, these new technologies are stymied by financial analyses that cannot provide estimated investment return adequate to override the oil and gas alternatives. But such analyses don't usually factor in the true cost of oil and gas, omit the subsidies, and are based on investor profits at the outer limit of expectation, percentages purportedly provided to some by hedge funds and the like, but far in excess of what most of us experience as acceptable basic return. The terrible irony is that such ocean alternatives have been additionally compromised recently by a financial argument based on the collapse of the oil price, thereby bringing the compared costs more against the alternatives than for the weakening conventional industry. It is as if all the market forces are lined up to protect the status quo against the change that would most probably drive the market faster and farther should the long term calculation be applied and the alternatives and their benefits prevail.

In my view, the most interesting of the existing alternative energy technologies is ocean thermal energy conversion (OTEC), which is based on acknowledgement of the ocean as an enormous potential heat pump that, like the device that might now be heating or cooling our homes, relies upon the conversion of the temperature differential in the water column and can provide a constant energy source, fueling itself and generating surplus, without most of the compromising negatives of present systems. The technology is not limited by the sun or wind; it operates 24 hours a day, year round, to produce cooling water in summer months or tropical areas and to generate electricity that can be stored, used to power itself, provided to adjacent or combined desalination or aquaculture projects, or distributed commercially beyond. Historically, the reasons against OTEC have been the same as against all alternatives. A small demonstration plant was funded by the US government decades ago using the first iteration of the emerging technology, and was promptly attacked as too little, too expensive, and too threatening to the oil producers then at the height of their market and political power. But much has changed. First, the technology has improved in sophistication, efficiency, and cost. Second, the other alternatives, wind perhaps excepted, have not proven to be viable. Third, the oil and gas supply has continued to run its exhaustive course, demand flattened in part by escalating price, production and labor costs, increased taxes, greater consumer conservation awareness, mandated more energy-efficient appliances and automobiles, a global recession, fluctuating share prices, CEO indecision, and massive penalties and insurance increases for coverage for the accidents, then disasters that have continued unabated simply as a function of an aging technology and diminished market. There are some promising examples, in both Scandinavia and the Caribbean where small projects, particularly for cooling, have been successfully installed. The OTEC time will come, and I am convinced that at some point soon the probability and profitability of OTEC will become evident and useful, and that coastal installation, however controversial and expensive, will be inevitable and successful.

Inventors are also looking to the ocean for new forms of fuel based on algae and other marine processes that can be mimicked, replicated, synthesized, and grown to scale as a new kind of biofuel with applications for automobiles, airplanes, and other large energy consuming machines and systems. J. Craig Venter, the American biochemist and entrepreneur who succeeded in sequencing the human genome and then privately sailed the ocean to find thousands of previously unidentified marine species, has been experimenting to this end with some support coming from the research and development funds of some energy companies.[232] Through his nonprofit research institute, Venter is exploring how bio-machinery created by genetic technology can perform many of our necessary manufacturing tasks with energy supplied not by expensive and polluting fossil fuels, but by the sun. Not without its controversies and dangers, this is nonetheless the stuff of invention, a projection of the invaluable human capacity for imagination, the "what if" thinking that might just create the story by which to change the world.

AIR. The most familiar aspect of the climate change dilemma is, of course, emissions into the atmosphere that have afflicted us perhaps with the most immediate, pervasive, and physical manifestations evident in coal- and oil-fired electric plants, the spread of invisible chemicals by prevailing wind over large geographical regions, the deposit of that acid rain into lakes and rivers, the killing of fish and wildlife in these areas, and the penultimate acidification of the ocean, remediable (if possible) over time far greater than the few decades it took to create the problem. My son recently returned from two years in Beijing, China, where he and thousands of others suffered from constant respiratory conditions, wore masks while outdoors, and kept their apartment and office windows closed with filters to clean the air within.

The larger "greenhouse effect" magnifies the problem globally. We have discovered, researched, and legislated in an attempt to correct this situation for decades. But again and again, those reluctant to accept the expense for stack scrubbers, adaptation to less-polluting fuels, increase in rates, legislative regulations, even penalties, have fought every initiative to control, restrict, or improve air quality, most times winning, and when losing relentlessly returning to overturn or dilute the regulation and cost. The American coal industry has fought change, ignored the health issues of its miners, thrown its waste into adjacent waterways, and procrastinated only long enough to see its political support decline and its market collapse. China, as in so many areas where its obsession with growth has caused it to emulate the proven bad practice of the earlier industrialized states, would appear to have reached a point where its reliance on coal has alienated the public and threatened the central government management with political and social instability like no other issue.

At some point the demand for public health overwhelms the compulsion for private profits. The US tobacco industry fought similarly until the statistics of lung cancer connected to nicotine, tar, and chemicals in cigarettes created a constituency and argument to force regulation, warnings, and a precipitate decline in tobacco consumption. A similar battle is ongoing worldwide, against continuing performance and policy that maintain the status quo.

Earth, fire, air, and water. These are the fundamental elements of Nature to which we must return to create "the new hydraulic society." It seems so clear. We have the incontrovertible need. We have the capacity and technology. We have the legal basis and economic alternatives. We have every reason to build our future around water cycles, circulations, conversions, and connections. But we appear not to have the political will or moral understanding to free us from our desiccated past.

Water: The Universal Healer

Water in the end is the universal healer. Without it in adequate supply we expire at every level of our being. This fact is the penultimate point that must be understood as we attempt to build new life on the detritus of the old. We have enumerated here the environmental consequences of past behaviors on both land and sea whereby we have grown and consumed more than the Earth can produce to sustain us. The social results are no less challenging. How then can we place water at the center of the new paradigm by which we can hope to feed and otherwise care for ourselves and for all the inhabitants of the only world we know? The future lies in the ocean.

We have discussed why the ocean matters and why we need a new way of thinking. We offered solutions to specific problems, cited examples of projects that are contributing to the impetus for change, and we have suggested new ways of conceiving, planning, and implementing through water conservation, management, and equitable distribution.

The present drought in California in the United States is the most highly visible realization of our lack of water awareness and its destructive undermining of the financial structure and social organization we have built in that most progressive state in that most successful global economy. If we fail in California, how can we succeed anywhere else?

At the most reductive level, the traditional water supply system in California has been overwhelmed by climate, industrial agriculture, and water-rich consumption that have been the envy of the world but can survive no longer without revolutionary change. If there is not enough water on the mountaintops to feed the watersheds, rivers, and reservoirs, then where will the requisite water come from?

In 2012, the San Diego County Water Authority signed an agreement to build the largest desalination plant in the United States.[233] The process is not new; it is applied today in some 21,000 desalination plants in over 120 countries, including Italy, Australia, Spain, Greece, Portugal, Japan, China, India, United Arab Emirates, Malta, Cape Verde, and Cyprus, producing more than 3.5 billion gallons of potable water per day. Saudi Arabia leads the world, meeting 70 percent of the daily needs of its population.

The San Diego project is proposed to come online in 2015 and to provide 7 percent of the Authority's demand by 2020—56,000 acre-feet of desalinated seawater per year. The plant is to be built and operated by Poseidon Water, a private investor-owned company that develops water and wastewater infrastructure. The contract is for 30 years, after which the Authority can purchase the plant for $1. The company is also building a 10-mile pipeline to deliver treated water inland to the Authority's aqueduct system where it can augment existing collected or natural supply to serve the needs of the 24 regional member water agencies serving 3.1 million people.

The plant occupies 6 acres of the 388-acre oceanfront site of the Encina Power Station that for 50 years has run on oil and natural gas, releasing emissions, and requiring a large dredged lagoon to hold seawater for cooling and to receive plant efflu-ent—a stagnant, stinking reminder of an old technology. The adjacent desalination plant will use a reverse-osmosis process with its source water coming from the generating plant cooling supply, treated and pumped under pressure through membranes to remove salt and other microscopic impurities.

In the past, the primary objections to desalination have been salt residue, corrosion, habitat destruction, and cost. The Poseidon plant has undergone comprehensive review by the Regional Water Quality Control Board, California Coastal Commission, California Department of Health, the City of Carlsbad, and other local, state, and federal agencies; each determined to protect its constituents and the environment. For every two gallons treated, one will be quality drinking water and the other diluted salt content for return to the ocean. The plant will run on Encina electricity to power high-speed pumps at market rates build into the contract. The approvals indicate that there will be no noise, no odor, and no environmental impact. Remarkably, the surrounding land has already been renewed by the prospect of the new plant and has been redeveloped by the Authority to transform the embayment into a viable environ-ment for marine life and community activities to include a YMCA camp, a fish hatchery, and an educational discovery center.

The San Diego region has been a center for the development of international desalination technology. The reverse-osmosis process was born from a local company in the 1960s. There are some 35 related companies in the area employing 2,200 people and generating over $200 million in annual revenue. According to the

Authority, the Carlsbad Project "will have significant economic benefit for the region, including $350 million in spending during construction, 2,400 construction-related jobs, and $50 million in annual spending throughout the region once the desalination plant is operational. For the region, the facility will create jobs, generate tax revenue, improve water quality and enhance water reliability with a new drought-proof supply."[234]

Drought-proof?

These hopeful numbers and language are the typical political arguments that have been used to justify new technology for a long time. The values inherent and the prediction of consummate solution may be forgiven as an evolutionary method to get a new idea in place, a demonstration of success, and additional volume into the pipelines. The financial estimates may or may not be predicable or accurate, but the ultimate return is *inevitable* when there is suddenly no more water available, we need its healing, and the cost is priceless.

Joseph Conrad, one of literature's greatest observers of the sea, writes in *The Mirror of the Ocean*:

> *Water is friendly to man. The ocean, a part of Nature farthest removed in the unchangeableness and majesty of its might from the spirit of mankind, has ever been a friend to the enterprising nations of the earth. And of all the elements this is the one to which men have always been prone to trust themselves, as if its immensity held a reward as vast as itself.*[235]

Laudato Si

In March 2015, Pope Francis, world leader of the Catholic Church, issued a papal encyclical, *Laudato Si—On Care of our Common Home*,[236] in which he addressed the moral imperative to steward our natural world for the benefit of succeeding generations, and issued a call that speaks beyond Catholicism to every person on Earth:

> *I urgently appeal, then, for a new dialogue about how we are shaping the future of our planet. We need a conversation which includes everyone, since the environmental challenge we are undergoing, and its human roots, concern and affect us all. The worldwide ecological movement has already made considerable progress and led to the establishment of numerous organizations committed to raising awareness of these challenges. Regrettably, many efforts to seek concrete solutions to the environmental crisis have proved ineffective, not only because of powerful opposition but also because of a more general lack of interest. Obstructionist attitudes, even on the part of believers, can range from denial of the problem to indifference, nonchalant resignation or blind confidence in technical solutions. We require a new and universal solidarity. As the bishops of Southern Africa have stated: "Everyone's talents and involvement are needed to redress the damage caused by human abuse of God's creation". All of us can cooperate as instruments of God for the care of creation, each according to his or her own culture, experience, involvements and talents.*[237]

On water and the ocean, the Pope writes:

> *Other indicators of the present situation have to do with the depletion of natural resources. We all know that it is not possible*

to sustain the present level of consumption in developed countries and wealthier sectors of society, where the habit of wasting and discarding has reached unprecedented levels. The exploitation of the planet has already exceeded acceptable limits and we still have not solved the problem of poverty.

Fresh drinking water is an issue of primary importance, since it is indispensable for human life and for supporting terrestrial and aquatic ecosystems. Sources of fresh water are necessary for health care, agriculture and industry. Water supplies used to be relatively constant, but now in many places demand exceeds the sustainable supply, with dramatic consequences in the short and long term. Large cities dependent on significant supplies of water have experienced periods of shortage, and at critical moments these have not always been administered with sufficient oversight and impartiality. Water poverty especially affects Africa where large sectors of the population have no access to safe drinking water or experience droughts, which impede agricultural production. Some countries have areas rich in water while others endure drastic scarcity.[238]

One particularly serious problem is the quality of water available to the poor. Every day, unsafe water results in many deaths and the spread of water-related diseases, including those caused by microorganisms and chemical substances. Dysentery and cholera, linked to inadequate hygiene and water supplies, are a significant cause of suffering and of infant mortality. Underground water sources in many places are threatened by the pollution produced in certain mining, farming and industrial activities, especially in countries lacking adequate regulation or controls. It is not only a question of industrial waste. Detergents and chemical products, commonly used in many places of the world, continue to pour into our rivers, lakes and seas.

Even as the quality of available water is constantly diminishing, in some places there is a growing tendency, despite its scarcity, to privatize this resource, turning it into a commodity subject to the laws of the market. Yet access to safe drinkable water is a basic and universal human right, since it is essential to human survival and, as such, is a condition for the exercise of other human rights. Our world has a grave social debt towards the poor who lack access to drinking water, because they are denied the right to a life consistent with their inalienable dignity. This debt can be paid partly by an increase in funding to provide clean water and sanitary services among the poor. But water continues to be wasted, not only in the developed world but also in developing countries that possess it in abundance. This shows that the problem of water is partly an educational and cultural issue, since there is little awareness of the seriousness of such behaviour within a context of great inequality.

Greater scarcity of water will lead to an increase in the cost of food and the various products which depend on its use. Some studies warn that an acute water shortage may occur within a few decades unless urgent action is taken. The environmental repercussions could affect billions of people; it is also conceivable that the control of water by large multinational businesses may become a major source of conflict in this century.

Oceans not only contain the bulk of our planet's water supply, but also most of the immense variety of living creatures, many of them still unknown to us and threatened for various reasons. What is more, marine life in rivers, lakes, seas and oceans, which feeds a great part of the world's population, is affected by uncontrolled fishing, leading to a drastic depletion of certain species. Selective forms of fishing which discard much of what they collect continue

*unabated. Particularly threatened are marine organisms which
we tend to overlook, like some forms of plankton; they represent a
significant element in the ocean food chain, and species used for
our food ultimately depend on them.*[239]

On the world we want to live in:

*When we speak of the "environment", what we really mean is a
relationship existing between nature and the society which lives
in it. Nature cannot be regarded as something separate from
ourselves or as a mere setting in which we live. We are part of
nature, included in it and thus in constant interaction with it.
Recognizing the reasons why a given area is polluted requires
a study of the workings of society, its economy, its behaviour
patterns, and the ways it grasps reality. Given the scale of
change, it is no longer possible to find a specific, discrete answer
for each part of the problem. It is essential to seek comprehensive
solutions which consider the interactions within natural systems
themselves and with social systems. We are faced not with two
separate crises, one environmental and the other social, but
rather with one complex crisis which is both social and environmental. Strategies for a solution demand an integrated approach
to combating poverty, restoring dignity to the excluded, and at
the same time protecting nature.*

*What kind of world do we want to leave to those who come after
us, to children who are now growing up? This question not
only concerns the environment in isolation; the issue cannot be
approached piecemeal. When we ask ourselves what kind of world
we want to leave behind, we think in the first place of its general
direction, its meaning and its values. Unless we struggle with
these deeper issues, I do not believe that our concern for ecology*

will produce significant results. But if these issues are coura-geously faced, we are led inexorably to ask other pointed questions: What is the purpose of our life in this world? Why are we here? What is the goal of our work and all our efforts? What need does the earth have of us? It is no longer enough, then, simply to state that we should be concerned for future generations. We need to see that what is at stake is our own dignity. Leaving an inhabit-able planet to future generations is, first and foremost, up to us. The issue is one which dramatically affects us, for it has to do with the ultimate meaning of our earthly sojourn.[240]

Let us also mention the system of governance of the oceans. International and regional conventions do exist, but fragmen-tation and the lack of strict mechanisms of regulation, control and penalization end up undermining these efforts. The growing problem of marine waste and the protection of the open seas represent particular challenges. What is needed, in effect, is an agreement on systems of governance for the whole range of so-called "global commons".[241]

On ecological conversion:

The rich heritage of Christian spirituality, the fruit of twenty centuries of personal and communal experience, has a precious contribution to make to the renewal of humanity. Here, I would like to offer Christians a few suggestions for an ecological spirituality grounded in the convictions of our faith, since the teachings of the Gospel have direct consequences for our way of thinking, feeling and living. More than in ideas or concepts as such, I am interested in how such a spirituality can motivate us to a more passionate concern for the protection of our world. A commitment this lofty cannot be sustained by doctrine alone,

without spirituality capable of inspiring us, without an "inte-
rior impulse" which encourages, motivates, nourishes and gives
meaning to our individual and communal activity.[242]

The Collaborative Age

Jeremy Rifkin, Lecturer at the Wharton School, University of
Pennsylvania, and prolific author and social thinker, offers
a comparable secular analysis in the conclusion to his *The Zero
Marginal Cost Society: The Internet of Things, The Collaborative
Commons, and the Eclipse of Capitalism*[243]:

> *For those who have lost hope in the future prospects of
> humanity and even our ability to survive as a species...let me
> ask this question: Why would we stop here and put an end to
> a journey that has taken us into ever more inclusive domains
> of empathic engagement and collective stewardship? If we
> have passed from mythological consciousness to theological
> consciousness to ideological consciousness to psychological
> consciousness and have extended our empathic drive from
> blood ties to religious affiliations to national identities and
> associational communities, is it not possible to image the
> next leap in the human journey—a crossover into biospheric
> consciousness and an expansion of empathy to include the
> whole of the human race as our family, as well as our fellow
> creatures as an extension of our evolutionary family?*
>
> *The collaborative sensibility is an acknowledgement that our
> individual lives are intimately intertwined and that our personal
> well-being ultimately depends on the well-being of the larger
> communities in which we dwell. That collaborative spirit is
> now beginning to extend to the biosphere. Children all over the*

world are learning about their "ecological footprint." They are coming to understand that everything we humans do—and for that matter every other creature—leaves an ecological footprint that affects the well-being of some other human being or creature in some other part of Earth's biosphere. They are connecting the dots and realizing that every creature is embedded in myriad symbiotic and synergetic relationships in ecosystems across the biosphere and that proper function of the whole system depends on the sustainable relationships of each of the parts. A younger generation is learning that the biosphere is our planetary community, whose health and well-being determines our own.

Their newfound openness is tearing down the walls that have long divided people by gender, class, race, ethnicity, and sexual orientation. Empathic sensitivity is expanding laterally as quickly as global networks are connecting everyone together. Hundreds of millions of human beings...are beginning to experience "the other" as "one's self." As empathy become s the ultimate litmus test for a truly democratic society. Millions of individuals, especially young people, are also beginning to extend their empathic drive...to include our fellow creatures, from the penguins and polar bears adrift on the poles to the other endangered species inhabiting the few remaining pristine, wild ecosystems. The young are just beginning to glimpse the opportunity of forging an empathic civilization tucked inside a biospheric community. At this stage, much of the anticipation is more hope than expectation. Still, there is an unmistakable feeling of possibility in the air.

Toward a New Hydraulic Society

The intent of this writing has been to suggest a means by which to transform knowledge, possibility, and empathy into a practical strategy that focuses and applies the sensibility and moral instruction of our most prescient leaders—and the efforts of citizens everywhere—in the specific design of a new system of structures and behaviors determined by the incontrovertible, infinite value of water.

Water delivered to nurture our bodies and minds is but the end result of a massive new reorganization of society around the cycles of water—from ocean to atmosphere, from our summits and glaciers via watersheds to the sea, and from the horizontal and vertical conveyors that circulate and filter that water as an eternal force for life.

Hydraulic means water in motion. That effort, measured by natural, economic, political, and social scales, is the force that drives civic action—movement—backward, in conflict, forward—a change—that determines the success of what we call civilization. We must move away from the failed methods and exhausted results of the past. We cannot drift. We must apply our collective energy and imagination, not just through science and technology, but also through shared values and collective action. The purpose here is simply to articulate what might be a functional idea, a re-invention that, if accepted, inspires our best selves toward a logical and authentic course for the future.

Some may doubt the viability of such an idea, deny its practicality and possibility in our world today—a world very much in conflict and transition. It is, however, that very vulnerability that offers the opportunity and imperative for change. Many examples of creative movement toward this new paradigm are included here, and there are many, many more evinced in the efforts of individuals in their towns, states, and national governments. Some individuals and some nations are more advanced in this direction than others. What is most encouraging is that these activities are local and simultaneously international, that they are not just confined to the most developed places, but are in fact being initiated and adopted in the developing world where policy and action can transcend the outmoded practice and technologies and ascend without complications to a future beyond. African nations, for example, can move to wireless communications beyond the wired infrastructure, to solar energy beyond oil and gas, to agricultural and irrigation methods that maximize available resources and production, and to fresh water supplies that are adequate, affordable, sustainable, and equitable for all. The associated reallocation of capital, recalculation of value, and re-organization of management structures and political entities around the realization of a new hydraulic society can guarantee an enduring democratic standard for individual and collective commitment as expressed in our response to a global imperative to conserve and maintain water in all its forms for the benefit of all mankind.

Ocean Light

I lived for 20 years in a megacity, with all its joys and frustrations. It is a place where life moves at hectic pace, innovation thrives, and people make, and lose, their fortunes. It is an ocean city, but you would hardly know it in that its port is mostly distant, and slowly its waterfront has transformed from a vital working place, to a derelict place, to a recreational place where people come to run and walk and socialize, special I suppose in a city that has so little time for socialization.

That waterfront is a place where residents come for light. I can remember walking in the deep canyons of the city's architectural heights and seeing a shaft of light illuminating the side of a glass façade, breaking through to surprise me, encourage me, that there is that freedom from darkness, from the weight of work or any other oppressing thing that might be on my mind as a city dweller. I was fortunate to work by the river and so perceived that ocean light more often than most with liberating effect.

Ocean light. It is different in so many ways. Obviously it is light reflected, relentless glare, or refracted fragments, or dull sheen—a mirror of the various filters of passing weather and the sun moving across the sky. Ocean light changes with the wind and tide and motion generated by forces oftentimes originated far away. An earthquake or a ship's wake can generate a shift in light many miles distant. A passing front, a raft of cloud, even the turning of a flock of birds can cause the light to change before our very eyes. The variety of light is an essential element of sea experience.

It seems to me that consciousness of light is not always top of mind. How many of us live in a lightless world? Artists and photographers, for example, live by light, attempting to re-create or capture its presence in a single frame. We learn to appreciate how light falls through a window on a woman's face. Or to admire how light on walls or natural features can transform a realistic cause into an abstract effect. We objectify light, subjectify light, calculate by the speed of light, and celebrate light in our religious beliefs as a force transcendent.

When we want to see something for what it is, we shine the light upon it. When have a brilliant idea or realization, we have seen the light. When we want to shout for joy, we trip the light fantastic. When we perceive love, we see that light in our lover's eyes. When we are aligned in time and space, we know "lightness of being." And when we ask for benediction, we invite "everlasting light to shine on me."

When I moved from the city to the rural north, my greatest concern was darkness. I live on a hill with a view of the ocean with the express purpose of accumulating every last lumen of light from the open summer days or the closing days of winter. I sympathize with folks who claim to suffer from some kind of light disorder, knowing full well my own need and concern that at some point there might not be enough to see me through. On those days, I will head to the shore to find the light that seems so abundant near to and on the sea.

How to explain this? We have experienced the cycle of light and dark on a daily basis over all time, and we have expressed this through self-realization in psychology, idea in philosophy, metaphor in literature, symbol in art, archetype in myth, parable in religion, progenitor/synthesizer in science, and regenerative healing treatment in health.

To find our political will and moral core, to act in the name of our heirs, to invent our way forward—through "hydraulic society" or any other powerful, revolutionary idea—we will all need the power of light to find our way from the once to the future ocean.

Light in the forest is illusive and mysterious. Light in the desert is harsh and destructive. Light on the mountain is amplified bright. Light on the ocean is dynamic and pure. When you feel dim or dark or down, find an ocean by which to re-create yourself in the fulsomeness and beneficence of redemptive light.

REFERENCES

I

1   Carson, Rachel. (1951) *The Sea Around Us*. Oxford University Press, Oxford & New York

II

2   Gilbert, Daniel. (February 24, 2014) Exxon CEO Joins Suit Citing Fracking Concerns. *The Wall Street Journal*. Rex Tillerson (ExxonMobil) www.wsj.com/articles/SB10001424052702304899704579391181466603804

3   Kurlansky, Mark. (1997) *Cod: A Biography of the Fish that Changed the World*. Penguin Books, New York

4   Encyclopedia of Earth (updated July 14, 2012) *Threats to Coral Reefs*

    www.eoearth.org/view/article/156613

5   United Nations. (1987) *Brutland Commission Report*

    www.un-documents.net/ocf-02.htm

6   Green Economy, Oxford Dictionaries

    www.oxforddictionaries.com/definition/english/green-economy

7   Svensson, Lisa Emelia, and Linwood Pendleton, eds. (2014) *Blue Economy: Transitioning to a New Blue Economy: Proceedings of the Economics of the Ocean Summit*. NI CP 14-01. Duke University, Durham, North Carolina

III

8   www.atlanticcouncil.org/blogs/new-atlanticist/ ending-americas-sea-blindness

9   Spaulding, Mark. (n.d.) *Ocean Foundation: Climate Change and Oceans*. The Consultative Group on Biological Diversity commissioned paper. A Mark Spaulding with Alaska Conservation Foundation and Ocean Foundation Collaboration

    www.oceanfdn.org/sites/default/files/ClimateandOceans_0.pdf

10 Intergovernmental Oceanographic Commission, Annual Report 1998. *International Year of the Ocean*

    unesdoc.unesco.org/images/0011/001169/116947Eo.pdf

11 Spaulding, Mark. (n.d.) *Ocean Foundation: Climate Change and Oceans*. The Consultative Group on Biological Diversity commissioned paper. A Mark Spaulding with Alaska Conservation Foundation and Ocean Foundation Collaboration

www.oceanfdn.org/resources/publications-reports/
climate-change-and-oceans-0

12   www.ipcc.ch/report/ar4

13   Pachauri, Rajendra K., Chairman of the International Panel on Climate
     Change. Edited by Chad V. Johnson, Harris L. Friedman. (2014) *The
     Praeger Handbook of Social Justice and Climate Psychology*, p. 21, ABC-CLIO,
     LLC., Santa Barbara, California

14   www.regions.noaa.gov/north-atlantic/wp-content/uploads/2013/07/
     CEANA-Final-V11.pdf

15   *The Population Division of the United Nations Department of Economic and
     Social Affairs, in its World Population Prospects: The 2010 Revision* (May 2011)

     www.un.org/en/development/desa/publications/world-population-
     prospects-2015-revision.html

16   *The United Nations World Water Development Report.* (2015)

     unesdoc.unesco.org/images/0023/002322/232273E.pdf

17   *The United Nations World Water Development Report: Water for a Sustainable
     World.* (2015)

     unesdoc.unesco.org/images/0023/002318/231823E.pdf

18   Vörösmarty, C. J., et al. (2005) United Nations Environment Program
     Ecosystems and Human Well being: Current States and Trends—Fresh Water

     www.unep.org/maweb/documents/document.276.aspx.pdf

19   Mejia, Abel, et al. (2012) United Nations World Water Development Report
     No. 4 (WWD). *Water and Sustainability* UNESCO Paris, France

20   United Nations Economic and Social Council. (February 1997)

     www.un.org/esa/documents/ecosoc/cn17/1997/ecn171997-9.htm

21   Prüss, Annette, et al. (May 2002) World Health Organization *Estimating
     the Burden of Disease from Water, Sanitation, and Hygiene at a Global Level*
     Environmental Health Perspectives Vol 110, No. 5

     www.who.int/quantifying_ehimpacts/global/en/ArticleEHP052002.pdf

22   *Bioscience.* (2008) Issue 58 (5): 403-414. doi: 10.1641/B580507

     www.worldwildlife.org/press-releases/world-wildlife-fund-and-the-
     nature-conservancy-release-first-ever-comprehensive-global-map-of-
     freshwater-systems

23   High numbers of fish species unique to Congo's Malebo Pool, the
     Amazon's Western Piedmont, and Cuba and Hispaniola, World Wildlife

Fund and The Nature Conservancy

bioscience.oxfordjournals.org/content/58/5/403.full.pdf+html

24   Bonello, Jenna. (May 8, 2008) World Wildlife Foundation and The Nature Conservancy WWF/TNC Press Release

www.worldwildlife.org/press-releases/world-wildlife-fund-and-the-nature-conservancy-release-first-ever-comprehensive-global-map-of-freshwater-systems

25   Valentine, Katie. (April 6, 2015) *CLIMATE: Despite Historic Drought, California Used 70 Million Gallons of Water for Fracking Last Year*

thinkprogress.org/climate/2015/04/06/3643184/california-70-million-gallons-fracking

26   Water Use in the US. (2010)

water.usgs.gov/watuse/wuin.html

27   H. John Heinz III Center for Science, Economics and the Environment. (2002) Cambridge University Press, New York

28   Kumar, C. P. (2003) National Institute of Hydrology Report. Uttaranchal, India

29   Mulholland, Patrick, et al. (March 13, 2008) *Nature*: International Weekly Journal of Science Stream

www.nature.com/nature/journal/v452/n7184/abs/nature06686.html

30   Shiklomanov, Igor. (1993) World fresh water resources. Peter H. Gleick (editor). *Water in Crisis: A Guide to the World's Fresh Water Resources,* Oxford University Press, New York

31   Howard and Bartram. (2003) *Right to Water,* World Health Organization

www.who.int/water_sanitation_health/en/righttowater.pdf

32   Water shortage headlines. (2015)

www.watershortagenews.com

33   www.allianceforwaterefficiency.org

34   www.allianceforwaterefficiency.org/WaterSense-Main-Page.aspx

35   The Global Water Contract. (2006)

www.gdrc.org/uem/water/WATER_MANIFESTO.doc

36   Coleridge, Samuel Taylor. (1798) *The Rime of the Ancient Mariner,* London

37   United Nations. (1967) *Report of the United Nations Water Conference, Mar del Plata.* United Nations Publications, New York

38   The Water Manifesto for a New Global Contract. (2006)
      www.world-governance.org/article75.html

39   www.gdrc.org/uem/water/WATER_MANIFESTO.doc (2006) p. 2

40   ibid.

41   ibid. p. 4

42   ibid.

43   ibid. p. 3

44   ibid. p. 4

45   ibid.

46   NOAA Fish Watch Western Bluefin Tuna. (2006)
      www.fishwatch.gov/seafood_profiles/species/tuna/species_pages/
      atl_bluefin_tuna.htm

47   ICCAT Report (2014-2015)
      www.iccat.int/Documents/SCRS/ExecSum/BFT_EN.pdf (2015) p. 14

48   www.parlevliet-vanderplas.nl/Home.aspx (*cached*)

49   Cabra, Mark, and Mort Rosenblum, (September 25, 2012) *New York Times.*
      In Mackerel's Plunder, Hints of Epic Fish Collapse
      www.nytimes.com/2012/01/25/science/earth/in-mackerels-plunder-
      hints-of-epic-fish-collapse.html?_r=0

50   Looting the Seas III: Free-for-all Decimates Public Fish Stocks in the
      Southern Pacific (January 25, 2012)
      www.publicintegrity.org/node/7900

51   New Zealand Ministries for Primary Industry: Atlantic Bluefin Tuna
      fs.fish.govt.nz/Page.aspx?pk=5&tk=96&ey=2014&fpid=50

52   www.greenpeace.org.au/
      blog/10-reasons-super-trawlers-welcome-australia

53   www.interpol.int/Crime-areas/Environmental-crime/Projects/
      Project-Scale

54   ibid.

55   National Oceanic and Atmospheric Administration. (February 9, 2015)
      United States continues global leadership to address illegal, unreported,
      and unregulated
      www.noaanews.noaa.gov/

stories2015/20150208-united-states-continues-global-leadership-to-address-illegal-unreported-and-unregulated-fishing.html

56   Service, Shannon. (October 27, 2014) *The Guardian*. Tuna firm's bungled IPO exposes China's flouting of global fishing rules

      www.theguardian.com/sustainable-business/2014/oct/27/toyo-reizo-shell-companies-fisheries-china-tuna-overfishing-oceans-ipo

57   ibid.

58   ibid.

59   Guilford, Gwynn. (April 30, 2013) *The Atlantic*

      www.theatlantic.com/china/archive/2013/04/china-is-plundering-the-planets-seas/275437

60   ibid.

61   ibid.

62   Greenberg, Paul. (March 21, 2009) *New York Times*. Cat Got Your Fish?

      www.nytimes.com/2009/03/22/opinion/22greenberg.html

63   ocean.si.edu/ocean-photos/sea-sponge-hiv-medicine

64   Oceans and Human Health. Highlights of National Academies. (2007)

      dels.nas.edu/resources/static-assets/osb/miscellaneous/Oceans-Human-Health.pdf p. 2

65   www.coml.org

66   www.fda.gov/Food/FoodborneIllnessContaminants/Metals/ucm393070.htm

67   Winner, Sherrie. (October 1, 2010) How Does Toxic Mercury Get Into Fish, *Woods Hole Oceanographic Institute Oceanus Magazine*. Vol 48, No. 2

      www.fda.gov/Food/FoodborneIllnessContaminants/Metals/ucm393070.htm

68   Ocean Genome Legacy

      http://www.northeastern.edu/cos/marinescience/tag/ocean-genome-legacy

69   CDC/gov/mmwr/preview/mmwrhtml/00036609.htm

70   http://www.nrdc.org/water/oceans/ttw/health-economic.asp

71   Harvell, C. D., and K. Kim, et al. (1999) *Science's Compass Review*. Emerging Marine Diseases, Climate Links and Anthropogenic Factors. University of Nebraska, Lincoln. Digital Commons

72   NOAA Ocean Service Education. (March 25, 2008)

oceanservice.noaa.gov/education/kits/estuaries/media/supp_estuar09c_pathogens.html

The National Academies Ocean Science Series: *Oceans and Human Health.* (2007)

dels.nas.edu/resources/static-assets/osb/miscellaneous/Oceans-Human-Health.pdf

73   ibid.

74   Megacities by the sea Demographia: World Megacities. (2015)

www.demographia.com/db-megacity.pdf p. 31

75   ibid.

76   Lui, Coco. (April 16, 2013) ClimateWire. *Scientific American*

www.scientificamerican.com/article/what-happens-when-asias-water-tower-dries-up

77   Kolbert, Elizabeth. (December 7, 2015) *The New Yorker.* Unsafe Climates

www.newyorker.com/magazine/2015/12/07/unsafe-climates

78   ibid.

79   Environmental Justice and the EPA

www.epa.gov/environmentaljustice

80   Climate Justice Initiative. (March 2001)

s3.amazonaws.com/corpwatch.org/downloads/cjfacts.pdf

81   The Oxford Institute for Energy Studies. (November 2014)

The Prospect and Challenges for Arctic Oil Development

www.oxfordenergy.org/wpcms/wp-content/uploads/.../WPM-56.pdf

82   Paschoa, Claudio. (December 27, 2013) *Marine Technology News*

www.marinetechnologynews.com/blogs/the-prirazlomnaya-rig-details-e28093-part1-700429

83   ibid.

84   *Ocean News and Technology.* (October 2014)

digital.oceannews.com/publication/?i=227039 p. 8

85   US Energy Information Administration. (October 2015) Unplanned supply disruptions tighten world oil markets and push prices higher.

www.eia.gov/finance/markets/supply-nonopec.cfm

86   Gallup Poll—Energy. (2014)

      www.gallup.com/poll/2167/energy.aspx

87   CBC Canada. (April 13, 2015)

      www.cbc.ca/news/canada/british-columbia/vancouver-oil-spill-coast-
      guard-fires-back-at-criticism-of-response-1.3030722 CNN May 23 2015

88   Most States Have Renewable Portfolio Standards

      www.eia.gov/todayinenergy/detail.cf

89   Fracking: SourceWatch. (March 2015)

      www.sourcewatch.org/index.php/Fracking

90   Exxon, Total Join Forces to Drill Uruguay's First Offshore Well

      www.reuters.com/article/us-uruguay-exploration-idUSKCN0SZ036201511
      10#PdimY5vivpS8Heuf.97

91   *Yale Environment 360.* (April 7, 2014) On Fracking Front: A Push to Reduce
      Methane Leaks

      e360.yale.edu/feature/
      on_fracking_front_a_push_to_reduce_leaks_of_methane/2754/

92   Toxic and Dirty Secrets: The Truth About Fracking

      www.ceh.org/legacy/storage/.../Fracking/fracking_final-low-1.pdf

93   www2.epa.gov/hydraulicfracturing

94   Stone, Les. Greenpeace USA *Fracking's Environmental Impacts—Water.*

      www.greenpeace.org/usa/global-warming/issues/fracking/
      environmental-impacts-water

95   The Academy of Natural Sciences of Drexel University—Delaware River
      Watershed Initiative (2015)

      www.ansp.org/research/environmental-research/projects/
      watershed-protection-program

96   Oil Tanker Spill Statistics—International Tanker Owners Pollution
      Federation. (2010) Oil Spills By The Numbers—Center for American
      Progress

      www.itopf.com/knowledge-resources/data-statistics/statistics

97   Phase-out of single hulled tankers. "Vessels operating in US waters must
      have *double* hulls by January 1, 2015"

      www.gpo.gov/.../CHRG-108

98   Civil Liability for Ocean Oil Pollution. (July 2015) *Journal of Environmental*

Law Vol 27, No. 2

www.oxfordjournals.org; www.congress.gov/bill/101st-congress/senate-bill/686

99   *American Anthropologist.* (2008) Why Katrina's Victims Aren't Considered "Refugees": Musings on a Dirty Word

Vol 108, Issue 4 (article first published online January 6, 2008)

100   Campaign to Ban Plastic Microbeads—5 Gyres Institute

5gyres.giv.sh/14ae

101   ibid.

102   *The Economist.* "Welcome to the Plastisphere." (July 18, 2013)

www.economist.com/news/science-and-technology/21581981-what-pollution-some-opportunity-others-welcome-plastisphere

103   Zettler, Erik R., Tracy J Mincer, and Linda A. Amaral-Zettler, (2013) Life in the "plastisphere": microbial communities on plastic marine debris, *Environmental Science & Technology,* Vol 47 (13), pp. 137–46

104   ibid.

105   NOAA's Office of Protected Resources. About

www.nmfs.noaa.gov/pr

106   Islay LIMPET Wave Power Plant. cordis.europa.eu/documents/documentlibrary/66628981EN6.pdf

107   European Wind Energy Association

www.ewea.org/offshore2015

108   Smithsonian Ocean Planet

www. seawifs.gssfc.nasa.gov/OCEAN_PLANET/HTML/ps_power.html

119   Global Wind Power

gwec.net/.../Global-Wind-2008-Report.pdf

110   *Financial Times.* Denmark Considers Wind a Les Volatile Option
www.ft.com/intl/cms/s/0/d3ccfc36-3a06-11e5-bbd1-b37bc06f590c.html#axzz3uEPLrFRm

111   Bureau of Ocean Energy Management

www.boem.gov/Renewable-Energy-Program/Renewable-Energy-Guide/Offshore-Solar-Energy.aspx

112   Vyawahare, Malavika. (August 27, 2015) *Scientific American,* Hawaii First

To Harness Deep-Ocean Temperatures For Power

www.scientificamerican.com/article/
hawaii-first-to-harness-deep-ocean-temperatures-for-power

113   Smithsonian/ NASA seawifs.gsfc.nasa.gov/OCEAN_PLANET/HTML/
        ps_power.html

114   energy.gov/eere/energybasics/articles/
        ocean-thermal-energy-conversion-basics

115   Kingston, William. (April 2011) Marine Technology Report, Tidal Energy:
        How it can be made to pay, p. 42

        www.seadiscovery.com

116   Catalysing Ocean Finance Vol 1. United Nations Development
        Programme

        www.thegef.org/gef/sites/thegef.org/files/publication/Catalysing%20
        Ocean%20Finance%20Vol%20I%20Final%20Oct1_1.pdf

117   www.oceaneconomics.org

118   The Ocean Health Index

        www.oceanhealthindex.org/news?category=blue%20economy

119   Safina, Carl. (2011) *The View From Lazy Point: A Natural Year In An
        Unnatural World*. Henry Holt & Co., New York

120   Blue Growth in the Middle Kingdom: An analysis of China's ocean
        economy

        cbe.miis.edu/cbe_working_papers/3

121   Patton, Kimberly C. (2007) *The Sea Can Wash Away All Evils*. Columbia
        University Press, New York

122   ibid.

123   Bas Verschuuren, Robert Wild, Jeffrey A. McNeely, and Gonzalo Oviedo
        (eds). (2010) Routledge. Earth Scan, New York

124   Intangible Cultural Heritage (2010)

        portal.unesco.org/culture/en/ev.php-URL_ID=34325&URL_DO=DO_
        TOPIC&URL_SECTION=201.html

125   ibid.

126   National Religious Partnership for the Environment

        www.nrpe.org/overview.html

IV

127 Sylvia Earle Hope Spots
www.mission-blue.org

128 Commons. Oxford Dictionary

www.oxforddictionaries.com/definition/english/commons

129 Ocean Commons. United Nations Environment Program (UNEP)

www.unep.org/esm/Default.aspx?tabid=129799

130 www.lighthouse-foundation.org/.../field_mpas_guide_april_2012.pdf

131 Royal Borough of Greenwich—Thames Barrier and Information
Center www.royalgreenwich.gov.uk/directory_record/2006/
thames_barrier_and_information_centre

132 Arcata's Wastewater Treatment Plant & The Arcata Wildlife Marsh and
Sanctuary

www2.humboldt.edu/arcatamarsh/overview.html

V

133 Democrats Clock An All-Nighter With Climate Talk. (2014)
www.wusa9.com/story/news/politics/2014/03/11/
democrats-climate-talk-senate/6284051

134 Soares, Mario. (1998) *The Ocean, Our Future.* Cambridge University Press,
Boston, Massachusetts

135 ibid.

136 *The Economist.* (July 21, 2012) Insatiable Longing

www.economist.com/node/21559308

137 Tanizaki, Junichiro. (1977) *In Praise of Shadows.* Leete's Island Books,
Sedgwick, Maine

138 Dursten, Diane. "Mottainai: The Fabric of Life. Lessons in Frugality From
Traditional Japan". Regional Arts & Culture Council. Oregon. 2011.

139 Paine, Lincoln. (2013) *The Sea and Civilization: A Maritime History of the
World.* Vintage Books, New York

140 Leopold, Aldo. (1949) *A Sand County Almanac.* Oxford University Press,
Oxford, United Kingdom

141 ibid.

142 ibid.

143 Lévi-Strauss, Claude. (1949) *The Elementary Structures of Kinship.* Beacon Press, Boston, Massachusetts

144 Murawski, Steve. (2012) *Science: Ocean Benefits in the Face of Acidification and Climate Change.* Panel Presentation at the Global Conference on Oceans, Climate, and Security. Boston, Massachusetts

145 ibid.

146 www.water.usgs.gov/edu/earthwherewater.html

147 Fatehpur Sikri archeological water

asi.nic.in/asi_monu_whs_fatehpursikri.asp

148 www.citypopulation.de/php/india-uttarpradesh.psp?cityid+0941511000

149 New York City Environmental Protection. New York City Green Infrastructure Program. www.nyc.gov/html/dep/html/stormwater/using_green_infra_to_manage_stormwater.shtml

150 ibid.

151 ibid.

152 Tata Communications completes world's first wholly owned cable network ring around the world. (2012) Tata Communications

www.tatacommunications.com/article/tata-communications-completes-worlds-first-wholly-owned-cable-network-ring-around-world

153 Tata Group Profile

www.tata.co.za/about-site/group-profile

154 McKibben, Bill. (2010) *Earth, Making a Life on a Tough New Planet.* Henry Holt, New York

155 ibid.

156 Genaze, Mathew R. (2010) *Towards a Hydraulic Society: An Architecture of Resource Perception.* UMI Dissertation Publishing/ProQuest. Masters Thesis. Architecture, Rice University, Ann Arbor, Michigan

157 Seawater Greenhouse. A New Approach: Restorative Agriculture.

www.seawatergreenhouse.com

158 Scott, Katie. (2012) Sahara Forest Project to be Built in Qatar

www.wired.co.uk/news/archive/2012-02-28/sahara-forest-project-pilot-gets-funding-and-go-ahead

159 Lowry, Natalie. Deep Sea Mining—Out of Our Depth

www.deepseaminingoutofourdepth.org/urban-mining-vs-deep-sea-mining

160 Jacobs, Jane. (1961) *The Death and Life of Great American Cities*. Random House, New York

161 History of the Arctic Council. (Arctic Council)

www.arctic-council.org/index.php/en/about-us/arctic-council

162 The Arctic Council: A Backgrounder. (Arctic Council)

www.arctic-council.org/index.php/en/about-us

163 Nichols, Wallace J. *Blue Mind: Your Brain on Water*

www.wallacejnichols.org/122/blue-mind.html

164 Amazing Surf Adventures

www.amazingsurfadventures.org

165 Lexivox.org. (October 15, 2012) Bolivia: Framework Law of Mother Earth and Integral Development for Living Well

www.lexivox.org/norms/BO-L-N300.xhtml

166 ibid.

167 Jackson Browne. "Before the Deluge"

Jackson Browne lyrics are property and copyright of their owners. "Before The Deluge" lyrics are provided for educational purposes and personal use only. Jackson Browne dba Swallow Turn Music c/o Gelfand, Rennert Feldman.

VI

168 www.weforum.org/events/world-economic-forum-annual-meeting-2015

169 Walton, Brett. (2015) World Economic Forum Ranks Water Crisis as Top Global Risk

www.circleofblue.org/waternews/2015/world/
world-economic-forum-ranks-water-crises-as-top-global-risk

170 Pouring Good Water After Bad: China's Water Stress to Worsen. (January 12, 2015)

www.uea.ac.uk/about/media-room/press-release-archive/-/asset_
publisher/a2jegmifhphv/content/pouring-good-water-after-bad-China-s-
water-stress-set-to-worsen-with-transfer-initiatives

171 Bloomberg News. (2015) China Water Stress May Worsen Even With Transfer Projects

www.bloomberg.com/news/articles/2015-01-12/
china-water-stress-may-worsen-even-with-transfer-projects

172 Heileman, Sherry, and Drake Rugundo, United Nations Environment

Program: Terminal Evaluation of the UNEP Project Adapting to Climate Change Induced Water Stress in the Nile River Basin

www.unep.org/eou/Portals/52/Reports/Nile%20Basin%20Final%20 Terminal%20Evaluation%20Report%20-%20Final%20Report.pdf

173 DHI Group

www.dhigroup.com/about-usp

174 DHI Group. Floods and Water Security: Supporting Climate Change Adaptation in the Nile River Valley

www.dhigroup.com/global/news/imported/2014/2/18/ modellingfutureflowsofthenileriver

175 Buiter, Willem. (2011) Water as Seen by an Economist

www.capitalsynthesis.com/wp-content/uploads/2011/08/Water-Thirsty-Cities.pdf

176 Citi. (2011) Global Themes Strategy: Thirsty Cities

www.capitalsynthesis.com/wp-content/uploads/2011/08/Water-Thirsty-Cities.pdf

177 Buiter, Willem. (2011) Water as Seen by an Economist

www.capitalsynthesis.com/wp-content/uploads/2011/08/Water-Thirsty-Cities.pdf

178 ibid.

179 ibid.

180 ibid.

181 Walton, Brett. (2010) Alaska City Set to Ship Water to India, US Company Announces

www.circleofblue.org/waternews/2010/world/north-america/ alaska-city-set-to-ship-water-to-india-u-s-company-announces

182 S2C Global Securing Sales of its Alaskan Water to India. (2010) Follow the Money. www.seeker401.wordpress.com/2010/07/19/ s2c-global-securing-sales-of-its-alaskan-water-to-india/comment-page-1

183 ibid.

184 Hidropolitikakademi Academy (2014) Alaska Wants to Sell the World a Drink

www.hidropolitikakademi.org/en/alaska-city-wants-to-sell-the-world-a-drink.html/2

185 H2O Coach: Good Water, Water to "Eat." What is Virtual Water?

(UNESCO-Venice Office Regional Bureau for Science and Culture in Europe)

www.unesco.org/new/fileadmin/MULTIMEDIA/FIELD/Venice/pdf/special_events/bozza_scheda_DOW04_1.0.pdf

186   Jenkins, Jesse. (2013) Energy Facts: How Much Water Does Fracking for Shell Gas Consume?

www.theenergycollective.com/jessejenkins/205481/friday-energy-facts-how-much-water-does-fracking-shale-gas-consume

187   Danish Hydraulic Institute. Developing a Water Management Plan for the City of Olomouc

www.dhigroup.com//media/shared%20content/global/references/emea/case%20stories/surfaceandgroundwater_cz_casestory_developing%20a%20water%20management%20plan%20for%20the%20city%20of%20oloumouc.pdf

188   Romero, Simon. (2015) Tap Starts to Run Dry in Brazil's Largest City
www.nytimes.com/2015/02/17/world/americas/drought-pushes-sao-paulo-brazil-toward-water-crisis.html

189   ibid.

190   ibid.

191   Danish Hydraulic Institute. Developing a Water Management Plan for the City of Olomouc

www.dhigroup.com//media/shared%20content/global/references/emea/case%20stories/surfaceandgroundwater_cz_casestory_developing%20a%20water%20management%20plan%20for%20the%20city%20of%20oloumouc.pdf

192   Fountain, Henry. (2015) *New York Times*. California Drought Is Worsened by Global Warming, Scientists Say

www.nytimes.com/2015/04/02/science/california-drought-is-worsened-by-global-warming-scientists-say.html

193   Nagourney, Adam. (2015) *New York Times*. California Imposes First Mandatory Water Restrictions to Deal with Drought

www.nytimes.com/2015/04/02/us/california-imposes-first-ever-water-restrictions-to-deal-with-drought.html

194   Barringer, Felicity. (2014) *New York Times*. In California, Spigots Start Draining Pockets,

www.nytimes.com/2014/05/09/

us/a-thirsty-california-puts-a-premium-on-excess-water-use.html

195   Wines, Michael. (2015) *New York Times*. Mighty Rio Grande Now a Trickle
      Under Siege

      www.nytimes.com/2015/04/13/us/mighty-rio-grande-now-a-trickle-
      under-siege.html

196   Gillis, Justin. (2015) *New York Times*. For Drinking Water in Drought,
      California Looks Warily to Sea

      www.nytimes.com/2015/04/12/science/drinking-seawater-looks-ever-
      more-palatable-to-californians.html

197   Urbina, Ian. (2015) *New York Times*. The Outlaw Ocean

      www.nytimes.com/interactive/2015/07/24/world/the-outlaw-ocean.
      html?_r=0

198   Agardy, Tundi. (August 9, 2105) *Ocean Zoning: Making Marine Management
      More Effective*. Routledge, New York

199   Wood, Mary Christina (2013) *Nature's Trust: Environmental Law or a New
      Environmental Age*. Cambridge University Press, New York

200   ibid.

201   ibid.

202   ibid.

203   ibid.

204   Sax, Joseph L. (1970) The Public Trust Doctrine in Natural Resource Law:
      Effective Judicial Intervention

      www.uvm.edu/~gflomenh/PA-CDAE395-VCAT/articles/sax.pdf

205   Wood, Mary Christina. (2013) *Nature's Trust: Environmental Law or a New
      Environmental Age*. Cambridge University Press, New York

206   Geiling, Natasha. (2015) In Landmark Case, Dutch Citizens Sue Their
      Government Over Failure To Act On Climate Change

      www.thinkprogress.org/climate/2015/04/14/3646690/
      pass-that-dutch-climate-change-action

207   Our Children's Trust. www.ourchildrenstrust.org

208   Our Children's Trust. (2014) Federal Climate Lawsuit Filed in 2011

      www.ourchildrenstrust.org/2011federalclimatelawsuit

209   ibid.

210   Our Children's Trust State Lawsuits

www.ourchildrenstrust.org/US/LawsuitStates

211   Wittvogel, Karl. (1964) *Oriental Despotism: A Comparative Study of Total Power.* Yale University Press, New Haven, Connecticut

212   Hilton, Isabel. (2015) *The New Yorker.* Nepal's Dangerous Dams

www.newyorker.com/news/news-desk/nepals-dangerous-dams

213   ibid.

214   ibid.

215   Kass, Stephen L. (2015) *The Environmental Struggle Within the Trans-Pacific Partnership*

www.clm.com/publication.cfm?ID=512&Att=93

216   ibid.

217   ibid.

218   Klein, Naomi. (2015) *This Changes Everything: Capitalism vs. the Climate.* Simon & Schuster, New York

219   ibid.

220   ibid.

221   Alperovitz, Gar, James Speth, Gustave & Guinana, Joe (2015) *The Next System Project: New Political-Economic Possibilities for the 21st Century,* p. 2

www.thenextsystem.org/wp-content/uploads/2015/03/NSPReport1_Digital.pdf

222   ibid. p. 5

223   ibid. p. 8

224   ibid. p. 19

225   McGlade, J., et al., UNEP. (2012) *Measuring water use in a green economy, A Report of the Working Group on Water Efficiency to the International Resource Panel.*

www.unep.org/resourcepanel/Portals/24102/Measuring_Water.pdf

226   Hoekstra, Arjen Y., Ashok K. Chapagain, Maite M. Aldaya, and Mesfin M. Mekonnen, (2011) The water footprint assessment manual: Setting the global standard, Earthscan, London, United Kingdom

www.waterfootprint.org/media/downloads/TheWaterFootprintAssessmentManual_2.pdf

227   Water Footprint Statistics (WaterStat). (2012) Water Footprint Network

www.waterfootprint.org/en/resources/water-footprint-statistics

228 Water Footprint Network (2012) Water Footprint Assessment Tool

www.waterfootprint.org/en/resources/interactive-tools/
water-footprint-assessment-tool

229 McGlade, J., et al. (2012) UNEP *Measuring water use in a green economy, A Report of the Working Group on Water Efficiency to the International Resource Panel.* www.unep.org/resourcepanel/Portals/24102/Measuring_Water.pdf

230 Water Footprint Network. Frequently Asked Questions

waterfootprint.org/en/water-footprint/frequently-asked-questions

VII

231 Illich, Ivan. (1986) *H2O and the Water of Forgetfulness.* Heydey Books, Berkeley, California

232 J. Craig Venter Institute. About

www.jcvi.org/cms/about/overview

233 San Diego County Water Authority. (2015) Seawater Desalination

www.sdcwa.org/seawater-desalination

234 San Diego County Water Authority. (2015) Seawater Desalination: The Carlsbad Desalinations Project

www.sdcwa.org/sites/default/files/desal-carlsbad-fs-single.pdf

235 Conrad, Joseph. (1906) *The Mirror of the Sea.* Harper and Brothers, New York

236 Francis, Pope Holy Father. (May 2015) *Laudato Si: On Care For Our Common Home. An Encyclical on Climate Change*

w2.vatican.va/content/Francesco/en/encyclicals/documents/papa-franchesco_20150524_enciclica-laudato-si.html

237 ibid.

238 ibid.

239 ibid.

240 ibid.

241 ibid.

242 ibid.

243 Rifkin, Jeremy. (2015) *The Zero Marginal Cost Society: The Internet of Things, the Collaborative Commons, and the Eclipse of Capitalism.* St. Martins-Griffin, New York

Agardy, Tundi. *Ocean Zoning: Making Marine Management More Effective*. London/ Washington, DC: Earthscan, 2010.

Allen, Thomas B. *Vanishing Wildlife of North America*. Washington, DC: National Geographic Society, 1974.

Barlow, Maude. *Blue Covenant: The Global Water Crisis and the Coming Battle for the Right to Water*. New York: The New Press, 2007.

Barlow, Maude, and Tony Clarke. *Blue Gold: The Fight to Stop Corporate Theft of the World's Water*. New York: The New Press, 2002.

Bascom, Willard. *The Crest of the Wave: Adventures in Oceanography*. New York: Harper and Row, 1988.

Blanchard, Gaston. *Water and Dreams: An Essay on the Imagination of Matter*. Dallas: Dallas Institute of Humanities and Culture, 1983.

Beatley, Timothy. *Blue Urbanism: Exploring Connections Between Cities and Oceans*. Washington, DC: Island Press, 2014.

Beebe, William. *Half Mile Down*. New York: Harcourt, Brace and Company, 1934.

Beston, Henry. *The Outtermost House*. New York: Henry Holt and Company, 1928.

Bollier, David. *Think Like a Commoner*. Gabriola Island, BC: New Society Publishers, 2014.

Boorstin, Daniel J. *The Creators: A History of the Heroes of the Imagination*. New York: Random, 1992.

Buchanan, Mark. *Nexus: Small Worlds and the Groundbreaking Science of Networks*. New York: W.W. Norton & Co., 2002.

Burroughs, Richard. *Coastal Governance*. Washington, DC: Island Press, 2011.

Carson, Rachael L. *The Sea Around Us*. New York, Oxford University Press: 1961.

Casey, Susan. *The Wave: In Pursuit of the Rogues, Freaks, and Giants of the Ocean*. New York: Doubleday, 2010.

Clark, Story. *A Field Guide to Conservation Finance*. Washington, DC: Island Press, 2007.

Clarke, Robin, and Jannet King. *The Water Atlas: A Unique Visual Analysis of the World's Most Critical Resources*. New York: The New Press, 2004.

Cosgrove, Denis, and Geoff Petts. *Water, Engineering and Landscape*. London/New York: Belhaven Press/Pinter Publishers, 1990.

Cousteau, Jacques-Yves. *The Silent World*. New York: Harper and Row, 1953.

Cousteau, Jean-Michel, and Phillippe Vallette. *Atlas de l'Ocean Mondial*. Paris: Editions Autrement, 2007.

Cramer, Deborah. *Great Waters: An Atlantic Passage*. New York: W.W. Norton & Company, 2001.

Dawkins, Richard. *Unweaving the Rainbow: Science, Delusion, and the Appetite for Wonder*. Boston: Houghton Mifflin, 1998.

Deacon, Margaret, Tony Rice, and Colin Summerhayes. *Understanding the Oceans*. London: University College London Press, 2001.

De Villiers, Marq. *Water: The Fate of Our Most Precious Resource*. New York: Houghton Mifflin, 2001.

Dudley, William. *Endangered Oceans: Opposing Viewpoints*. San Diego: Greenhaven Press, 1999.

Duncan, David James. *My Story As Told By Water*. San Francisco: Sierra Club Books, 2001.

Fagan, Brian. *The Great Warming: Climate Change and the Rise and Fall of Civilizations*. New York: Bloomsbury Press, 2008.

Fagan, Brian. *Elixir: A History of Water and Humankind*. New York: Bloomsbury Press, 2011.

Farber, Thomas. *On Water*. New York: The Ecco Press, 1994.

Fenical, William. *From Monsoons to Microbes: Understanding the Ocean's Role in Human Health*. Washington, DC: National Academy Press, 1999.

Fernandez-Armesto, Felipe. *Civilizations: Culture, Ambition, and the Transformation of Nature*. New York: Simon & Schuster, 2002.

Field, John, Gotthilf Hempel, and Colin Summerhayes. *Oceans 2020: Science, Trends, and the Challenge of Sustainability*. Washington, DC: Island Press, 2002.

Flader , Susan L. *Thinking Like a Mountain*. Columbia: University of Missouri Press, 1974.

Foster, John Bellamy. *Marx's Ecology: Materialism and Nature*. New York, Monthly Review Press, 2000.

Genaze, Mathew R. *Towards a Hydraulic Society: An Architecture of Resource Perception*. Ann Arbor, UMI Dissertation Publishing/ProQuest, 2010.

Glover, Linda, and Sylvia Earle. *Defying Ocean's End: An Agenda for Action*. Washington, DC: Island Press, 2004.

Greenberg, Paul. *Four Fish: The Future of the Last Wild Food*. New York: Penguin Books, 2010.

Hall, Donald, ed. *The Oxford Book of American Literacy Anecdotes*. New York: Oxford UP, 1981.

Hawken, Paul. *Blessed Unrest*. New York: Penguin Books, 2007.

Hawken, Paul, Amory Lovins, and L. Hunter Lovins. *Natural Capitalism: Creating the Next Industrial Revolution*. New York: Little Brown and Company, 1999.

Helvarg, David. *Blue Frontier: Saving America's Living Seas*. New York: W.H. Freeman and Company, 2001.

Herenden, Wyman H. *From Landscape to Literature: The River and the Myth of Geography*. Pittsburgh: Dusquesne University Press, 1986.

Hiss, Tony, and Christopher Meier. *H2O: Highlands to Ocean*. Morristown: Geraldine R. Dodge Foundation, 2004.

Illich, Ivan. *H2O and the Waters of Forgetfulness*. Berkeley: Heyday Books, 1985.

Jackson, Jeremy, Karen Alexander, and Eric Sala. *Shifting Baselines: The Past and Future of Ocean Fisheries*. Washington, DC: Island Press, 2011.

Klein, Naomi. *This Changes Everything: Capitalism vs. The Climate*. New York: Simon & Schuster, 2014.

Koeppel, Gerard T. *Water for Gotham: A History*. Princeton: Princeton University Press, 2000.

Longhurst, Alan. *Ecological Geography of the Sea*. Burlington: Academic Press, 2007.

Lopez, Barry. *Arctic Dreams: Imagination and Desires in a Northern Landscape*. New York: Charles Scribner's Sons, 1986.

Lucero, Lisa, and Barbara Fash. *Pre-Columbian Water Management*. Tuscon: University of Arizona Press, 2006.

Mack, John. *The Sea: A Cultural History*. London: Reaktion Books, 2011.

McKibben, Bill. *Eaarth: Making a Life on a Tough New Planet*. New York, Henry Holt and Company, 2010.

McKibben, Bill. *The End of Nature*. New York: Random House, 2006.

Moore, Kathleen, and Michael Nelson. *Moral Ground: Ethical Action for a Planet in Peril*. San Antonio: Trinity University Press, 2010.

Nelson, Richard. *The Island Within*. San Francisco: North Point Press, 1989.

Outwater, Alice. *Water: A Natural History*. New York: Basic Books, 1996.

Paine, Lincoln. *The Sea and Civilization*. New York: Alfred A. Knopf, 2013.

Pauly, Daniel, and Jay Maclean. *In a Perfect Ocean: The State of Fisheries and Ecosystems in the North Atlantic Ocean*. Washington, DC: Island Press, 2003.

Pearce, Fred. *When the Rivers Run Dry: Water—The Defining Crisis of the Twenty-First Century*. Boston: Beacon Press, 2006.

Pelling, Mark, and Sophie Blackburn. *Megacities and the Coast*. Washington, DC, Earthscan, 2013.

Petrella, Riccardo. *The Water Manifesto*. London: Zed Books, 2001.

Reiter, Lawrence, Henry Falk, Charles Groat, and Christine Coussens. *From Source Water to Drinking Water*. Washington, DC: National Academy Press, 2004.

Rifkin, Jeremy. *The Zero Marginal Cost Society*. New York: Palgrave Macmillan, 2014.

Roberts, Callum. *The Ocean Of Life: The Fate of Man and the Sea*. New York: Viking Press, 2012.

Rolens, Mats, Helen Sjoberg, and Uno Svedin. *International Governance on Environmental Issues*. Dordrecht: Kluwer Academic Publishers, 1997.

Rothfeder, Jeffrey. *Every Drop For Sale*. New York: Penguin Putnam, 2001.

Safina, Carl. *Song for the Blue Ocean*. New York: Henry Holt and Company, 1997.

Sampath, Padmashree Gehl. *Regulating Bioprospecting: Institutions for Drug Research, Access and Benefit-Sharing*. Tokyo: United Nations University Press, 2005.

Scarborough, Vernon L. *The Flow of Power: Ancient Water Systems and Landscapes*. Santa Fe: School of American Research, 2003.

Schalansky, Judith. *Atlas of Remote Islands*. New York: Penguin Books, 2010.

Schell, Jonathan. *The Fate of the Earth*. New York: Alfred A. Knopf, 1982.

Schlee, Susan. *The Edge of an Unfamiliar World: A History of Oceanography*. New York: E. P. Dutton & Co., 1973.

Searles, Baird, and Martin Last. *A Reader's Guide to Science Fiction*. New York: Facts on File, Inc., 1979.

Sedlak, David. *Water 4.0: The Past, Present, and Future of the World's Most Vital Resource*. New Haven: Yale University Press, 2014.

Shiva, Vandana. *Water Wars: Privatization, Pollution, and Profit*. Cambridge: South End Press, 2002.

Shubin, Neil. *Your Inner Fish: A Journey into the 3.5 Billion-Year History of the Human Body*. New York: Random House, 2009.

Soares, Mario. *The Ocean Our Future: The Report of the Independent World*

Commission on the Future of the Ocean. Cambridge: Cambridge University Press, 1998.

Soloman, Steven. *Water: The Epic Struggle for Wealth, Power, and Civilization.* New York: HarperCollins Publishers, 2010.

Steinberg, Philip E. *The Social Construction of the Ocean.* Cambridge: Cambridge University Press, 2001.

Toomer, Jean. *Cane.* Ed. Darwin T. Turner. New York: Norton, 1988.

Tuan, Yi-Fu. *The Hydrologic Cycle and The Wisdom of God.* Toronto: University of Toronto Press, 1968.

Verschuuren, Bas, and Robert Wild. *Sacred Natural Sites: Conserving Nature and Culture.* London/Washington, DC: Earthscan, 2010.

Williams, Chris. *Ecology and Socialism: Solutions to Capitalist Ecological Crisis.* Chicago: Haymarket Books, 2010.

Wittvogel, Karl A. *Oriental Despotism: A Comparative Study of Total Power.* New Haven: Yale University Press, 1957.

Wood, Mary Christina. *Nature's Trust: Environmental Law for a New Ecological Age.* New York: Cambridge University Press, 2014.

Woodward, Colin. *Ocean's End: Travels through Endangered Seas.* New York: Basic Books, 2000.

World Bank. *Changing the Face of the Waters: The Promise and Challenge of Sustainable Aquaculture.* Washington, DC. The World Bank, 2007.

World Bank. *Scaling Up Marine Management: The Role of Marine Protected Areas.* Washington, DC: The World Bank, 2006.

PETER NEILL is the founder and director of the
World Ocean Observatory (W2O), an Internet-
based place of exchange of information and
educational services about the health of the ocean.
The W2O focuses on the full spectrum of ocean
issues: climate, fresh water, food, energy, trade,
transportation, public health, finance, governance,
security, recreation, and culture. W2O serves as a
means to advance public awareness and political
will and to create an informed and inter-connected
community of "Citizens of the Ocean."

Peter Neill is the author of three novels and several
books on maritime art, literature, and history;
is former Director of the Maritime Program at
the National Trust for Historic Preservation; and
served as President of the South Street Seaport
Museum, New York. He lives in Sedgwick, Maine.